inside fashion design

Second Edition

Sharon Lee Tate

illustrated by Mona Shafer Edwards

1817

HARPER & ROW, PUBLISHERS, New York
Cambridge, Philadelphia, San Francisco,
London, Mexico City, São Paulo, Sydney

Sponsoring Editor: Fred Henry
Project Editor: Nora Helfgott
Designer: Robert Sugar
Production Manager: Jeanie Berke
Compositor: TriStar Graphics
Printer and Binder: The Murray Printing Company

Inside Fashion Design, Second Edition

Library of Congress Cataloging in Publication Data

Tate, Sharon Lee.
    Inside fashion design.

    Includes index.
    1. Costume design.   I. Edwards, Mona Shafer,
1951–   II. Title.
TT507.T38   1984   746.9'2   83-4358
ISBN 0-06-046583-2

contents

6

Sources of Inspiration   159

7
Principles and Elements of Design

8
Drawing a Working Sketch

9
Bodices, Blouses, Jackets, Coats

10
Skirts

11

Dresses   295

14
Collars

preface

Designing women's apparel is an exciting and demanding profession that requires special skills and abilities. The successful designer is usually a skilled artist and, sometimes, a qualified patternmaker and dressmaker. This person must be able to direct people and interpret fashion trends. The designer must extract the exact information from the many reports and predictions introduced at the beginning of a season and interpret them in the context of a particular product. Finally, above all, the successful designer must create a garment that will sell. To sell, the garment must appeal to a group of customers and must be capable of being produced at a price competitive with a particular market.

FEATURES

Inside Fashion Design, Second Edition, first describes the job of the designer and how the designer functions in the context of an apparel manufacturing firm in Chapters 1 and 2. People who plan a career in any aspect of fashion should know the mechanics of the creation and production of the commodity they sell and promote. Fashion people must also know what is involved in creating and manufacturing a line. Chapter 3 presents a comprehensive overview of how to organize a line, including discussions on work sheets, cost sheets, color, and markets. The designer's duties in choosing fabrics for a line is an important aspect of the job, as is studying fibers and materials. Chapter 4 is an intensive discussion of fabricating a line and includes a lengthy textile dictionary of pictures and descriptions of more than 100 fabrics. Chapter 5 describes kinds and ways of trimming a garment and features up-to-date topics like studding and airbrush painting. Chapter 6's sources of inspiration should stimulate interest in discovering the vast research sources available to the designer, including domestic and foreign publications, museums, home furnishings, and fashion shows.

Chapter 7, principles and elements of design, illustrates the illusions clothing can create to alter the basic human proportions. This knowledge is as important to a person who must buy and sell apparel as it is to someone who creates it. An enjoyable feature of this chapter is art that asks readers to determine proportions; the pictorial "answers" are hidden from the question art. Chapter 8, on basic drawing, is an excellent introduction to an extended course on fashion drawing and illustrations. Chapters 9 to 14 (jackets, skirts, dresses, and so on) further illustrate proportion and style. Each of these chapters includes historical information about various types of garments and serves as a springboard to a more detailed study of historic costume.

APPLICATIONS

Inside Fashion Design, Second Edition, thus provides people with a general interest in fashion an understanding of the way apparel is created and manufactured. Readers will also be able to increase their visual and verbal vocabulary of terms basic to all fashion careers. To anyone seriously considering apparel design as a career, this book details the specific talents and skills required and how to develop them. Many important areas that should be studied in greater depth, such as textiles, fashion drawing and illustration, historical costume, color, and draping and pattern work, are brought together so readers can see how they interrelate to become the tools of the professional apparel designer. (I have deliberately omitted a complete discussion of draping and pattern work because it should be intensively studied and practiced in a laboratory situation. A knowledgeable teacher is the most useful guide in these areas. Also, there are many excellent books on draping and pattern work available.)

SPECIAL NOTE

Designing women's apparel is a career in which both men and women can excel. Creativity and skill are the ingredients of success, not the sex of the designer or craftsperson. Men and women have equal ability to function in most of the occupations in an apparel factory—even the traditional male dominance in the cutting room is breaking down. Thus I have used the she/he pronouns interchangeably in the book, with the understanding that both sexes can build careers in manufacturing, designing, and promoting women's apparel.

ACKNOWLEDGMENTS

I would like to extend many thanks to the following teachers and professionals who helped in the preparation of *Inside Fashion Design,* Second Edition: Sue Banks, Grayce Baldwin, Norma Carnahan, Elanore Kennedy, Vilma Matchette, Mary Stephens, and Vivian Tellefsen.

Special appreciation to Larry Kastendiek and Kim Tucker for their excellent photographs, and extra thanks to the manufacturers and their staffs, who so graciously appeared in the photographs: Grayce Baldwin Consults; Judy Baldwin; Margie Balun; Gail Baizer; Michael Calderón; *California Apparel News;* California Girl; Camsco, Charm of Hollywood; Joan Christy; Cotton, Incorporated; Dea Eldorado; Leslie Fahn; Raymond Fahn; Fernando Flores; Hoechst Fibers; *IM;* Elanore Kennedy, Marin Kirkland; Lidz Brothers; Ted Levy; Ray Matsanaga, Mr. Pleat; Albert Orfaela; Sam Patti; Shirley Raab; Raj of India; *Report West,* Earle Ross; Kathy Saba; John Scott; Bernard Wassink; and Warren Zeretsky.

In addition, I am very grateful to Elaine Beckman, Elle Joie Originals; Nancy Bryant, Oregon State University; Frances Harder, Seattle Central Community College; Mary Kearns, Stephens College; Dr. Michelle Morganosky, University of Illinois; Diane C. Smith, San Diego Mesa Community College; Vivian Tellefsen, The Fashion Institute of Design and Merchandising; Dr. Jo Ellen Uptegraft, University of Oklahoma; Martha Webb, Miami-Dade Community College; and Paula Wepprich, Stephens College. All took a great deal of time and added their expertise to the second edition. Their comments and suggestions helped me greatly.

Sharon Lee Tate

Author's Conference

1.
the apparel factory

The garment industry is characterized by both small and large manufacturing firms. A businessperson with a good idea or the ability to sell a product can capitalize on his or her talent and pay small-business people to complete the manufacturing process. In fact, almost all phases of production and selling can be contracted to small outside firms. This saves the creative person from large investments in plant facilities and machinery. Also, a small apparel firm tends to have more styling flexibility and more merchandising innovativeness. Because the small manufacturer does not have to support a large factory and keep many machines busy, he or she can follow a trend quickly and then pull out as the fashion item saturates the market. Often small firms specialize in servicing a small group of retailers who want exclusive, more expensive styling.

During the past two decades, many small apparel firms have developed into giants, with sales in the millions of dollars. These large firms have departments that handle almost all the manufacturing, selling, and promotional aspects of garment production. Frequently these firms have several divisions that produce noncompetitive lines. Some firms produce men's, women's, and children's apparel.

Larger firms have several advantages over smaller firms. Larger manufacturers can buy fabrics before they are offered to the general market because they cut in large volume and order large amounts of yardage well before the season begins. Often the larger manufacturer has a well-established credit rating that facilitates ordering stock yardage. The design departments can order special colors and prints, and occasionally they style the fabric they use because the manufacturer also owns a knitting operation or prints his or her own fabric.

There are several disadvantages in a large firm. Though the large manufacturer can control internal operations, the firm still must design garments that sell. For that reason, the larger firm must not become complacent about its position in the market. Many times the large manufacturer's styling policy will not be flexible enough. And change in the demand of the consumer will leave the inflexible manufacturer with much unwanted merchandise. (Several seasons of poor styling can be disastrous for an apparel producer of any size.) Finally, finding the proper executive and sales talent to manage all phases of a large manufacturing organization may be difficult.

MAJOR DEPARTMENTS IN AN APPAREL FIRM

The average apparel firm is divided into three major departments: design, production, and sales.

1. *The design department* is headed by the designer, who is responsible for producing somewhere between four and six collections of garments per year: fall-winter; holiday (an optional season depending on category of merchandise); cruise-spring; summer; and transitional or early fall. Many progressive manufacturers avoid truly seasonal lines by working with a loose seasonal feeling and constantly adding and subtracting garments.
2. *The production department* is responsible for mass producing the line in various sizes and colors and filling orders placed by retailers.
3. *The sales department* markets the line produced by the design department and acts as an intermediary between buyers and the designer.

In all three departments, the designer is actually a participant.

Orders and shipping, a subdepartment managed in most firms by the sales staff, works between sales and production. This subdepartment collects and processes orders, verifies the store's credit rating, and compiles orders for the production head. The production head can then work out delivery schedules to meet the completion dates (deadline for shipment to stores) set by the house and the customers. Sometimes a buyer will have the "muscle" to override a completion date set by the house. This buyer is probably important to the manufacturer because he or she buys such large quantities of the manufacturer's merchandise. Thus the manufacturer feels he must honor the buyer's request for an earlier shipping date. Normally, though, the production head will schedule according to the availability of fabric from the mill, and completion dates for the house follow automatically from fabric delivery dates. If the completion date is not met, the retailer has the right to cancel the order and refuse delivery of any goods.

CONTRACTING

Contracting is hiring a factory or service to perform a specific part of the manufacturing process. The range of contracting services offered in an apparel-producing center spans all phases of production and design. Whether operations in a small- to moderate-sized firm will be done out of the shop is determined by how much investment capital is available, the talent of the person starting the firm, and the age of the business.

When a person strong in design teams up with a person who can supervise the production aspects of the business, the two may hire a sales organization to represent them in their home market and the territories. They will pay the salesperson a commission based on the volume of the product sold. The partners can also contract out the pattern work, cutting, and sewing. If a good salesperson began manufacturing, he or she might farm out everything but the actual selling and shipping of the garments. This person would have to purchase the fabric and assume the responsibility for choosing which styles to make into samples and cut for shipping.

The contractor is generally responsible for completing by a specific time the work agreed upon. Furthermore, the contractor must make the garments to a previously agreed-upon standard. Because the contractor assumes no responsibility for styles that do not sell, his or her risk is smaller than the manufacturer's.

As a firm matures and gains some working capital, the manufacturer will hire people to work exclusively for the firm. Especially important is an in-house designer. This designer is more likely to create a product uniquely in the image of the firm than a freelance designer who cannot benefit from close contact with the day-to-day operations of the firm.

There are both advantages and disadvantages to contracting out work or maintaining an inside shop. To overcome the disadvantages, the manufacturer and the contractor *must* work closely together on the product and allow each other a fair share of the profits. The production person is the contact between the contractor and the manufacturer.

Inside Shop

ADVANTAGES

1. Greater quality control of product.
2. More accurate scheduling; special jobs more easily handled.
3. Less physical movement of goods and personnel.
4. Depreciation of facilities and machinery yields tax benefits.

1. Large, fairly consistent payroll to maintain.
2. Greater monthly rent, repair, and overhead costs.
3. More time and effort devoted to union and employee demands.
4. During seasonal slow periods, workers have to be laid off, or an artificial work flow of promotional garments is created.
5. Large amounts of capital (money) tied up in machinery and facilities.

Contractor or Outside Shop

ADVANTAGES

1. Great production flexibility when a contractor is hired only as production requires. During the busy season, almost all firms have to contract out some aspect of the sewing operation.
2. Some contractors specialize in operations requiring special machines or talents (examples: a pleater, a beltmaker). These services are used by most firms at some time.
3. A highly paid technician whose work is seasonal, such as a patternmaker or grader, does not have to be maintained during a period of no work.
4. No direct negotiations with labor or unions.
5. No capital investment or maintenance necessary.

DISADVANTAGES

1. Less control over quality of product.
2. Delivery and deadlines sometimes missed.
3. Communication problems (many contractors speak a foreign language).
4. Extra physical movement of goods, resulting in greater chance of shortage or possible style piracy.

Foreign Production

Manufacturers may produce merchandise in a foreign country. This is called *offshore* production. The foreign sewing shop receives a sample garment, construction specifications, and a production pattern or marker from the manufacturer. The fabric may be sent to the contractor, who cuts and sews it, returning finished garments to the stateside manufacturer. Another method is to cut the fabric domestically and send the cut pieces abroad to be sewn. There are some advantages to this method because customs rates may be lower. The manufacturer must carefully weigh the advantages of inexpensive labor against shipping costs, customs fees, and the cost of coordinating the offshore production.

MANUFACTURING A READY-TO-WEAR GARMENT

Let us follow all phases of production of a style that has sold successfully. To the left of the operation described is the person who would be in charge of the job in an average firm. The larger the manufacturer, the more staff members participate in each operation. In a small factory, one person might perform several of the jobs described.

CUTTING TICKET

Style No. _7268 P_   Date _5/3_   19 _83_

Color	4 3	6 5	8 7	10 9	12 11	14 13	16 15	18 17	Total
Red Floral Pattern #4959		35	40	40	40	35			190
Actual Cut									
piece 1 – 151½ y.		38	40	40					
piece 2 132 y.					38	35			191
Total		38	40	40	38	35			
Gray Floral Pattern #4959		35	40	40	40	35			190
Actual Cut									
piece 3 153 y.		38	40	40					
piece 4 136 y					39	35			
Total		38	40	40	39	35			192

Cutting Ticket   The number of garments to be cut in each size and color is determined by compiling from the individual store orders all the pieces that have been sold. These totals are recorded on the cutting ticket. The cutter lays up the fabric and may slightly alter the number of garments cut depending on the exact yardage that can be cut from each bolt (also called piece) of fabric. Additional garments may be cut to supply reorders and replace possible damaged garments. The minimum pieces to be cut are set by the manufacturer, based on the kind of garment and its price.

Plan Cutting and Production

Production person

Compiles orders for a specific style and lists the style by size, color, and fabric on a cutting ticket.

Figures the amount of stock yardage required. Checks that fabric is in house and ready for cutting.

May do final costing of the garment after marker yardage has been determined.

Follows up on all phases of production and corrects problems arising during production.

Findings buyer

Orders findings (lining, zippers, thread, seam tape, and so on).

Orders trimmings (buttons, belts, special trims, and so forth).

Checks in items and stores them as they arrive. Dispatches items, including labels and care instruction labels, to contractors as needed.

Stock Yardage Ordering and Receiving

Owner or production person

Orders stock yardage. This may be anticipated by the manufacturer before a style has been sold. If a fabric looks like a good seller, the manufacturer will take an early position (place a tentative order) on a given amount of yardage to receive delivery at the proper time. The textile firm may let the person decide on the color or print (assort) at a date that is nearer the production season. Later assorting prevents errors.

Checks with the mill if delivery is delayed.

Quality controller

Checks stock yardage for flaws. Usually each bolt is unrolled and inspected, then marked in the selvage (fabric edge) to alert the cutter to avoid flaws. If the yardage is too badly damaged, the manufacturer will try to return it to the mill.

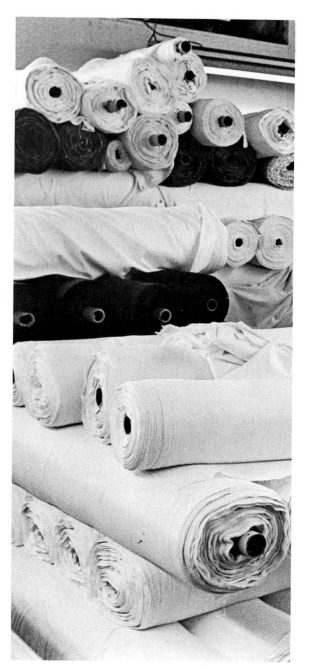

Stock Yardage Stock yardage is ordered as early in the season as possible to ensure delivery.

Pattern Work

Production patternmaker

Remakes the first pattern (made by the design department) to conform

Production Patternmaker The production patternmaker remakes the designer's pattern into a garment that is as simple to construct as the style will allow. The stock garment must also conform to the company's commercial fit.

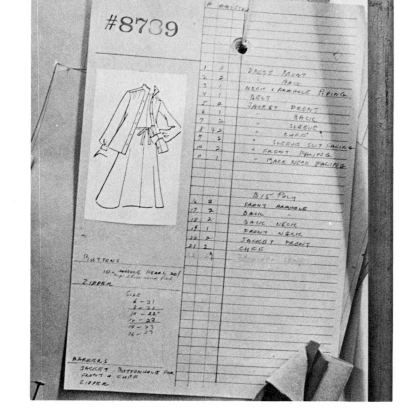

Production Pattern Each production pattern is identified with a pattern chart that lists the pieces needed to construct the garment. A working sketch, a swatch of the fabric, and all trimming specifications are also included.

to the company fit (the company's concept of the average customer).

Production pattern is simplified as much as possible to eliminate sewing problems and waste.

Grader   Changes the measurements of the sample pattern and makes a set of patterns for the size range the garment will be sold in.

Grading the Pattern   The grader usually uses a machine to move the pattern pieces as she outlines the pieces in the large and small sizes. Each piece of the production pattern must be graded.

Computer Grading and Marker Making The screen of the scope projects the pattern pieces stored in the computer memory that can be modified by using the stylus (the penlike instrument) into various styles. The functions box to the left of the screen pivots the pattern and enables the operator to enlarge and reduce the image of the pattern on the screen as needed. (Courtesy of Camsco.)

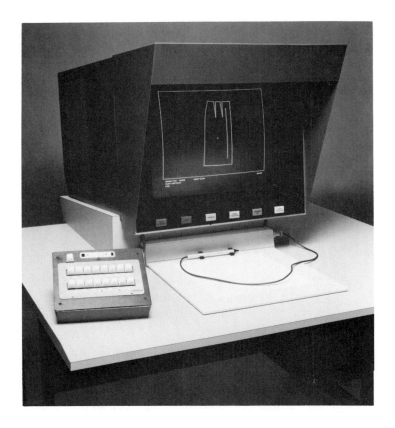

Marker maker	Outlines on marking paper exactly how the pattern pieces from the production pattern should be cut from the fabric. The pieces are arranged and interlocked to save as much fabric as possible. The outline on the marking paper is called the *marker*.

Patternmaking, grading, and marker making is now being done by computers. These advanced technology systems convert the physical pattern pieces into special shapes that are stored in the computer's memory. These pattern pieces may be called up on the computer screen and modified by a skilled pat-

Marker A marker may be made by outlining each pattern piece with a pen or by photographing the pieces on light-sensitive paper with a photo marker, as this photo shows. The dark areas indicate the pieces to be cut. The large holes in the pattern pieces allow the pieces to be hung on a pattern hook.

Spreading Fabric is laid on the cutting table in many layers. Cutting costs are lower when many garments can be cut at the same time. These layers are aligned on nails so the stripes will match at the side seams.

ternmaker to form new styles. The new sample pattern is printed out full scale so it can be sewn into a garment and tested. When the pattern development system (PDS) has a completed and perfected pattern, it is graded according to "grade rules" specified by the manufacturer. These rules are the measurement increments that change the size of the pattern with a prearranged formula. The graded pattern pieces are greatly reduced in size on the computer screen so the marker maker can arrange them in the most economical layout for the given fabric width and pattern. Then the full-size marker is printed out ready to cut.

Computer operators must be skilled patternmaking technicians. This computer technology greatly speeds up the time it takes to produce, grade, and mark a garment. Considerable fabric savings are also possible with this new system.

Cutter and spreader	Lays up the cut.
	The fabric is spread evenly, layer upon layer, according to the size, color, and amount designated on the cutting ticket. Spreads the marker on the stack of fabric.

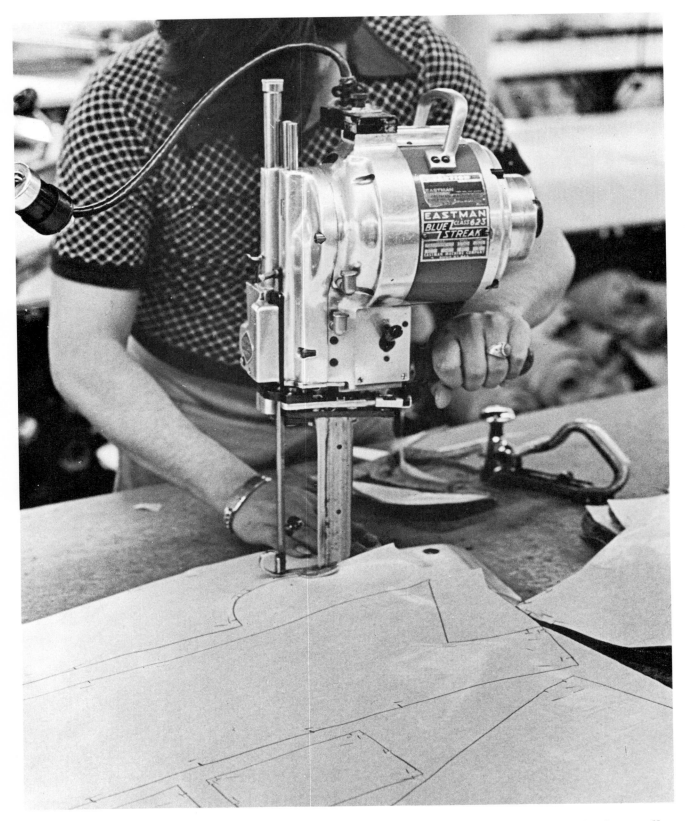

Cutting The cutter cuts this stack with a blade. This marker has been made by hand. The small lines at the edges of the pattern pieces are notches that guide the sewer as the garment is constructed.

Finished Cut　All pieces that have been cut are tied together and labeled with the style number, size, and pattern piece.

Rewrites the cutting ticket to indicate the number of pieces cut from each bolt. The shades of color are separated during the spreading process.

Cuts the stack of fabric with a cutting knife (a hand-held machine resembling an electric saw).

Bundling

Bundling worker

Organizes the pieces of each unit. Garments can be bundled according to item, group, or section methods.

1. Item. All pieces that make up one garment are placed together and sewed by one operator. (Used most often in moderate- and better-priced garments.)
2. Group. Ten to 20 garments are put in one bundle that the operator sews. This method is usual-

Bundling As each garment is assembled in a bundle for the sewers, the bundler includes thread, work tickets, zippers, and other findings.

ly used for simple, inexpensive garments or staples.

3. Section. An operator works on one area of a garment (shirt collars, for example). Then the completed areas of the garment are assembled. Typical method for a staple garment or a garment with a special trim. The trim can be sent out to be completed while work continues in house on other pieces of the garment.

Recuts any damaged pieces.

Puts the necessary findings with each bundle.

Attaches production tickets for future operations. As an operator finishes working on a piece, he or she will remove one segment of the ticket as proof of having completed that phase of construction. The operator's pay will be based on the number of tickets he or she has collected.

Attaches labels and care instructions.

Special Trims (Not Always Used)

Contractor specializing in trims

Trims, as well as appliqués and pleats, are done at this time. The section to be trimmed is separated from the bundle and reunited with it after the trim is applied.

Construction Operations

Operator:
straight
  sewing
  machine
overlock
  (or sew-
  overlock
  machine)
blind stitch
  (supervised
  by a floor
  supervisor)

The method of construction is determined by the kind of garment and its price. The two main methods of construction are these:

1. Section work. The operator specializes. Each operator on the assembly line sews only one part of the garment.

2. Complete garment construction. The whole garment is sewed by one operator. Special effects (like overlocking the seams, hemming, and buttonholes) are done by separate workers. This

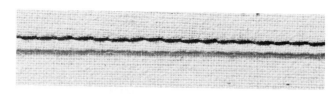

The single-needle stitch is the most versatile machine. It produces a straight stitch that can be lengthened or shortened and is used for joining the garment pieces, some hemming and finishing areas, and many special trims like quilting and trapunto.

Single-Needle Lock-Stitch Machine   This machine sews a straight seam in a simple stitch. Another name for this machine is single needle.

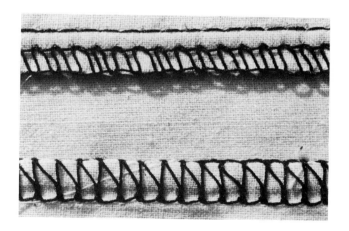

The top example shows an overlock stitch. This is often used for knits because it will stretch and therefore be more compatible with the knit. The lower example shows a sew overlock stitch. This machine joins the two pieces of fabric, overlocks the edges and trims off the excess fabric for a clean, neat seam. Overlocked seams do not always press flat because two thicknesses of fabric are stitched together. This makes them less desirable for tailored clothing.

Sew Overlock Machine   This machine overlocks the edges of the fabric, trims the seam, and sews the seam with a straight stitch, all at the same time.

Blind Stitch Machine The hem is finished with a stitch that is barely visible on the right side of the fabric. Many times clear polyester thread is used so it will not have to be changed when garments of different colors are being sewed.

The example to the left shows the back side of a hem. The righthand example shows the right side of the garment. Contrast thread has been used to show the stitches. Thread the same color as the fabric would be less noticeable.

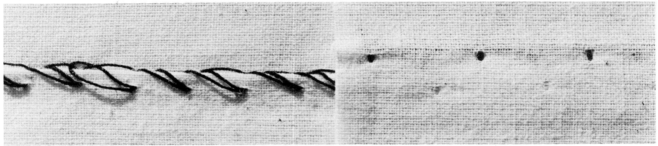

Floor Supervisor The floor supervisor regulates the flow of work through the factory and solves any construction problems that may arise.

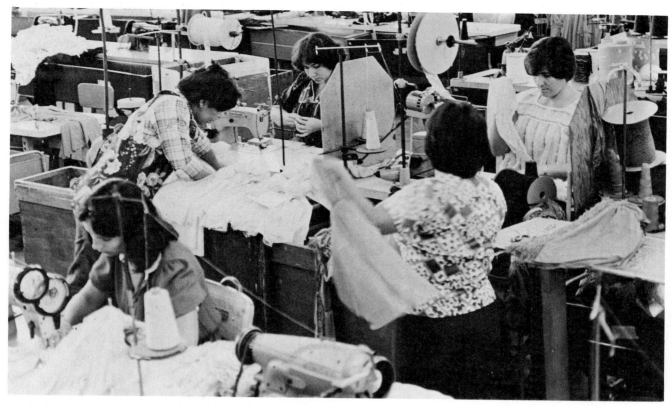

Sewing Factory   A large factory is a busy place with operators sewing at machines placed side by side and floor workers, or conveyor belts in more modern factories, moving the garments from the sewers to the special machines. (Courtesy of Chic Lingerie.)

method is most often used for better garments, especially tailored jackets.

Workers in a factory are paid by the number of pieces they do in a day. The price paid for the individual task is determined by the difficulty of the task and the time it takes to complete it. This is called *piecework*. Workers detach the segment of the work ticket that corresponds to the task they do to complete the garment. At the end of the pay period, the number of tickets each worker turns in determines that worker's salary.

Time and motion engineer

The two methods described above can be combined to complete the garment as inexpensively and quickly as possible. To determine the most efficient method, a time and motion engineer may devise the construction system.

STYLE	STYLE	STYLE	STYLE	STYLE	STYLE	STYLE	STYLE	STYLE	STYLE	STYLE
SIZE QTY.	SIZE QTY.	SIZE QTY.	SIZE QTY.	SIZE QTY.	SIZE QTY.	SIZE QTY.	SIZE QTY.	SIZE QTY.	SIZE QTY.	SIZE QTY.
	RATE	RATE	RATE	RATE	RATE					
13478 CONTROL	13478 Press	13478 Button Sew	13478 Button Holes	13478 Facings	13478 Lace Collar	13478 LACE FRONT	13478 FRONT 1	13478 SLEEVE OVERLOCK	13478 SLEEVE CONTROL	13478 COLLAR CONTROL
	Press	Button Sew	Button Holes	Facings	Lace Collar	Lace Front	Front 1	Slv. Overlock	Make Sleeve	Make Collar

HOLLYWOOD BLOUSE, INC.

S-1756—6-78—AJ-48

Trim	Blindstitch	Closing	Set Sleeves	Set Collar	Neck Overlock	Lace Front	Front 1	Slv. Overlock	Make Sleeve	Make Collar
STYLE	STYLE	STYLE	STYLE	STYLE	STYLE	STYLE	STYLE	STYLE	STYLE	STYLE
SIZE QTY.	SIZE QTY.	SIZE QTY.	SIZE QTY.	SIZE QTY.	SIZE QTY.	SIZE QTY.	SIZE QTY.	SIZE QTY.	SIZE QTY.	SIZE QTY.
RATE	RATE	RATE	RATE	RATE	RATE	RATE	RATE	RATE	RATE	RATE
13478 Trim	13478 Blindstitch	13478 Closing	13478 Set Sleeves	13478 Set Collar	13478 Neck Overlock	13478 Lace Front	13478 Front 1	13478 Slv. Overlock	13478 Make Sleeve	13478 Make Collar

Piecework Ticket   Each worker tears off a section of the work ticket that identifies the work done on the garment. At the end of the pay period, the total of tickets turned in determines the worker's wage.

Hand Finisher   Final trims and findings are sewn by hand to better garments.

Presser   Garments may need underpressing (opening seams and pressing facings) during construction. After all sewing processes are completed, the garment is given a final or "finish" pressing.

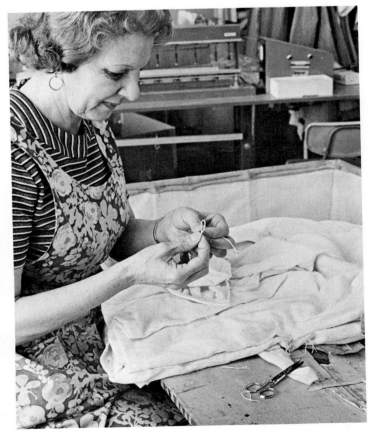

Presser	Does underpressing (opening seams, pressing facings, and so forth) when needed during the sewing operation. Finishes pressing the garment when completely sewed.
Hand finisher	Sews on special buttons, tacks, cuffs, hems, and so on. (This person works only on more expensive garments.)

Quality Control The garment is checked before it is sent to the shipping department. Hang tags are attached at this time.

Quality controller	Trims threads, checks for sewing errors, hangs garments on hangers, attaches hang tags, covers each garment with a plastic bag. The retailer's sales tag may be placed on the garments at this point.

Shipping

Head shipper	Pulls orders for the stores (selects the sizes, styles, and colors specified on the orders) and carefully ships garments according to the retailer's instructions. Designates the carrier (which company will deliver the shipments).
Packer	Packs shipments into boxes or garment bags.
Billing department	Sends bills and invoices to the stores.

Pulling Orders The specific garments that stores have ordered are pulled for shipping.

Packing Garments are packed into boxes or hanging containers for shipment to the stores.

Departments Not Directly Involved with Construction and Shipping

SHOWROOM

Head of sales
Road sales-
    people
Showroom
    staff
Stylist
Model
Clerical
    people

Generally a showroom is centrally located in the apparel mart. Occasionally, if the factory is in the apparel district, it will contain an in-house showroom. Sales activities are carried on here for buyers who visit the manufacturer. Usually the sales staff contacts out-of-town accounts by mail and telephone on a regular basis to check on sales and prevent problems. Salespeople may also call on buyers in the store.

ADVERTISING AND PROMOTION

Advertising
    manager
Copywriter
Artist-photog-
    rapher
Fashion
    coordinator

Marketing bulletins, advertising allowances, and trade journal advertisements are planned and executed by this department. In general, only the largest companies maintain a staff in this area. Smaller manufacturers will hire specialists on a free-lance basis as the need arises.

ACCOUNTING

Accountant
Bookkeeper
Clerical
    people

In charge of billing, credit checks, collection of delinquent accounts, and all other bookkeeping.

Responsible for payroll, commissions, and general tax accounting.

Pays contracts, bills, and so on.

FINANCE DEPARTMENT

Investment
    counselor
    (tax adviser)

Advises on major capital expenditures. In public companies, this department handles legal problems and stockholder activities.

Factor

A finance company that buys a manufacturer's accounts receivable (retailers' orders that have not yet been delivered and paid for). The finance company takes as a commission a percentage of the total dollar amount and gives the manufacturer the balance of the money.

Sales Warren Zeretsky, national sales manager, shows a garment to a buyer reviewing the line at the California Girl showroom.

In this way, the manufacturer has ready cash with which to operate while the garments are being made and shipped. Sometimes the factor will take over the billing and financial aspects of the business.

MACHINE SHOPS

Machinist

Manufacturers who have many trimming machines, particularly lingerie and bathing suit manufacturers, use a machinist to install various attachments on the heads (machines) they already own. Additionally, this department may print labels, boxes, and so forth. Some manufacturers periodically hire an independent sewing machine repair service to keep the machines operating and to make miner modifications in machine setups.

THE DESIGNER'S ROLE IN PRODUCTION

The designer must understand the production procedures of the factory. If the designer is to produce a garment compatible with the price range and technical limits of the production system, he or she must understand the whole production process. This is particularly important when selecting fabrics. Often a factory cannot sew a delicate fabric, or new machines or techniques will have to be used on a new fiber or fabric construction. Generally, the designer will recognize potential problems when he or she constructs the sample in the design room. The designer should test how each new fabric reacts to pressing, washing, or dry cleaning. Often a manufacturer will have a washer and dryer on the premises to test washable fabrics. The designer will pass on all this information to the production person, who may modify the sewing or pressing techniques for stock goods.

The designer plays an important role in the sales department too. He or she will often conduct sales meetings to inform the salespeople about the reason for the styling of the line and the specific fabric information they will need to sell the merchandise to buyers. Designers may have contact with store buyers to discuss fashion trends and consumer reactions. Visits to the stores to see how the garments fit a variety of sizes and figures is important for all designers. Sometimes the designer is promoted as a personality and makes public appearances at fashion shows or in retail stores.

All this interaction between the designer and the sales and production departments of a manufacturing plant is easy to understand when you remember that a designer's primary job is to create a product that sells. *No matter how large or small the manufacturer, to stay in business season after season, the firm must make a salable garment.*

The Major Steps in Manufacturing a Garment

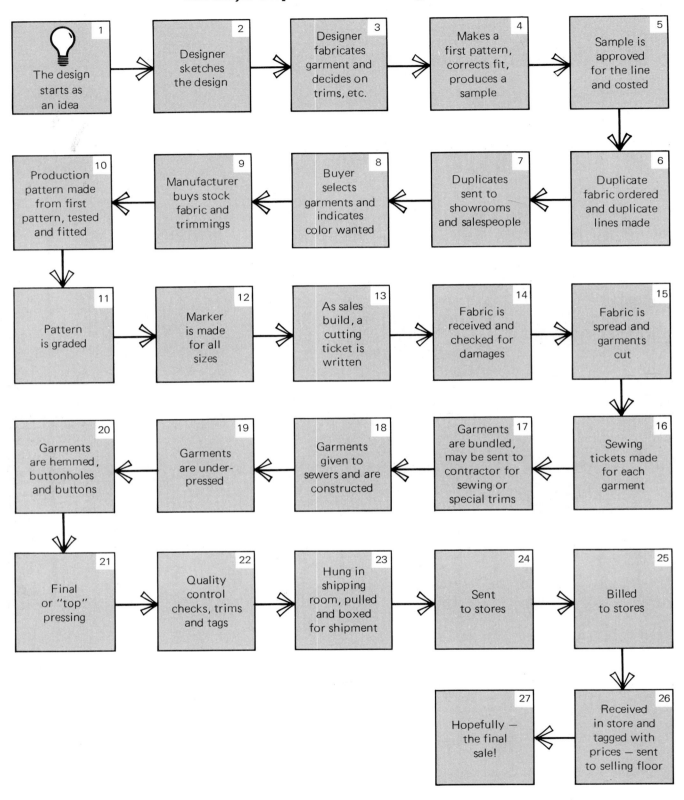

1. The design starts as an idea
2. Designer sketches the design
3. Designer fabricates garment and decides on trims, etc.
4. Makes a first pattern, corrects fit, produces a sample
5. Sample is approved for the line and costed
6. Duplicate fabric ordered and duplicate lines made
7. Duplicates sent to showrooms and salespeople
8. Buyer selects garments and indicates color wanted
9. Manufacturer buys stock fabric and trimmings
10. Production pattern made from first pattern, tested and fitted
11. Pattern is graded
12. Marker is made for all sizes
13. As sales build, a cutting ticket is written
14. Fabric is received and checked for damages
15. Fabric is spread and garments cut
16. Sewing tickets made for each garment
17. Garments are bundled, may be sent to contractor for sewing or special trims
18. Garments given to sewers and are constructed
19. Garments are under-pressed
20. Garments are hemmed, buttonholes and buttons
21. Final or "top" pressing
22. Quality control checks, trims and tags
23. Hung in shipping room, pulled and boxed for shipment
24. Sent to stores
25. Billed to stores
26. Received in store and tagged with prices — sent to selling floor
27. Hopefully — the final sale!

REVIEW

Word Finders

Define the following words from the chapter you just read:

1. Bundling
2. Capital
3. Contractor
4. Cutting ticket
5. Factor
6. Findings
7. First pattern
8. Grader
9. Inside shop
10. Marker
11. Piecework
12. Presser
13. Production pattern
14. Production person
15. Production tickets
16. Quality controller
17. Section work
18. Selvage
19. Showroom
20. Trimmings

Discussion Questions

1. List two advantages a large manufacturer has over a smaller manufacturer.
2. Discuss the advantages and disadvantages of an inside shop as compared with an outside shop.
3. Large or small, what must an apparel manufacturer do to stay in business?
4. Why should a designer be familiar with production procedures?

2.
what does a designer do?

What exactly does a designer do? No two designers will answer this question in the same way because each designer does so many different things. As a rule, designers work for a wholesale apparel house or manufacturer, and their duties include a range of interrelated jobs.

Usually the designer is directly responsible to the head of the company or the division. The head of the company directs the overall operations that allow the company to function. He or she is in charge of all office and sales personnel as well as the functions considered the business side of the operation. In addition, depending on the size of the company, the head may work closely with the designer in choosing fabrics and finalizing the styles selected for the line.

The average apparel firm is divided into three major departments: design, production, and sales departments. The designer is actually a participant in all three departments. The best way to present a picture of the designer at work is to trace the creation of a line. The line begins as a series of ideas in the designer's mind, ideas that are made concrete in the design process, then sold to the retailer, and finally sold to the customer. Let us trace the process.

RESEARCHING COLORS
AND FABRICS

The first step in creating a new line is to research fashion and consumer trends. The numerous excellent sources of fashion information will be discussed in great detail in Chapter 4 (which explores fabricating a line and sources of inspiration). Generally, the designer will begin by investigating color trends. Information on color trends for the coming season usually comes from fiber companies and professional color services like Pat Tunskey. On the basis of these general predictions, the designer selects the colors he or she feels will make the line unique and salable. Once the color story is set, the designer begins to review textile lines.

Often someone from management, perhaps the head of the company, the merchandise person (head of sales), or the stylist, will assist the designer in selecting fabrics and colors. Those people participating in the selection will exchange information on new fibers and processes while trying to incorporate new fabric trends appropriate to the firm's view of cost and styling. Fabric, of course, is a great source of inspiration, and the excitement it generates often starts the chain of creation.

Frequently a style is carried over from one season to the next because it sold well. Manufacturers tend to run (continue) with a hot number as long as the style will sell, but only when a style has proved itself by continuous reorders. The designer must know which styles have become hot items. He or she will then refabricate the style to make it more attractive to buyers. (*Refabricate* means putting the "good body" into another fabric.) Many times a designer is asked to incorporate parts of a good body into a similarly styled garment or version of the original.

CREATING STYLES

Once fabrics have been selected, the designer begins to create styles for the line. The refabrications and versions of good bodies from the last season may provide the basic styles or staples of the new line. Then the designer begins styling the new garments.

Most designers work within the narrow constraints of the category that has been assigned to the manufacturer by the stores to which that firm has successfully sold. For example, a missy, moderate dress manufacturer may be further defined by retailers as

Reviewing Textile Lines   Kathy Saba of Palazzo Fabrics shows the line to designer Grayce Baldwin. Often a designer will have to see a line several times during the season as new colors and patterns are added.

Creating Styles John Scott, designer for Campus Casuals, sketches many more designs than will appear in the line. After evaluating and editing, he will fabricate the best ideas for the line.

specializing in print dresses made in easy-care fabrics. Usually it is very difficult to change this reputation drastically, because customers come to a manufacturer expecting to find a special kind of merchandise. Often buyers will allocate money to the specific category of merchandise and the manufacturer who has a reputation for producing it well. This can be a dangerous trap for a manufacturer. Overspecialization is disastrous if the category of merchandise sold goes out of fashion. To avoid overspecialization, the manufacturer should diversify the product line so that it is current with trends in the fashion market.

The designer must think of the customer who will want the particular category of merchandise. Visits to retailers who sell the merchandise well will help in the creative process, because the designer will have a concrete idea of what the customer wants and what the customer's figure problems are. Some designers visualize an "ideal customer," a person who wears the garments well. Good designers never lose sight of the individual who will ultimately have to find the garment attractive enough to purchase it, no matter how large the manufacturer or the stores who sell the merchandise. In addition, the following specific requirements for a good style must guide a designer as he or she sketches or drapes the actual garments.

Aesthetic Appeal

The garment should be attractive to the specific customer for whom it was created. Customers' aesthetic requirements differ with every size, price, and age range, but everyone is looking for a stylish garment. Therefore, the fabric in every garment should be attractive and fashionable in print and color. Most customers touch a garment immediately after being visually attracted to it, so the hand (feel) of the fabric is as important as its appearance.

Hanger appeal is very important in the customer's first evaluation of a garment. Clothes that do not present themselves well on a hanger (a halter dress, for example) benefit from being displayed on a mannequin. A garment that looks attractive on a hanger has a much better chance of selling than a garment that does not.

The designer should create each garment for a specific kind of occasion. For example, a showy garment is fun to look at and display, but where would it be worn? Accessorizing a garment is important too, and the designer can help the customer pick accessories by adding a belt or trim that suggests a color for shoes and bag. A garment that can be accessorized easily and yet is suitable for a range of activities is likely to sell.

Price

The garment should be an obviously good value for its price. If the price is too high, the customer will probably not try it on, even if she likes the style. When the designer styles a garment, he or she must consider the price of every detail, from the initial cost of the fabric to the trims and construction methods. Ultimately, the garment's success or failure may depend on cost.

The price of a garment is relative to the prices of the garments that surround it in the store and compete with it in the market. The manufacturer's sales department tries to sell the line to the department or store that has the most compatible merchandise, both in price and "look" of garments. Generally, a line will not sell well in a department if it is either the most expensive or the cheapest offered. Furthermore, the designer must be careful not to select a fabric or print that is used by other manufacturers for a lower-priced garment.

Timing

A design should both fit into a general fashion trend and satisfy the customer's desire to be unique and fashionable. Again, how these requirements are met varies greatly for different customers. During the same period, the young junior customer may be buying authentic work overalls, the young missy (contemporary) customer may be looking for copies of European prêt-à-porter (ready-to-wear), and the designer customer may be looking at Paris couture. Many excellent products have hit the sale racks because they were too early or too late for the fashion taste of the moment. The designer must be aware of general fashion trends and, more important, the trends that are influencing that particular market.

Fit

Once the customer has selected a garment to try on, the chance of selling that garment improves. Now the way the garment looks on the customer's figure is crucial. The customer wants the garment to fit and make her look taller and more slender. If the designer has created a garment to fit a slender, tall model, many average customers with figure problems will be disappointed when they try on the garment. The garment that conceals figure problems, flatters the face and body, fits well, and is pleasingly proportioned will be a success—and success means a garment that sells!

Care and Durability

Most customers will examine a garment to see if it is well made. Easy care, particularly wash and wear, is an important part of making a satisfactory garment, and a satisfactory garment is one that performs well and looks beautiful. If the designer chooses a wash and wear fabric but lines the garment with a fabric

32

Fitting Fitting the first sample is a critical part of design. The garment should fit the customer's figure, but it should also look good on the hanger so the customer will be tempted to try it on.

that must be dry-cleaned, that is defeating the fabric's purpose. The successful performance of the garment also depends on the designer's care in selecting trims and findings. Many chain stores recognize the importance of durability. A chain store may give the manufacturer specific instructions about how the garment should stand up to washing and ironing.

Usually the responsibility for performance is shared by the production and design departments. If a fabric performs badly, the manufacturer may choose not to use it. If the fabric is faulty but is already made into garments, the manufacturer may attempt to place the responsibility on the textile mill that sold the fabric. Care and durability are particularly important in designing and selling children's apparel, uniforms, and work clothes.

With aesthetics, timing, fit, and other considerations in mind, the designer plans the styles. The number of models or pieces in the line depends on the type of garment, the price range of the house, the method of distribution, and the number of lines made by the house. A particular number of garments will be planned for each type of fabric selected and for each category of garment in which the house specializes. A certain portion of the line will be conservative staples, and a certain portion will be more fashionable. The designer chooses the belts, buttons, and other trimmings. The choice of both fabric and trimmings is influenced by price as well as appropriateness.

Draping Usually only half the garment is draped to begin the pattern. Joan Christy, designer for C. G. Sport, is making corrections before the pattern is made by her assistant.

Draping as Inspiration Some designers prefer to drape their own garments. Ray Matsunaga of Chic Lingerie uses a piece of elastic to control the gathers for this drape.

Patternmaking Not all designers make their own patterns as Ray Matsunaga is doing, but designers should have a working knowledge of patternmaking so they understand garment construction well enough to work with patternmakers.

DEVELOPING A LINE

The techniques used to develop a line vary. One designer may make sketches that are turned over to an assistant who will make the sample first in muslin (an inexpensive plain fabric) and then in the chosen fabric. Another designer may work entirely with muslin or with the final fabric, draping it on a dress form or even on a live model. If a dress form is used, the designer drapes and pins the muslin into a three-dimensional form that is really a soft sculpture. When the designer is satisfied with the look and fit of the drape, the fabric is removed and the shape is transferred to a flat pattern. This pattern is made into a complete muslin (the first drape is often done on only half the figure, and a complete garment is necessary to check the fit). After corrections, the pattern is cut out of the sample fabric and made into the finished sample. Some designers prefer to *work on the flat*, also called *flat patternmaking*, which is a method of developing a style by making changes according to geometric rules in a basic block or sloper (a simple pattern with standard ease), and then completing the test muslin.

The choice of method depends on the designer's preference and training and the type of garment. Whatever the method, the result must be a garment that fits a human body. A model may show the style to buyers who come to the showroom to choose garments from the manufacturer's line and place orders for their stores. Less expensive garments are shown on a hanger. Designing is truly experimental. Every designer makes a great many unsuccessful numbers. A good number has the fortunate combination of the right fabric, the right cut, the right trimming, the right price, and the right margin of profit.

In Developing a line designers must combine the

THE DESIGN ROOM

The designer's primary responsibility is the creation of seasonal collections, but he or she is also head of a department and has executive functions. The designer is expected to take charge of the personnel in the design (or sample) room. The designer must cooperate with the sales force, the production department, and merchandisers, so creating a line is a team effort.

Assistant Designer This assistant is using the flat pattern technique; that is, she is translating from the sketch to the first pattern without draping the design first.

The designer usually has a staff in the design room to help develop ideas and execute sketches for the line. The designer must coordinate all staff activities and make sure the flow of work is constant. The number of people employed in the design room depends on the volume of work. The more functions a designer can perform in the design routine, the more valuable the designer will be to the firm.

A typical design room staff is described in the following list. Each job will require at least one person, depending on the amount of work to be completed.

1. Assistant designer. This person is usually a good patternmaker. The assistant may work on the flat, drape in muslin, or combine the two methods, but he or she must make an accurate pattern that translates the designer's working sketch into an actual garment.

2. Sample and duplicate cutter. The cutter uses the designer's first pattern to cut sample garments and duplicates out of sample fabric. Duplicates are extra samples used by the salespeople and other showrooms to sell the line. The design department frequently supervises the construction of the duplicate sample line. Duplicates are also called *dups*.

3. Sample maker. This person constructs the sample garment and may press and hand finish the sample. The sample maker works with the designer and assistant designer to fit the sample perfectly to the model. Usually the sample maker has had much experience in factory sewing methods and can spot potential difficulties. She or he can alert the designer to sewing problems that can be solved by the production pattern person or the staff of the design room. The success of a designer's styles depends on a good sample maker. For this reason, the sample maker is generally paid by the week, not by the piece, because the number of samples completed is much less important than a carefully made sample.

4. Sketcher. A sketcher may be employed to make working sketches for the designer and illustrations for the final promotion of the line. Working sketches are pencil sketches made from the designer's rough idea of the garment. The sketches are used in the sample room. The sketcher must interpret precisely the silhouette (shape and outline) of the garment and draw all seamlines and trims. Illustrations are smart fashion sketches and are used in the showroom book or for adver-

Sample Cutter The sample cutter cuts one garment. If the first sample is successful, duplicates will be cut for the out-of-town salespeople.

Sample Construction The construction of the sample takes much more time than the construction of the same garment in production. Care must be taken at this stage to produce an attractive sample. The sample should not be sewed hastily.

tisements. Usually these sketches are color renderings, emphasizing the texture and/or print of the fabric. Because manufacturers are trying to cut costs, the designer most often does the working sketches and sketchers are hired only to make illustrations.

5. Miscellaneous duties. These include shopping for findings and trimmings, supervising the making of duplicates, running the design room in the absence of the designer, filling out cost sheets, and supervising the receipt and storage of sample fabrics. In a large house, these duties may be the responsibility of one full-time employee; otherwise, the duties are part of the assistant's job.

6. Free-lance models. These models try on samples so the designer can fit and evaluate the garments. Models are also used to show the salespeople and buyers the samples during sales meetings and market weeks. The fitting model also works with the production patternmaker to perfect the fit of stock garments.

Beginners are rarely hired as designers. The responsibilities a designer must assume are so great that any manufacturer with an investment at stake

Samplemaker The samplemaker is an important member of the design team. She will test the first pattern to make sure it can be constructed properly. John Scott is working closely with his samplemaker to perfect a garment.

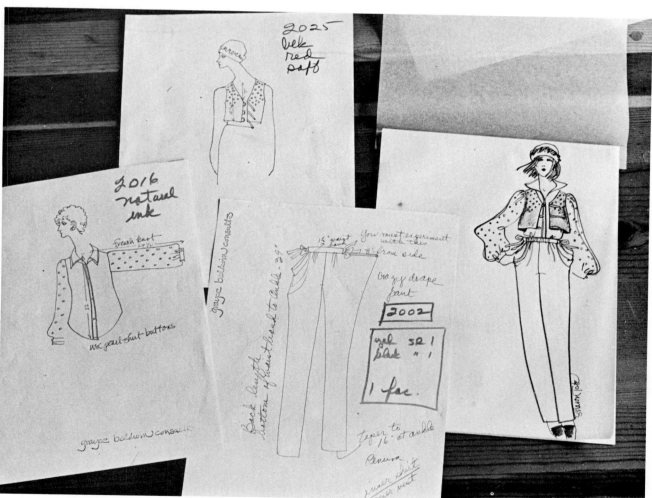

Working Sketch Frequently the working sketch will include measurements, colors, and other style notes. In contrast, the illustration is drawn to show the garments at their fashionable best. The illustration does not show all technical details.

will require an experienced person to head the design department. Occasionally a small or struggling house will hire a novice, but as a rule the beginner is hired as an assistant to the designer. In this capacity, he or she will perform a variety of services, depending on talent and training. The different jobs undertaken in the design room are an excellent starting place for a student who wishes a career in designing.

MERCHANDISING THE LINE

After all styles are finished, usually right before the season and before the styles are shown, the line is appraised and merchandised. This is also called weeding out the potentially unsuccessful styles. Many of the numbers may be discarded. If they cannot be fitted into one of the price lines featured by the house, even some of the most attractive numbers may be discarded.

How a line is merchandised depends on the policy of the house. The designer may show the line to the company head, who will review each piece. The company head decides whether the consumer will be willing to pay the price that will make the garment a profitable item. In one successful firm, if the head of the company is doubtful about a style, he asks the fitting model for her views. Models sometimes develop great sensitivity to the line because they show garments day after day and overhear the buyers' frank remarks about styles. In large firms, the salespeople are asked to participate in weeding the line because they also have great sensitivity to buyer reaction. The production person should be the technical advisor at the merchandising meeting so he or she can evaluate the practicality of the designs to cost and product. The designer and merchandiser round out the evaluation team at a typical merchandising meeting.

Some houses merchandise the line on the advice of several favorite buyers whose consistent success with the line proves their familiarity with customer reaction. Generally, weeding by any method reduces the line to relatively few garments. For production to be economical, only a few styles can be developed, but only a few really good numbers are needed for a house to have a successful season. Generally as the price of the line increases, the number of pieces in it also increases. High-priced lines contain many styles because these customers demand exclusiveness above all else.

PATTERN DEVELOPMENT

The designer's involvement in the development of the production pattern varies greatly from company to company. At one extreme, the designer may never see the final product because all production procedures are separate from the design room. At the other extreme, the designer may be responsible for making the production pattern and supervising the grading and marker making. The latter system is prevalent in small firms.

Typically the designer is called upon to make aesthetic decisions about the production garment when changes in pattern or proportion must be made to make the garment fit better or make it easier to produce. The designer may be asked to advise the production area on how to reduce the yardage in a garment.

Once the line has been merchandised and the styles chosen, the designer usually gives the first sample to the production patternmaker. It is necessary to make patterns for each garment in each size offered. Missy lines offer their garments in sizes 6 to 16, and junior lines are sized 3 to 13. Pattern devel-

Production Patternmaker   Production patternmaker Marin Kirkland makes a first production sample. Usually several garments have to be made to perfect the fit and constructions details.

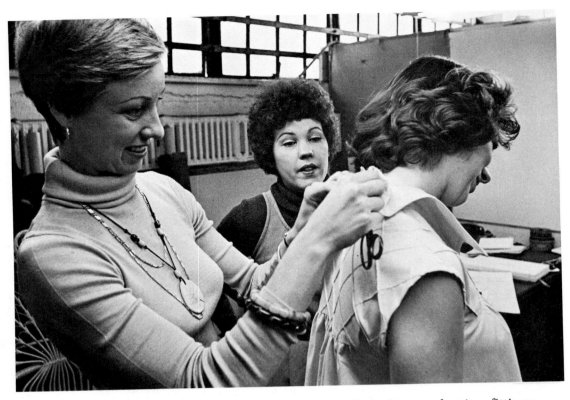

Production Fitting   The designer will often be included in production fittings. Ideally the stock garments will have the same appeal that made the sample sell. Margie Balun joins a discussion of the fit of a production sample.

Patternmaking Tools   Patternmaking tools include rulers, brush for cleaning the pattern, pushpins and a weight to secure the pattern as it is traced, French curve for smoothing the curved lines, various pencils and markers, Scotch tape, rabbit punch for holes that allow pattern pieces to be hung on a pattern hook, large stapler for putting together double pattern pieces, transparent rulers, tape measure, pins, notcher for marking the pattern, hole punch for marking darts, paper shears, tracing wheel for marking, fabric shears, seam-ripping scissors, and staple remover.

opment is such an expensive process that production patterns are not made until the line has been weeded and successful styles have been established through early sales. In most cases, the first pattern used for the original sample is made to fit a model who is not a perfect commercial size. Showroom models have the idealized proportions used in fash-

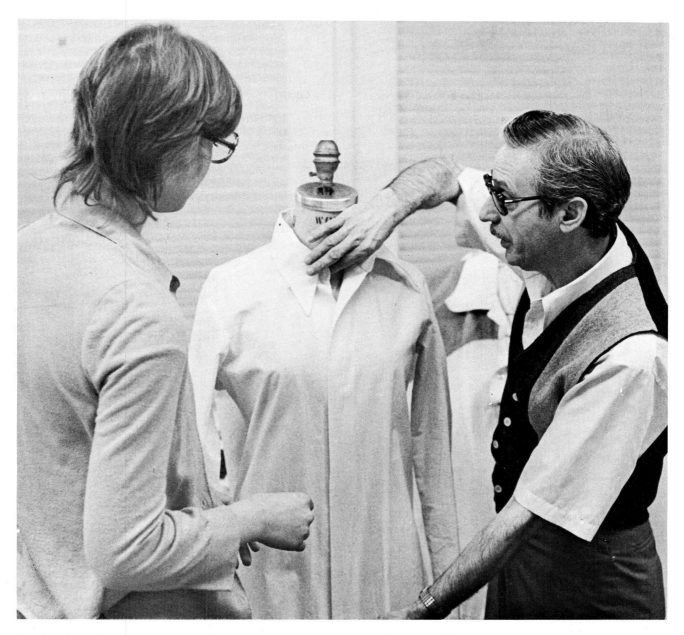

Production Conference Production man Sam Patti works closely with the patternmaker to anticipate any problems that may arise in cutting, making, or sewing.

ion drawings—broad shoulders, narrow hips, long legs—so they can show samples with great elegance and chic.

The more expensive houses use tall women for models, popular-priced houses may use shorter models, and the least expensive, or budget, houses show the garments on hangers.

The production patternmaker cuts an accurate or perfect pattern for each sample chosen for the line. He or she may look at the sample garment on a dress

Showroom Personnel: Selling The showroom personnel have two important responsibilities—selling the line and guiding the buyers in their selections.

form and take measurements or look at the original sample room pattern. The result is a pattern in the stock pattern size (whatever regular size the house uses as a standard). Usually this is a size 10 or 12 in the missy range and a size 7 or 9 in the junior range. The patternmaker can drape or use the flat method to duplicate the sample. Additionally, the pattern-maker tries to simplify the pattern because a factory seamstress will be constructing the garment later, not a skilled sample maker.

The patternmaker has a stock sample cut and made in the factory to "prove" the new pattern. Fre-

quently he or she will have to make several production samples before the fit and the pattern are perfected. The production sample is fitted on a fitting model, a woman whose measurements are the commercial measurements for the stock size. The stock sample is compared with the original designer sample to see that the duplicate fits properly and that the duplicate is as smart as the original. If the designer has a good understanding of garment construction, the sample will be designed with seams in the proper places. Otherwise, the patternmaker may have to change the lines of the garment so it can be cut in a standard way and laid out economically.

The designer usually joins the head of production, the head of sales, and the production pattern person to discuss the final garment that is chosen as the style for stock (garments that are manufactured and sent to the stores).

DISTRIBUTION

The sales department consists of the head of sales (also called a merchandise person) and the salespeople who work under his or her direction. Often included on the staff is a showroom girl. The showroom girl is in charge of the showroom and the models, maintains the line in good shape, and keeps up the book of sketches and swatches. She compiles and records all orders placed, handles special orders and trim replacements, and manages other details relating to retail stores and their orders.

Buyers from retail stores in all parts of the country are invited to visit the showroom for seasonal showings. Between showroom visits, buyers replenish their stock in the following three ways:

1. A buyer may reorder runners (styles that sell well and have been recut several times) by phone, following up with written confirmation order (called *paper*).
2. Company salespeople regularly visit established customers, taking some numbers from the line—especially new styles added since the line opened—as well as a book of illustrations and a complete set of swatches. In low-priced houses, most contact with buyers may be made this way.
3. As a rule, a retail store is affiliated with a buying office. In this way, groups of retail stores in different cities can join in a loose federation to obtain up-to-date information on the market. When

Showroom Personnel: Sales Records The showroom personnel must also maintain accurate sales records. They follow up with the stores that have purchased the styles as orders are shipped. Reorders are handled through the showroom staff.

45

buyers go to New York or California, their buying office may brief them on "resources," as the wholesalers are called. If needed, buying office representatives may help out-of-town buyers in the market. Buying offices constantly review the local market and the lines in their price and size area. They furnish member stores with information on new items and new resources by publishing bulletins and presenting fashion shows during market weeks. Furthermore, a buying office may purchase merchandise for member stores between the regular buyer's visits.

The designer will often begin a new season by presenting the line to the sales staff and explaining the styling and theme at a sales meeting. Often the designer will join the sales staff when they are working the line with a buyer who makes many purchases or who represents a prestigious store. Sometimes the buyer will arrange an in-store promotion when a designer visits. A newspaper advertisement or fashion show (called a *trunk show* if the merchandise shown is for the next season) will be planned to bring in more customers than usual. This gives the designer an opportunity to see the garments on a variety of customers.

A sales-oriented manufacturer will go to great lengths to provide services for retail customers. An initial order may not be large because the buyer is waiting to see how well the stock is made and how it sells on the floor. The numbers that *check* (sell well) are reordered in greater quantity, so small initial sales may lead to profitable sales later. The styles that do not sell are ignored and then marked down for the sale racks. A buyer learns what types of garment sell best and who manufactures the garments by analyzing sales records. The records show how many pieces have sold in each style, size, and color. Armed with this information, a buyer will return to a manufacturer to reorder hot items and try new styles. The manufacturer and the retailer establish a good relationship based on their understanding that good styling means profits for both.

CUSTOM DESIGN

The smallest manufacturing firm is the single designer or seamstress who creates garments for private customers. This person handles all the aspects of the business we have outlined. This is an awesome task

Eli Sobel · Image Makers

117 w. 9th street, los angeles, california 90015 (213) 627-5921

mailing address: p.o. box 15265, los angeles, california 90015

DEPT — MODERATE DRESSES

DELY: 9/15 Comp
TERMS: 8/10 EOM

#8374/$40.00

2 pc. soft bateau neck,
long fitted sleeve,
elastic waist skirt,
dropped yoke, softly
gathered —
100% Polyester Matte Jersey.
3 asst. prints-Black with
Multi Brights
6-16

CASEY MORTON, BUYER
SANDY RICHMAN, M.M.

CAREER DRESSING
BY
Mel Naftal
120 E. 8th St.
Los Angeles, CA

Buying Office Bulletin Bulletins cover new resources and noteworthy styles. Bulletins help the buyers preview what the local market will have to offer during the next buying trip. (Courtesy of Eli Sobel–Image Makers and Mel Naftal.)

for one person, even though that person may produce a limited amount of merchandise. Many designers prefer to work on a small scale because they are not hampered by the creative limitations imposed by mass production. Custom designers enjoy enhancing the appearance of clients directly without the barriers of a salesperson and a store.

The custom designer should have a good grasp of patternmaking to have flexibility in creating designs. A knowledge of fitting is essential. Usually the custom designer pads out a commercial dress form to represent a client's figure. A good sketch artist can save many long hours of sales time by sketching garments for clients before they are fitted in the first muslin.

Purchasing fabrics is usually a problem for the small designer because he or she often does not purchase enough of one fabric to buy wholesale. Good fabric stores will often sell small amounts of fabric at a discount to an independent designer because the designer will purchase a great deal of fabric over the year. In addition, a custom designer can obtain a resale number from the state in which he or she works that allows that designer to purchase materials at a discount and eliminates sales tax on items for resale.

The custom designer often hires a skilled seamstress to assist in producing the actual garments. A good accountant is a great help to the independent and will often assist the designer in determining a fair markup figure to charge so the business will be profitable.

Sales are best promoted by word of mouth. A satisfied customer will bring friends to the designer who creates attractive garments. Some custom designers will participate in fashion shows for women's groups. This is an expensive but effective way to solicit clients. Often people who are hard to fit in commercial garments make valuable return customers. Advertisements in local newspapers and magazines will also attract clients.

MANUFACTURING CATEGORIES

Buyers return to their established resources for a specific type of styling, so a designer may be successful at one house and unsuccessful at another. For a designer to be successful, his or her natural taste must find expression. A person develops a taste level by constant exposure to fine merchandise in stores, in publications, and on the streets. Good taste is the ability to recognize styles that will appeal to a specific segment of the market. The beginner should try to develop a feeling for one kind of apparel, a kind he or she particularly enjoys creating. However, before the designer begins to concentrate on one area, he or she should gain experience in several different areas. Fortunately, the beginner has a wide choice of areas in apparel design.

Successful designers do not design commercial garments for themselves. Designers create a product for a specific customer and are usually most successful when they view the customer objectively and do not impose personal design restrictions on their product. For example, the designer with a figure problem should not design a line just to camouflage that problem. The woman designer who is sensitive to a specialty customer, the petite woman or a large size figure, should identify with the design problems involved in creating apparel to flatter these figure types without confusing the problems with those of her own figure. Often men are successful designing women's apparel because of their objectivity. More and more women designers are entering the men's wear field for the same reason.

The following list describes the many categories of apparel. Remember that this list is even further divided by price ranges—budget, moderate, better, and designer—so there are many areas of apparel production available to creative designers.

Age and Category: Size divisions in women's apparel

    Women, half-sizes, large women, talls
    Missy and junior
    Junior petite, subteen
    Children (3 to 6x and 7 to 14), toddlers, infants
    Contemporary

Use Divisions in Apparel: Garments generally made for each price level

    Daytime dresses
    Cocktail and evening wear, formals
    Sportswear, separates, knits
    Coats and suits, rainwear, outerwear
    Specialized garments
        Uniforms, work clothes
        Active sportswear, bathing suits
        Bridal wear
        Maternity
        Theatrical costumers

Missy Dress The missy dress is more sophisticated than the junior dress. It is designed to be worn by a more mature customer.

Contemporary Garment The contemporary garment has less structure and is generally more body-conscious than a missy garment.

Intimate apparel
    Sleepwear
    At-home, robes
    Lingerie, slips
    Foundation garments, girdles, bras

Miscellaneous:

    Blouses, shirts, tops
    Accessories (shawls, scarves, and so forth)
    Shoes, bags, gloves, neckwear, and so on

Millinery

Missy and junior are the two major divisions in women's apparel. Missy garments are styled for a mature figure—that is, a woman with a back neck-to-waist measurement of about 16½ inches for a size 10. This customer has a full bust and slightly larger hips than a comparable junior size. The term *missy* defines a size range as well as a type of styling that is usually conservative or very basic. Actually, a vast range of styles is included in missy garments, from basic (sometimes called "dumb" because frequent repetition has made the styling predictable and easy for many women to wear) to high fashion. The term *contemporary* is used to describe garments made in the missy size range but with the most current styling.

A junior garment is cut with a shorter back neck-to-waist measurement than the comparable missy size. The customer who wears this kind of garment tends to be younger than the missy customer. Like the missy category, the junior category has a range of looks, from young apparel designed for a schoolgirl to more sophisticated styling designed for the young career woman. The career category is often called *contemporary junior*, and the styles fit a figure shorter and younger than the missy figure.

Double-ticketing is the practice of using both junior and missy sizing on a ticket. The garment may be labeled 9/10 or 11/12. This was first done in an effort to capture a greater range of customers. Usually the garment will fit a standard missy or junior figure. There is no way of regulating how a garment fits, and therefore there is a tremendous range of standards for each size. Mass merchandisers like Sears and J. C. Penney have tried to eliminate size differences among the manufacturers who sell them merchandise by making them all conform to the same body measurements for each size ordered. The independent manufacturer prizes its "fit" as just right for its particular customer, so size standards in the industry as a whole vary greatly.

It is most important for a manufacturer to define the customer. If a line lacks price and consumer definition, the buyer will not know where to sell the merchandise. Department stores especially plan their departments to carry particular items within a particular price range. The items are allocated on the basis of image (or styling reputation) and price. A specific image will concentrate the impact of the merchandise and give the designer a focal point for styling.

Consider the many jobs described in these two chapters. Apparel firms of every kind and in every price range need many specialized people to make them function. Many manufacturers hire a staff designer. For a young person who has developed skills in designing, patternmaking, sewing, and other areas of production, the opportunities are abundant. The desire to work hard in an exciting, fast-paced, ever-changing industry, the ability to master technical skills, and the determination to cultivate a sense of taste are the necessary ingredients for a successful career in apparel manufacturing.

INTERVIEWING FOR A JOB

Portfolio and Résumé

A *portfolio* is a representative collection of a designer's best work. The material should represent the kind of work the designer wants to be hired for, but not be so narrow that more general jobs are eliminated in the eyes of the interviewer. A manufacturer will often ask a prospective designer to design some garments that would be appropriate for its line. This is a fair request as long as the designer does not leave the sketches with the manufacturer before being hired for the job.

A résumé is a brief summary of work experience and education. The résumé is headed with name, address, and phone number. Work experience should be listed by date and employer. List the most recent job first, include a brief description of the job and specific duties. List schools attended and awards and degrees received. Type neatly on one page. Professional résumé services will write and print a résumé for a fee.

The student should collect school projects and review them with an instructor before graduation to evaluate the strengths and weaknesses of the portfolio. Ask for suggestions for filling gaps in your work. Students are wise not to be too specific about the type of design they want to do after leaving school. A period of apprenticeship as an assistant designer to gain a concrete idea of the requirements of a specific job will enable you to develop more realistic career goals.

Research a company before an employment interview. Shop a manufacturer's line and then select designs from your pool of work that are suitable or slightly more fashionable than the apparel produced by that company.

Select material from your designs that looks as though it was done by one person. Make sure you show enough variety to emphasize your strengths. A portfolio is often judged by its weakest example, not its strongest. Show from 12 to 15 pieces of work. Make sure the illustrations are clean and neatly mounted or matted. Published material is especially effective because it shows that your designs were significant enough to be advertised by retailers.

The job seeker is evaluated in many ways. The total package is important. Dress in a businesslike manner for the interview. Stress your desire to participate in the team effort needed to make the company a success. A huge portfolio is awkward to look at and spoils the image of the person carrying it. A portfolio should be a neat, flat case of a reasonable size containing your well-edited designs. Actual garments can be taken to show sewing skills if that is important for the job, or slides of garments can be added to the portfolio.

Preparation for the Interview

To avoid excessive nervousness, prepare carefully for the interview. Here are some important tips:

1. Know the exact time and place of the interview. Make an appointment to speak with the proper person. Arrive on time or a few minutes early. Know the interviewer's full name (and how to pronounce it) and title.
2. Investigate the company. Shop the line of a manufacturer, or at least a store that carries the kind of merchandise it makes.
3. Prepare questions to ask the interviewer. Accepting a job is a two-way street. Ask about growth potential and advancement possibilities.

4. Fill out an employment application neatly (in pen) and completely. Bring two copies of your résumé and leave one with the application. Give the other one to the interviewer.

5. Greet the interviewer by name. Shake hands firmly. Smile and be as relaxed as possible. Listen and respond alertly to questions. Look the interviewer in the eye as you speak.

6. Do not chew gum or smoke.

7. Ask about the requirements of the job as early in the interview as possible. Then you will be able to relate your skills and abilities to those requirements. Be prepared to answer questions about your goals and abilities. Show your portfolio as reinforcement for your career goals.

8. Answer questions truthfully and as to the point as possible. Do not overanswer questions. Do not make derogatory remarks about present or former employers.

9. Ask for the job if you are interested in accepting the position. Accept an offer on the spot if you want the job. If necessary, arrange a specific time to think it over. Call the interviewer with a response even if you have decided not to take the job.

10. Thank the interviewer for his or her time and consideration. In several days, follow up with a note summarizing your interest in the job.

REVIEW

Word Finders

Define the following words from the chapter you just read:

1. Buying office
2. Check out
3. Completion date
4. Double-ticket
5. Drape
6. Duplicate
7. First pattern
8. Fitting model
9. Hand
10. Hanger appeal
11. Illustration
12. Muslin
13. Portfolio
14. Prêt-à-porter
15. Refabricate
16. Resource
17. Résumé
18. Run with a hot number
19. Sample maker
20. Showroom girl
21. Silhouette
22. Stock pattern
23. Version
24. Weed the line
25. Working sketch

A typical junior garment.

Discussion Questions

1. List and discuss the requirements for a successful style.
2. What are the designer's responsibilities outside the design room?
3. How does a buyer contact the manufacturer between trips to the market?
4. Explain the two meanings of the term *missy*.

3.
organization of a line

Organizing a line is one of the designer's most important functions. To coordinate a group of styles so that the styles reflect a theme, the designer must have a feeling for merchandising apparel. Actually, the designer's organizing groups is very similar to the buyer's selecting merchandise for the store. The buyer must consider a variety of customer likes and dislikes and offer customers a range of colors, sizes, and styles. This range or selection is called an *assortment*. The designer does the same thing as the buyer when he or she plans a line by the group method. Generally, the designer offers more selections than the average buyer will buy. The designer realizes that because of price considerations, some pieces will fall out (not be sold in sufficient quantity to be cut), so he or she must design enough pieces to give buyers a choice. Sometimes a designer tries out a styling idea just to get buyers' reactions. Although the experiment may be a failure, it could be a success because the style is unique or high-fashion for the market.

There are several ways of organizing a line of merchandise. The more typical are (1) item lines and (2) groups of styles constructed from one fabric or the same combinations of fabrics. Some manufacturers combine the two approaches.

ITEM LINES

These lines are the simplest to define and understand. They consist of hot items—that is, items that have checked out in the stores or sold well at the buyer level for other manufacturers. The item house will sell each item alone, without a coordinated group, and try to sell a large volume so the house can order enough fabric to get a good price and delivery date. Many times the fabric has already proved its ability to please customers.

Often the item house is a *knock off* house; the house makes direct copies of other garments. A knock off house can offer a lower-priced garment because it reduces overhead. One way to reduce overhead is to shop the stores for hot items and eliminate a designer. The item house may purchase designs from free-lance designers who are paid a commission. The advantages of buying from an item house are lower prices and usually rapid delivery. Often a buyer will find a good item at a high price and buy it in small quantity. Then the buyer will have the high-priced garment copied by an item house and order it in volume at a lower price.

An item house has to be fast in production and promotion. The person who selects items for the line must be aware of current best sellers, so he or she

constantly shops the stores. Speed is essential in this kind of operation because usually the house carries the item for as long as it continues to sell at retail. Many item houses are found where merchandise is sold in volume, such as in discount stores, catalog and mail-order houses, and large chain retailers.

Item houses can also sell expensive garments. Usually higher-priced houses are built around one or two items that are interesting enough to be used as attention-getting garments in a department store or boutique. Manufacturers who import handmade garments from countries with *cottage workers* (people who work on garments in their own homes) are typical of item houses that handle expensive and unique items.

GROUP LINES

Group lines are organized around fabric groups. Depending on the type of line and the importance of a fabric, some garments are designed for each fabric. This type of organization has the following advantages:

1. The most seasonable fabric groups can be cut first and shipped to the stores before late-season fabrics. For example, a dress house tries to ship heavyweight cottons for early spring selling because the weather is still quite cool in February and March. The dress house follows this group with single-knit synthetics and then a lightweight cotton-polyester voile for early summer selling.
2. If several styles in a group do not sell, other styles will usually be strong enough to carry the fabric. Often the designer will fill in groups after they have been shown to buyers for a few weeks. The styles that have not sold will be dropped, and new numbers will be added to strengthen the group.
3. Several garments can be offered to a buyer for multi-item newspaper advertisements and window and floor displays. When a sportswear or coordinate company uses the group line method, it can add items to the basic units to generate sales.
4. When a line is unique, a buyer will frequently buy enough garments from different groups by the same manufacturer to fill an area of the store or department. This creates a visual impact, and the "department within a department" draws the

customer who seeks a special look. The customer will find preferred merchandise stocked in depth and will not be forced to search through racks of less exciting garments.

5. Because several items in each group probably will be good sellers, the manufacturer can order the fabric in quantity. With sufficient quantity, a manufacturer can recolor prints, demanding its own colors, and perhaps bargain for a better price per yard. Some manufacturers order enough yardage to confine a print, type of fabric, or special color to their price and style category.

6. By varying the type and cost of the groups, greater variety of price and styling can be incorporated in the line. The less expensive fabrics can be made into more complicated garments and be more lavishly trimmed.

7. A *story* or styling theme is best developed by designing similar items in one fabric. A strong style story is easy to advertise, and advertising money can be solicited from fiber companies on the basis of fashion-right garments and large fabric purchases.

8. A good body with a strong sales record can be offered in several different fabrics at various prices to cover a range of shipping dates. The overhead for reorders and previously developed styles is much less because the patternmaking and grading have been done already.

9. Well-developed groups, consistent in color story and styling, will look as if they have been created by one person—they will have an image and identity. You must remember this point when you consider merchandising single-unit items like dresses, coats, and suits, which do not have to coordinate within a group. A manufacturer strives to create a strong identity because many lines are so similar. When a buyer walks into a showroom, he or she should feel the strong visual presence of a well-developed theme.

Merchandise must be presented to many people before it reaches the individual consumer, and a well-organized line is easy to sell at each level of the merchandising process. The designer must present the line to her boss and the salespeople. She should motivate them with her own enthusiasm. If the salespeople understand the designer's motivation, they can incorporate her fashion research and theme development into their sales pitch when they present the line to buyers. In turn, buyers can repeat the information to salespeople in their stores, which may help motivate store personnel to sell the merchandise to the consumer. The consumer must be stimulated to take the garments to the fitting room, try them on, and finally purchase them.

The designer should plan a line so all styles have a consistent visual image. The colors should be seasonal, fashion right, and offer enough diversity to encourage buyers to purchase many items from the line. The styling within each group should have variety, yet each piece should develop the same theme. A *theme* is a styling detail, trim, or color story that is used consistently throughout the group. Variety of styling means that there should be, for example, different sleeve treatments or a selection of details and necklines. No piece should be so similar to another that the second piece "steals" a share of the first piece's potential sales. The group may have a *price leader,* a garment slightly less expensive than the others. This garment might be a repeat of a proved body, in which case the garment is less expensive because the production pattern and grading phase of production have already been paid for. Then again, the price leader may take less yardage or be easier to sew than other styles in the group. Often the price leader becomes the best seller just because it is the least expensive style in the group.

The designer cannot accompany each garment to the stores and explain his fashion story to salespeople and customers, so the garments must speak for themselves. As mentioned, the garment must stimulate the customer to take it off the rack and into the fitting room. Garments that are not single-unit items should suggest coordination visually because this is the only way to bypass an uncreative salesperson and stimulate an unimaginative customer. If these garments by themselves make a strong visual statement, the customer will find it easier to coordinate them. For example, the consumer should be able to add a shirt and a jacket to a pair of pants to create an outfit.

Developing a Group: Coordinated Sportswear

> Category: Junior contemporary
> Price range: Moderate
> Theme: Men's wear fabric and styling in gray and black flannel combined with a gray pinstripe and accented with a Fair Isle sweater group

Season: Early fall (delivery to stores, July 30 complete—selling time, August through October)

This styling demonstrates organization, not current fashion. Trends, hot items, and fashion change constantly vary the type, size, and price range of a line. The number of items in a group depends on the size of the line and the importance of the fabric as predicted by the manufacturer. The availability of fabric and the shipping date in relation to the season will influence how many pieces are made.

This group has been designed in smaller coordinated units that may be worn as mixed or matched

Black flannel
wool blend

Banker's stripe
wool suiting

Tweed sweaters

Fair Isle Sweaters

gray flannel
wool blend

Blouses in
poly/cotton
blend

Coordinated Group

61

outfits. The matched outfits will have a formal, dressier look that will be easily understood by the more conservative customer. Mixed, or mismatched, outfits have a trendier look for a more experimental customer. Study how the garments may be combined, then look at the diagram on page 61, which shows how the group has been planned. When a group has many optional combinations and appeals to both conservative and innovative customers, sales can be increased.

Developing a Group: Dresses

Category: Missy
Price range: Moderate
Theme: Color blocking on white grounds in cotton poplin
Season: Summer (delivery, March 30 complete—selling time, April through June)

A dress group does not require the coordination a sportswear group does. The dresses should have variety and a loose theme, making them easy to display and advertise together. For example, a buyer could advertise the two-piece blouson with either of the one-piece dresses.

Often a selection of "print bodies" (styles simple enough to be made in a variety of prints) are grouped together. These print groups may be sold assorted— that is, the buyer selects bodies, then various prints from a specific group are randomly cut in the bodies. A specific body in a specific print may also be sold.

PLANNING THE COLOR STORY

The master colors selected for a line should include

1. Some fashion colors
2. Some staple colors (typically a shade of blue and a shade of pink, neutrals like black and white, and so on)
3. Warm colors
4. Cool colors
5. Neutrals and darks

The colors should reflect

1. The season. They should be appropriate but differ from last season's colors.
2. The market they are designed for. For example,

California colors typically are lighter and brighter than colors selected for New York lines.

3. The type of merchandise. Specialized apparel, like bathing suits or bridal gowns, will differ radically from other RTW (ready-to-wear) areas.

4. The color groups should be varied enough to offer the buyer a range of appropriate and attractive colors throughout the shipping season.

Usually the designer chooses eight to twelve colors for the master color story. Each color is not used in each group, but each color is used at least once in the line. Frequently staple fabrics are offered in three or more colors, and novelty fabrics and prints are offered in two. The actual color selection depends on the individual designer's taste. The designer will re-

Print Dress Group A print dress depends on a strong silhouette and few details or trims. A group should offer a variety of sleeve and neckline styles.

view all color predictions for the coming season and choose colors that are appropriate for her line.

Occasionally a designer will ignore the market's general trend and make a very personal statement through the use of unusual colors. This plan succeeds only in a better-priced line, where a strong designer image appeals to a fashion-conscious customer. The designer will have to develop fabric converters who are willing to work with special colors. But the extra trouble is worth it if the color story is unusual and used consistently in exciting, well-designed garments.

When choosing colors, the best guide is: *Whatever choice you make, be consistent, offer enough variety, and develop the color theme in all groups.*

Fabric Boards

The designer should organize all fabrics chosen for each group on a *fabric board* and record all the necessary style information beside each swatch. This will become the central reference for fabric and styling decisions as the line develops. Use white illustration board and tape the fabric samples to it as they are selected. A sportswear fabric board should be about 20 by 30 inches because of the many components required in each group. A dress board can be smaller; 10 by 15 inches is usually adequate. After the fabrications are approved by management, all the fabric and trim information can be transferred to a list and given to the stock fabric purchasing person.

Note the following information on each board:

1. Season and year group is planned for; name of the group.
2. Name of the mill, name and phone number of both the regional and the New York (or principal) salesperson.
3. Style and quality number, pattern and color name and number, width of the fabric, fiber content and fiber mill, price (you may wish to code the fabric price if the board is used to discuss the line with buyers).
4. Trims and their style numbers, sources, and prices.
5. *Croquis* (the painted swatch of a print before it is printed on the fabric), and the finished swatch of the print.
6. *Lab dips* (small patches of colored fabric submitted to the designer to establish a match with other fabrics in the group) and their color numbers.

COUNTRY CLOTH

Charter — Los Angeles = "Exacta" - Tony Richardson 627·3232
New York = Jerry Hertz = 212·391·8110

#28151   58/60   HANK SALM   Hank Salm =
                                    L.A -
                    60 cotton   Mike Bernette
                    40 polyester   624·8311
                #3·45   N.Y
                    800 yard minimum Hank
                    warp per color   212·489·3736

PLAID SHIRTING

CHARTER CHAMBRAY
50% Polyester (DuPont)
50% Cotton
#50-21

Alexander Barloe
#2·35
100% polyester (TRIVERA)
683·
623·
Color 18
blue/yellow
58/60

HANDLOOM 3466·MI

(for color only)

CUSTOM BLAZER STRIPE

HANDLOOM· 3466·MI2

Stock Color

bold yellow #36

LA = Jim Weiss → 689·8211
NY = Barnie Feldman - 212·469·8320

STRIPE SHIRTING →

PRINT SHIRTING

Bibb
50 cotton/
50 poly
44-45" #1.12
yellow-white = Color 7
#4320 (stock colors)

Stock color

pink #24

Stock color

Bibb — color 5

LA = Joe Borea → 628·5144
NY = Fred Henry → 212·623·8413

(croquis - for color)

HAMPTON   58/60
"SHADOWS" 100% polyester
Custom color - #2·35

Steve Braun
(LA) - 623·3033

Sandra Couture
(NY) 212·921·2490

HAMPTON
(for color only)
"SHADOWS"
Pink/WHT - color 1

ALEXANDER BARLOE
683·623· Color 82

Chambray blue #30

→ 100 yard dye lots — 2 week turn time on stock colors — 6 for custom colors

HAMPTON
"SHADOWS"
Blue/white
Color 2

Bibb = color 1   Bob Everson - 469·1210 (local mill)

MELODY
100% cotton
58/60
off white
custom dip
#483-6
$1.25

SOLID SHIRTING

Custom dip - off white
#846-3

minimum dye lot = 900 yards

24 l.

BUTTONS   629·8642
FASHION NOVELTY - BERT COHN
"RIA" - pearl only - not dyable
18 l = $7.00 per gross
24 l = $8.75 "   "
30 l = $11.50 "   "

7. Clip or tape duplicate fabric orders to the back of the board. As you check on duplicate delivery, note the shipping date on the order. Check regularly with the fabric supplier to make sure the duplicate yardage will be delivered in time to produce and ship the duplicates.

Fabric boards may be used when discussing the line with other members of the merchandise development team so they are constantly aware of what has been planned and purchased for each group. Fabric boards can also be used when discussing future fabrications with buyers prior to the completion of the line. They form a valuable record of how each season was planned and what colors and fabrics were run, and they should be kept as a reference.

Designer Work Boards

A designer creates many garments for each group that are discarded before the group is finalized and sold to the stores. To keep track of all the styles, the designer should work up a *style board* for each group. Again, use white illustration board, a large size for coordinated sportswear and a smaller size for item lines. Divide the board into small boxes by categories when doing a sportswear board. Jackets, skirts, pants, blouses, and novelty items like sweaters would be typical categories. Sketch all the items you design for the group and want to present at the merchandising meeting. Use the board as a guide during the meeting to record changes that are to be made to pieces that are accepted in the line. Cross out rejected garments. Use this board as a guide in the design room so the pattern and sample makers can remember which garments have been made into a pattern and cut and sewn. Keep track of all the items in each group by numbering the styles to go into the group. The work board is a handy tool to use when deciding

◄ **The Fabric Board** Swatches of all the fabrics that comprise the group should be taped to the fabric board. Often the designer will have to cut small pieces of the base goods colors off the swatches and leave them with other fabric resources to match the colors of the base goods to the shirting prints and solids. If all the phone numbers of the resources are included on this master board, follow-up is easy. Often a designer will take these boards to New York from a regional market to complete the fabric story.

COUNTRY CLOTH

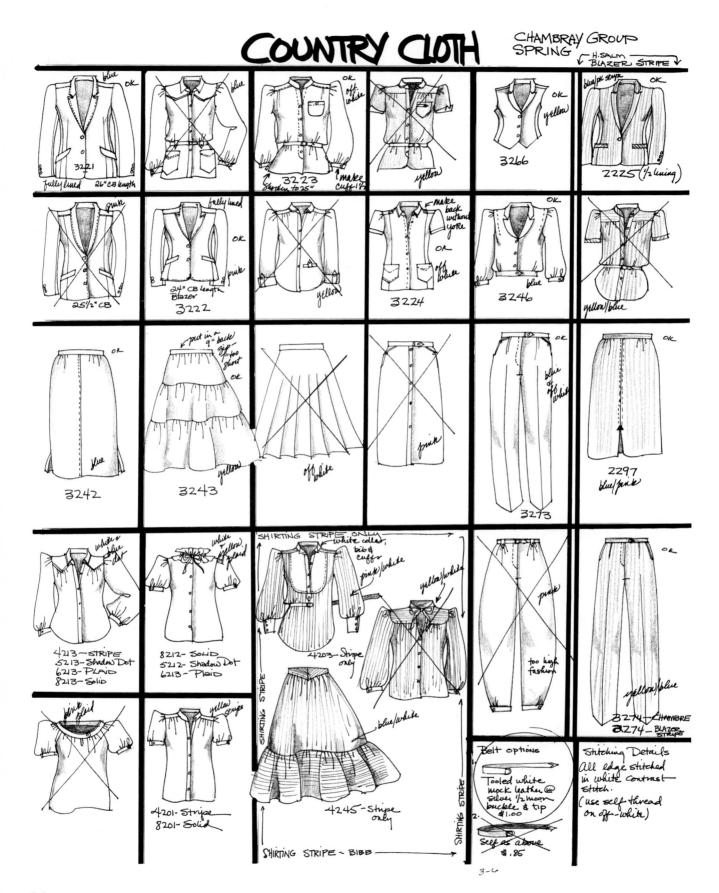

blue   OK
3221
fully lined   26" CB length

blue

OK
off white
3223
shorten to 25"   make cuff 1½"

OK
yellow

OK yellow
3266

blue/pk stripe   OK
2225 (½ lining)

pink
25½" CB

fully lined
OK
pink
24" CB length
Blazer
3222

yellow

make back without yoke
OK
off white
3224

OK
blue
3246

yellow/blue

OK
3242
blue

put in a 9" back zip. Too short
OK
3243
yellow

off white

pink

OK
blue & white
3273

OK
2297
blue/pink

white & blue dot
4213 — STRIPE
5213 — Shadow Dot
6213 — PLAID
8213 — Solid

white + yellow plaid
8212 — SOLID
5212 — Shadow Dot
6213 — Plaid

SHIRTING STRIPE ONLY
white collar, bib & cuffs
pink/white
4203 — Stripe only

yellow/white
blue/white
4245 — Stripe only
SHIRTING STRIPE
SHIRTING STRIPE — BIBB

pink
too high fashion

OK
yellow/blue
3274 — CHAMBRE
3274 — BLAZER STRIPE

pink plaid

yellow stripe
4201 — Stripe
8201 — Solid

Belt options
1. Tooled white mock leather w/ silver ½ moon buckle & tip $1.00
2. Self as above $.85
3 — 6

Stitching Details
All edge stitched in white contrast stitch.
(use self thread on off-white)

68

in which colors to duplicate all the samples that go to the salespeople.

These two reference tools, the fabric board and the designer work board, will have all the necessary information to write up the cost sheets on each item in the line. Use them to compile all the details, like number and size of the buttons, special trim prices and sources, description of the sample and its style number.

ORGANIZING THE GROUPS TO FORM A LINE

The number of groups depends on the size of the manufacturer, the season, and other considerations. The fabrics should vary in price so that the manufacturer can produce a variety of garments in a general price range, although the firm will want to emphasize its strong price point. The higher the fabric price, the less complicated the garment must be. Garments requiring more yardage than average must be cut from the less expensive fabrics so that no garment will exceed the price range of the line.

The fabric groups should vary in weight and type as well as in price. Just as similar styles can steal sales from one another, similar fabric groups will share sales and detract from one another. Competing fabrics can be made to work in the same line if the designer offers separate color ranges and groups with completely different themes.

Staple fabrics, also called *base goods* (solid colors or classical patterns like gingham), are usually offered in a large range of colors and styling, unlike the range for novelty groups. Many considerations

---

◀ **Designer Work Board** All the workers in the design room use the board to guide them through the cutting, patternmaking, and sewing of the samples. In this way, no pieces are lost. The designer can take this board to the merchandise meeting and note corrections that must be made on the first samples before they can be duplicated. Then the line can be numbered and the colors for the duplicates worked out from this master sheet. Notice how two belts were developed for the group so the merchandising team could have a selection. Preparation and anticipation of problems will save a designer a great deal of time in reworking the sample line.

may alter this typical way of organizing a line, so flexibility in planning is important. Very small lines may offer only two or three fabric groups but many styles within the groups. They try to capture a segment of the market in depth, thereby creating an impact, rather than selling random styles that will be scattered throughout a store or department. If fabric resources are limited, a manufacturer may decide to offer only one or two kinds of fabric. This method is particularly successful with prints. One or two fabric groups and many prints can be expanded into an entire line.

EVOLUTION OF A GROUP

Trace the evolution of the styles in the group illustrated. Notice the styles that drop out when the group is weeded. Best sellers develop after the line has been shown for several weeks. During the first week or two of selling, fill-in styles may be added and weak styles dropped. From this final group, the best sellers will emerge, but they must be proved in the store to become reorders. This process usually takes several months, depending on the time needed to produce the garments, ship them to the store, and analyze customer reaction. Because of this time lag, best sellers are frequently refabricated and offered in the next line.

COSTING A GARMENT

When a sample goes into production, the designer must complete a cost sheet that provides basic information on the sample. The designer should carefully fill in the information about fabric, interfacing, trims, and so on. Then the same sheet will be reworked by the production person to determine labor costs and the amount of fabric the garment will require when it is cut from the production marker. The production person is more interested than the designer in the cost of labor.

Analyzing a Cost Sheet

INFORMATION AREA

1. Date. Important in determining if the fabric price on the cost sheet is still accurate. The cost of piece goods fluctuates with supply and demand.

Missy Dresses • Fall • Matte Jersey solids 100% polyester Colors = Burgundy Royal Pearl grey	One piece peplum dress	one piece with shirred waist	wrap tie with asymmetrical closing	"sweatshirt" neckline 2 piece blouson		
reaction at Market week	poor	good	excellent	excellent		
reaction in store	not cut	good +	average — customer probably confused with wrap tie	excellent — consistent reorder at retail		
next season:	dropped	run again in different fabrics & prints as a promotional body. sells well at retail for 3 additional seasons (shorten sleeves for Spring!)	dropped	develope "versions" and re-fabricate in several different prints and novelties	shorten sleeves and offer again for Spring →	offer as summer promotion at lower prices in many prints

natural waist one piece

shift

Float with short sleeves

Short sleeve 2 piece Blouson

DATE _8.8.83_   STYLE No. _8074_

DESCRIPTION _"Sweatshirt" neckline blouson_   SEASON _Fall '84_

With Elasticized shirring on back belt   SELLING PRICE: _41.00_

SIZE RANGE _6-14_   COLORS _Burgandy, Royal, Silver = "Mad Plaid"_

MARKERS _44/45"_

MARKER YARDAGE: ALLOWANCE: _-0- Japanese goods_

SKETCH

1. MATERIAL	YARDS	PRICE	AMT.
Merry Mary "Mad Plaid"	_2½y_	_3.90_	_9.75_
Base = 3.75 + .05 delivery + .10 inspection			
~~Inter~~ Lining _Pellon TD47_	_⅕y_	_.55_	_.11_
TOTAL MATERIAL COST			_9.86_

2. TRIMMINGS	QUANT.	PRICE	AMT.
Fashion Novelty Buttons _#410 - 18 line_	_4_	_2.00gr_	_.06_
Pads			
Embroidery			
Belts			
Zippers _10"_	_1_	_.13_	_.13_
Pleating, Tucking			
Elastic Shirring "Mr Pleat"	_1_	_.55_	_.55_
TOTAL TRIMMINGS COST			_.74_

10.60 Total material

3. LABOR			
Cutting _$75 (based on 200 unit minimum)_			_.38_
Labor _(Mr Soo)_	_$7.00_		_7.00_
Marking $45-			_.23_
Grading $70-			_.35_
Payroll Taxes & Health Fund			
Trucking			
TOTAL LABOR COST			_7.96_

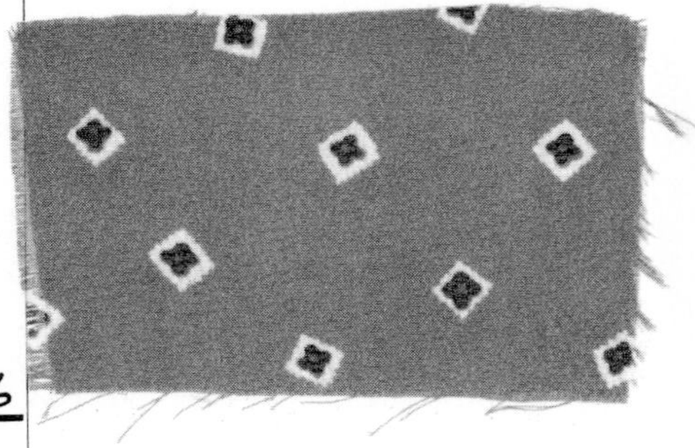

4. TOTAL COST			_18.56_

REMARKS

MATERIAL SWATCH

ADAMS PRESS, 830 SO. BROADWAY, L. A. 14, MADISON 7-2151   FORM NO. 32

The cost of sample yardage may differ from the cost of stock yardage if a larger quantity is being purchased. Often a larger purchase means a lower price.

2. Description. A word description of the style. Sometimes a dress will be given a nickname by the designer or salesperson.

3. Size range. Sizes in which the style will be offered.

4. Colors. Colors in which the style will be offered.

5. Style number. For each garment, manufacturers develop a numbering code that represents the season, fabric, and pattern. For example, a manufacturer will choose the 8000 series for the fall season and break down the style number as follows:

Fall season ⟶ 8 0 7 4

8000 = basic fabric group (gauze in this example)   designates the number of the pattern

The same body in a different fabric would be numbered like this:

Holiday season ⟶ 9 0 7 4

9000 series = brocade   same body as above

6. Season. *selling* season of the garment (not when the garment was designed).

7. Selling price. the garment's selling price is usually determined before production costs.

8. Marker. Specifies the width of the marker, which is usually 1 inch narrower than the fabric to compensate for slight variations in fabric width.

9. Marker yardage and allowance. The total marker length is averaged to determine the amount of fabric needed to cut all sizes. Fabrics with damages and the end cut fallout (small lengths of fabric not long enough for another garment piece) will generally add 5 percent to the marker yardage. This additional amount is added to the marker yardage when estimating the order for piece goods and when calculating the final amount of fabric used for each garment.

MATERIALS SECTION

1. Base goods. An additional amount must be added to the base price of the fabric to cover yardage shipping fees. This amount can be as high as 10

cents per yard if the fabric is being shipped from coast to coast. Fabric that is being imported from the Orient or Europe will often have to be shipped air freight. This adds 15–20 cents per yard depending on the source of the fabric. Many manufacturers add a fee per yard to cover inspection and storage of the fabric.

2. Accessory fabrics. Linings and interlinings are included here as well as descriptions of the quality and amount required. These fabrics are usually stocked locally, so no freight charge is necessary.

TRIMMINGS

Added trimmings are listed here. Included are all fabric treatments, such as applied trims, pleating, topstitching, and the obvious added elements, such as zippers, belts, and snaps. Usually the thread is supplied by the sewing contractor, but this custom may vary with the individual factory. The total for trimmings is added to the basic material cost.

LABOR

This area of cost sheet is most often completed by a production person with current knowledge of production costs. The production person will know the limits of the factory and can decide which phases of production will be done in house and which will be contracted out. All these factors will affect the cost of labor on the garment. A production person can manipulate the labor factor to increase the per-unit profit.

1. Cutting. The manufacturer sets a minimum cut figure. This is the smallest number of garments the firm will cut. If the number of orders for a style is less than the minimum cut figure, the style is dropped from the line. Generally, the lower the garment's cost, the higher the minimum cut figure will be. A volume cutter of budget blouses may set the minimum cut at 300 units. A manufacturer of expensive evening garments may set the minimum cut at 50 or 60 units and make the prices high enough to compensate for the higher per-unit cutting cost.

   Use this formula to determine the per-unit cutting price:

$$\underset{\text{price of cutting}}{\$45} \quad \underset{\div \quad \text{units cut}}{\div \quad 100} \quad \underset{= \quad \text{price per unit}}{= \quad 45¢}$$

2. Production pattern. Some manufacturers figure the production pattern as a direct cost instead of as overhead, especially if the production pattern is contracted out. If the pattern is done in house, the cost is difficult to determine. But a contractor is paid a specific amount for patternmaking. This is a variable in costing a garment.

3. Grading and marking. These costs are similar to the production pattern cost because they are paid only once. The cost will not be duplicated if the style is recut. Grading and marking can be contracted out or done in house. Therefore, the cost per garment depends on whether the manufacturer figures these expenses as overhead or direct costs. Frequently, a manufacturer will consider these direct costs. Then when a style becomes a reorder, these costs become "earned" profit. Another manufacturer may choose to ignore these costs on a first cut, especially when the firm feels the garment could develop into a hot item if the price is as low as possible. The per-unit profit would be smaller, but the firm might be able to cut more garments and make a smaller per-unit volume.

4. Labor. This figure includes all direct labor on the garment. Besides the sewing process, labor costs include bundling, pressing, hemming, trimming, and sewing on buttons, snaps, and loops.

On any garment, a wide variety of construction details must be controlled. The production person must set standards for construction that are compatible with the garment's final price and the general competition from other manufacturers. The production person must find contractors who can meet production standards, but at a competitive price. If a contractor accustomed to cheap, rapid production is given a complicated, high-priced garment, the garment may be constructed too poorly to sell. The good production person carefully matches the contractor's skills and the standards necessary for production at a competitive price. To ensure that the contractor is doing a good job, the production person must inspect the garments (or lot) during construction. When the garments have been completed, a final inspection is made. The contractor is expected to correct any sewing mistakes made by the factory workers.

Sewing costs are figured in two ways:
a. By using sewing costs for similar garments. Generally, the more garments a factory

makes, the lower the cost per unit. The operators become used to a style and work out difficulties after the first lot is completed. Often the best sewers in the factory are given a few garments of the new style. With the help of the floor supervisor, they analyze the construction and determine the fastest way to sew the garment. Then they teach the other sewers their methods.

b. Analysis of the style's fabric and elements. When a completely new style is given to a factory, the floor supervisor will do a detailed analysis of the construction elements. This supervisor may suggest less expensive construction methods to the production person. A trial garment is made, and the sewing cost is computed for each operation in the garment's construction. If the factory is a union shop, the union representative may join the supervisor and contractor in determining the price to be paid for the garment. Both the manufacturer's production person and the contractor should agree on this sample before a lot goes into production.

5. Trucking. The cost of shipping each garment to the retail store. A retailer may ask the manufacturer to pay a warehouse fee. This is an allowance given the store because the whole order is shipped to one place, saving the manufacturer the expense of shipping orders to branch stores, which the retailer will do. If many branch stores are involved, paying the warehouse fee may save the manufacturer high shipping costs.

TOTAL COST

A final, total cost can be calculated in two ways. The first way is this:

Total cost + mark-on desired = wholesale price

The mark-on percentage for moderate garments ranges from 45 to 60 percent. Budget cutters may figure a lower mark-on, whereas manufacturers of expensive garments may take a higher mark-on to cover higher production, design, and advertising costs.

Mark-on is the amount added to the garment's basic cost that covers a company's overhead. Overhead includes the sales commission (which ranges from 7 to 10 percent) and terms. The terms in apparel are usually 8/10 EOM—that is, 8 percent of the selling price is refunded to the purchasing store if the goods

are received in a given month, and the invoice is paid within 10 days of the end of the billing month. Also included in overhead are rent, machinery depreciation, salaries of personnel not directly involved with construction, taxes, billing, bookkeeping and accounting, advertising, and profit. In other words, overhead is the cost of running a business.

The second way of figuring the final price is to use the reciprocal formula. Divide the total cost figure by the reciprocal percentage:

Total cost ÷ reciprocal figure = wholesale cost

To determine the reciprocal, subtract the desired mark-on percentage from 100; the result is the *reciprocal percentage*. For example, suppose you have a 55 percent mark-on on a $18.56 item. Subtract 55 from 100 to get 45, which is your reciprocal figure. You are dealing in percentages, so the reciprocal percentage in the formula is .45. Now insert your reciprocal percentage into the formula to get the wholesale cost:

Total cost ÷ reciprocal figure = wholesale cost

$$\$18.56 \div .45 = x \qquad \frac{\$18.56}{1} \times \frac{100}{45} = \$41.24$$

$$\frac{\$18.56}{1} \div \frac{.45}{100} = x$$

Thus, $41.24 would be rounded to $41.00 or $41.50.

MERCHANDISING THE COST OF A GARMENT

A manufacturer will always cost a garment before establishing the wholesale price. But another factor is as important as the dollar cost of the garment: *Does it look the money?* A garment must compete in an established marketplace. If it does not look as if it is worth its price, the garment's sales appeal will diminish. For example, if two basic shirts made in a similar fabric and style are placed on a rack together and they differ in price by a dollar, the less expensive shirt is more likely to sell. In particular, basic items must be carefully priced to be competitive. Innovative styling can often be the major factor that allows a manufacturer to get more money for an item. The customer may resist a cheaper item if there is a more fashionable or more carefully constructed garment as an alternative.

Another reason for merchandising the cost of a garment (that is, lowering or raising the wholesale price to affect the sale) is to create a good seller. When the manufacturer sees a garment that is stylish and fairly easy to produce, it may use a lower mark-on when figuring the cost or manipulate the fixed costs as described above (see the section on grading and marking). The manufacturer is gambling that the lower cost will stimulate sales and the added volume will generate the needed profit to make the item worth reordering.

In addition to all these price considerations, the manufacturer must continually be aware of how its items fit into the price structure of the stores and departments that sell the merchandise. To maintain a constant retail customer, the manufacturer's line should display a consistent price structure and visual image.

FOREIGN LABOR MARKETS

The elements of costing a garment are fairly constant for both domestic and foreign apparel. The foreign manufacturer must consider the cost of materials, labor, and overhead. Unlike the domestic manufacturer, the foreign manufacturer must add freight, customs duties, and an import agent's fee to the basic components of the garment's cost. An inexpensive labor force and a ready supply of materials are the major reasons for a domestic manufacturer to explore foreign apparel production.

Frequently, the designer is an important element in the success of foreign manufacturing. The American designer should have the ability to design garments that will appeal to the domestic consumer. The foreign manufacturer, however, may fail to grasp the subtleties of construction, styling, and fabrication necessary to sell garments in the United States.

To design foreign-made garments successfully, a designer should analyze the strengths and weaknesses of the foreign country—for example, the material supply and the quality of labor. Things that are difficult to do in America's mass-production-oriented industry may be easy to do in a foreign country where small manufacturers dominate the market. India, for example, is geared to custom dyeing and printing of cotton goods. Hand detailing, such as embroidery and beading, is done inexpensively by cottage laborers.

Duty and quota are two additional cost factors that must be considered when importing garments. *Duty* is the fee that must be paid to United States customs to import an item. The amount of the duty for each specific item is set by the government in an attempt to balance the cost of inexpensive labor abroad with the higher wages paid in the United States. This is a way of protecting American industry and making domestic prices more comparable with those of garments made offshore. Duty is highest on items that have a competing domestic industry.

Quota refers to the type and number of garments that are allowed to be imported into the United States from each foreign country during the calendar year. The amount allocated to each country depends on the kind of quotas they have applied and the domestic production that must be protected by the American government. Quota is assigned to the foreign government, which in turn assigns it to manufacturers who request it. Quota is usually not a cost factor for a garment unless there is a limited amount of a hot category available. Then the quotas may be sold by a factory producing less of an item to another factory that has many orders. This will increase the price. Quotas are usually assigned to individual manufacturers based on what they shipped in previous years. Thus, it is very easy for a manufacturer that goes out of business or reduces its production to earn a great deal of money by selling its quota to another manufacturer that is producing a great deal and does not have enough quota to send all its product to the United States.

A foreign market may be desirable because labor is inexpensive, but it can also be worthwhile because highly developed technicians and sophisticated machinery are available. Areas of the Orient have cornered the full-fashion knitwear industry. American manufacturers design lines of sweaters and knit apparel to be manufactured in the Orient because the factories are so excellent and the costs so low.

Garments and accessories are imported from Europe because European lines have prestige, not because they are inexpensive. The customer who is seeking an unusual high-fashion garment often prefers to wear a European designer label. High-priced shoes and leather goods are imported from Italy and France. Spain and Portugal export less expensive shoes, often of Italian design. France and Italy are both noted for high-fashion designer labels. England and Ireland are noted for fine woolens, hand-knit sweaters, and linens. American buyers attend the

large prêt-à-porter shows in France and select merchandise for the affluent American customer, or European manufacturers like Gucci and Hermès sell directly to the customer through branch stores. Design is the forte of the European manufacturer, so the fashions are sold directly to the retailer. Hong Kong lacks well-known design talent and depends on American designers for guidance in styling merchandise, and so needs the manufacturers to export merchandise successfully on a large scale.

Countries tend to specialize in a specific quality and type of merchandise. The specialty evolves gradually as a market begins to experiment with a product, usually at a fairly inexpensive level. Factories develop, employees are trained, and gradually more sophisticated machinery and production techniques are introduced. Wages may increase as the employees acquire skills. Buyers will take their business to the foreign market that produces a garment to American specifications, has adequate production capacities, and delivers the garments on schedule at a price lower than the domestic price.

Constant supervision and creative design guidance are the two vital ingredients in successful dealings with foreign production. Often language and business customs are so radically different from accepted American practices that many mistakes are made. For this reason, manufacturers will take a higher mark-on when producing in a foreign country. The mark-on covers any problems that may arise.

REVIEW

Word Finders

Define the following words from the chapter you just read:

1. Cottage labor
2. Designer work sheet
3. Direct labor cost
4. Duty
5. 8/10 EOM
6. Fall out
7. Group line
8. Item line
9. Knock off
10. Mark-on
11. Master color story
12. Merchandising
13. Novelty fabric
14. Price leader
15. Quota
16. Reciprocal
17. Staple fabric
18. Style theme
19. Supervisor
20. Volume cutter

Discussion Questions

1. Describe the merits of organizing a line by the group method.
2. Plan a fall color story for a junior sportswear manufacturer. Keep the following points in mind: be consistent, offer enough variety, develop the color theme in all groups.
3. Describe two types of item houses.
4. Working from an actual garment, fill in a cost sheet. Estimate yardage, trims, and labor costs.

mix
and
match

4.
fabricating a line

The designer's responsibility in choosing fabrics for the line can vary quite a bit, depending on the house. For example, a designer can be assigned fabrics to work on after management has selected all the piece goods for the line. In another house, the designer may select and purchase both sample and stock yardage. Generally, the designer's responsibility will fall between these two examples. Sometimes the designer will review lines with a stylist or the owner of the house, but most manufacturers encourage the designer to make the aesthetic decisions about fabric. Frequently, the manufacturer will have had a bad relationship with some textile firms, and the designer will be discouraged from ordering their samples. Similarly, manufacturers with poor credit ratings will be unable to purchase piece goods unless they pay cash.

Timing yardage purchases is an important aspect of apparel manufacturing. Generally, piece goods salespeople encourage manufacturers who are buying substantial amounts of yardage to commit (buy a specific amount or a particular fabric) early in the season to ensure delivery at the promised time. Manufacturers try to wait for buyer reaction to fabric and styles, which means waiting until a number of garments from each group have been sold. The pressure from both directions—the salespeople wanting commitments for fabric and the production supervisor or owner wanting salable garments—often falls on the designer.

The designer usually reviews all fabric lines he feels have any relevance to his product, even lines that are above or below his typical price range. This wide sampling is important because the designer must know what competitors and other firms in the market are choosing. In other words, when the designer thoroughly researches all fabrics offered during a season, he will have an overview of all textile trends and innovations. Fabrics beyond the usual price range are important because the designer can use an inexpensive fabric as a lining or an expensive fabric as a trim in a limited area.

Occasionally, the designer will find a new fabric that promises to be a good seller, in which case he will sample it and test the most suitable sewing methods by making the fabric into a stock garment. When a new product is satisfactory, management will commit itself immediately for some amount of yardage but specify (assort) colors and prints at a later time. New fabrics are usually in short supply at first, so an early order ensures that a manufacturer will have the first chance to ship that fabric to stores in his product area.

A designer needs to know who else has sampled a fabric, and he tried to avoid fabrics that have been chosen by competitors or fabrics used in lower-priced lines. This is especially true for novelty and print fabrics. Staple fabrics may be used in competitive lines where styling determines success.

When a designer finds a fabric she wants to sample, she will order a *sample cut* of 3 to 5 yards. She should note available colors and request a color card. At this time, she should also ask about projected delivery dates for duplicate and stock yardage. *Stock yardage* is the large amount of fabric needed to cut garments ordered by the stores. Stock yardage is usually purchased by a purchasing agent specializing in fabrics. If the designer anticipates dyeing or printing a special color, she should ask for minimum yardage requirements.

It is important for a designer to see as many lines as possible. The piece goods salespeople are well acquainted with events in the market place, and they often have information that can aid a designer in the choice of fabric or print. One well-known designer in the California swimwear market saw at least once a season each salesperson who called on her. She sampled what she thought would be appropriate for her product. Because she saw everyone and rarely turned a person away, this designer was called first whenever a salesperson had a new or different fab-

MILL NAME *COLLINS + AIKMAN*

New York Contact _*JIM THOMPSON*_ Phone *212-953-4309*

Los Angeles Rep _*LES WEINGARD*_ Phone *213-683-1960*

Season _____

NAME OF PATTERN #	FIBER CONTENT	PRICE	WIDTH	DELIVERY & COMMENT
VEL·DU·YORK	*100% COT.*	*5.50*	*60"*	*SWATCH CARD ENCLOSED*
FANCIES: {	*all priced @ 6.25 all 60"*			*SWATCHS TO COME: SAMPLES ATTACHED*
HEATHER	*100% COT*	*6.25*	*60"*	

flannel here — also in a faded denim blue velvet.

SPACE FLORAL due in January →

VEL CHECK more in January →
Colours on white ground due }

coming : PIN STRIPE, ½" spaced stripe, paisley, bouquet & fleur de lis — I will send you my samples

Textile Information Sheet   The designer should keep a record of the lines reviewed. If it is possible to keep swatches of fabrics that are potentially interesting, they should be included in this record. If a special fabric request develops during the season, the designer can review the notes and discover who has the desired fabric. This sheet is an example of a form that organizes the information a fabric salesperson presents to a designer. (Courtesy of Grayce Baldwin *Consults.*)

ric. This gave her a tremendous edge over the other local designers who had discouraged salespeople at one time or another. The cardinal rule for a designer should be this: *See all the textile representatives you possibly can during a season. Judge their products' relevance to the designs you are planning. Be flexible, yet practical.*

The designer selects samples on the basis of price, aesthetics, fashion, and the fabric's suitability for the line. Frequently, a beautiful fabric cannot be used because it is too similar to another fabric in the line. The designer should look for different weights and textures, crisp fabrics and goods for draping, thin

Fabric Inspiration Designer Margie Balun sketches print bodies based on the fabric groups she has selected for early fall.

blouse weights and heavier "bottom" weights (suitable for skirts and pants). The fabrics in the line should be balanced between novelty goods and base goods. *Novelty fabrics* include prints, fancy woven patterns, textured and fancy knits, and textured wovens. *Base goods* are fabrics in solid colors and traditional patterns that can be used in many different styles.

The fabrics in a line should have a price range. The lower-priced fabrics can be made into more complicated styles. Higher-priced goods should be reserved for simple silhouettes.

If a sample fabric works well when it is made into a garment and if the garment is accepted as an item or group in the line, the sample garment must be duplicated. *Duplicates (dups)* are extra sample garments that are sent to road salespeople and showrooms in other markets. In many companies, the designer is responsible for ordering the duplicate yardage and supervising the construction of the dups. Each time the designer orders the fabric, he or she should check delivery date and price. The delivery date is determined by the turn-time of the fabric producer. *Turn-time* includes the time it takes to knit or weave the fabric, dye and finish it, and ship it to the manufacturer. Turn-time depends on many factors and can range from immediate delivery for yardage that is on hand in the producer's warehouse to several months. The designer should inquire about turn-time and relate it to the cycle the manufacturer can work with.

Ordering of piece goods for stock cutting is usually handled by the manufacturer after the number of confirmed sales and the number of projected sales for the item have been calculated. A contract for the yardage purchase is drawn up between the fabric company and the manufacturer.

Designers frequently travel to New York from Los Angeles, St. Louis, Dallas, Denver, San Francisco, and the other regional design areas. In New York, designers can see the newest fabric developments for the coming season They can discuss their ideas and color schemes directly with textile designers and technicians. Textile designers and principals also visit regional manufacturing areas to meet and work with designers.

Several firms have located creative and manufacturing plants on the West Coast to give firsthand service to the California market, but the total amount of yardage produced in California is not comparable to

Reviewing a Textile Line Designer John Scott carefully reviews the linen colors shown him by textile representative Manny Kovak. Fabric choices are based on aesthetics, suitability for the garment being manufactured, availability, and price.

the amount produced on the East Coast. Regional textile plants tend to be in close contact with the market they service because client contact is greater and local design talent is used.

THE TEXTILE FIRMS

There are two major types of textile firms. The first is the vertical textile firm. The company owns the mill or knitting factory that produces the *greige goods* (unstyled and unfinished base fabric, also spelled *grey* or *greig*), converts (styles, prints, and finishes) this yardage into fashion fabric, then markets it. The converter is the second type of fabric firm. The converter buys greige goods from large mills, employs designers and technicians to style the goods, and rents facilities where the greige goods are printed, dyed, and finished. Then the converter markets the finished fabric. The vertical textile firm owns the physical plant and the styling and marketing facilities. The converter owns people (that is, pays their salaries) and yardage. All other functions are contracted out.

The main contact between the textile firm and the manufacturer is the textile salesperson. Textile firms vary greatly in the size and complexity of their marketing operations, and textile salespeople vary accordingly. A salesperson may

1. Work for one division of a large firm that services only one kind of manufacturer (largest textile firms).
2. Handle an entire medium-sized textile house and sell to a variety of manufacturers, probably in one geographic area (medium-sized textile firm).
3. Handle several smaller converters and cover the entire market for goods in a particular price range. Usually this person will work in a limited geographic area and choose nonconflicting lines whose base goods differ in price or type (small firm with a specialized product).

Most textile firms try to specialize in one type of fabric and gear their product to a specific market—for example, women's wear in one price range. Even larger companies with a diversified product tend to group similar fabrics under one division to concentrate selling activities. Fashion can affect this grouping, however. Currently, men's wear designers are using many fabrics formerly thought to be suitable for women's wear and women's wear designers are using men's fabrics.

Among textile manufacturers, the trend is toward larger companies. Larger firms create divisions that specialize in one type of fiber, one price range, a particular type of a base goods, or a specific market. A division is broken down further into marketing areas based on price of the final product, manufacturer's geographical location, category of merchandise, and retail divisions.

Servicing the accounts assigned to him is the textile salesperson's first job. He shows the designer his line at the beginning of each season and whenever a new fabric or print is added. The designer should make every effort to see the line without interruption. She should get away from the workroom and the telephone so she can view the line without distractions and keep her current designs confidential.

The textile salesperson should not edit the line or prejudge a designer's selection. Often a designer is looking for a specific item and should see all available fabrics. The designer should select sample cuts of fabrics she would like to experiment with and judge realistically how the fabric will adapt to her line. She should check delivery time for stock goods, minimum yardage for special colors, and yardage for print recolors.

For colors that have not been included in the textile manufacturer's line, minimum yardage requirements depend on the method of dyeing or printing. Yarn-dyed and solution-dyed fabrics require the most yardage if a color is to be dyed to order. The yarn is dyed and then woven in the yarn-dyed fabric method. Solution-dyed fabrics are synthetics that are dyed in the liquid state, before the liquid is made into thread. Piece-dyed goods have a lower requirement for a special color because the piece (usually several hundred yards) is dyed after weaving. Each manufacturer will have different minimum yardage requirements for special colors, depending on what production facilities are available, the fabric blend, and the fabric price.

The fabric printing method is important when a designer is considering recoloring a print. For example, a roller print to be recolored requires a very large run or the price will increase. Machine screens are more flexible. They can be recolored if the minimum yardage ordered is somewhere between 1500 to 2000 yards. Heat transfer prints usually can be recolored at a minimum of 1000 yards per color.

Croquis A painting, or croquis, is made if a customer requests a color change in a pattern. Then the croquis is approved by the manufacturer and printed in the form of a strike-off.

When a designer wants a special color combination in a print, he or she asks the textile salesperson to have the art department make a painting or *croquis.* A croquis is rendered in paint on paper, and it shows the print in the new color combination. The designer may give the salesperson swatches of the desired colors, describe the colors, or adapt colors from another print. The artists in the textile firm's art department paint the croquis and the designer or the manufacturer approves it.

Then a *strike-off* is made; that is, the textile company produces on base goods a short run of the new color, usually no more than 1 yard. Usually the strike-off is not finished because the manufacturer's main concern is what the pattern will look like when it is printed on fabric. Generally, the purchase will have to be made before the manufacturer can receive yardage in the new color range. Just as in dyeing goods, the typical minimum yardage will vary according to market conditions and the textile firm.

Some textile firms specialize in flexible production, styling the product to meet the demands of the individual customer. Usually they receive a higher price for their product. Other firms specialize in a standard product at a competitive price. They require large fabric commitments if they are to do a special fabrication. Some companies have a division supplying the designer market that does special prints and colors which for one season are confined to one designer. The textile firm absorbs some production costs in these cases because it offers the fabrics to the general market at a lower price the following season. This method benefits both the designer firm and the textile manufacturer. The former has a unique product, a new and personal fabrication unlike any other on the market. The textile manufacturer gains prestige by selling to a high-priced resource, tests the product at the consumer level without making huge yardage commitments, and advertises the "exclusive" designer quality of the fabric and styling.

After the designer has sampled the fabric and made it into garments for the line, duplicate yardage must be ordered. In some firms, the designer will be responsible for this order; in other firms, it is the responsibility of the production department. After the duplicate yardage order, the designer has little to do with fabric ordering unless he or she works for a very small shop or is a principal in the house. Most often, the head of production and the fabric salesperson set up delivery dates, damage allowances, shipping terms, and the final price per yard.

Negotiations for advertising allowances usually begin at this point. Advertising allowances are given by the textile mill or the company that provided the converter with the fiber. The money is for advertisements that feature the name of the mill or the fiber. Generally, the manufacturer will also contribute some money and the retailer will make up the difference. The larger textile firms and fiber companies also run ads on the trade level.

There are several reasons why a designer may be called back into conference with the manufacturer and the textile representative. He or she may be needed

1. To review the fabric line if additional patterns and colors must be selected.
2. If problems develop with sewing methods on a particular fabric or if the sample maker is unable to solve a construction problem.
3. To refabricate styles when yardage commitments cannot be met and substitutions must be made.

Many times, a designer is working on two lines at once—preparing a future line while solving the problems of the line about to be shipped.

Frequently, the designer is called upon to choose promotional patterns. These are off-priced goods offered to manufacturers near the end of the season. Often they are print goods the textile firm has not been able to sell. The designer will select a group of prints that will be offered in "assorted" proven bodies. The manufacturer cuts the chosen fabrics and sells them at a lower price than the regular stock.

A good textile salesperson will attempt to develop a working rapport with many designers. He or she knows that each person may change jobs many times. If the salesperson has developed a good working record with a designer and has a good product to sell, the salesperson will have a successful future no matter where the designer is working.

The designer should always be open to the products and information a textile salesperson has to offer. The designer should consider the product's suitability to the line he or she is creating. By taking notes on available textile products, the designer will have information for future reference. Although the designer should be open to suggestion, she or he should not be motivated unrealistically by a good sales pitch or by the fabric representative's friendship.

Cooperative Fiber Advertisement
Hoechst Fibers promotes its fiber, Trevira, which is used by converter Razor Mills to make "Razette." This advertisement appeals to trade and retail consumers. (Courtesy of Hoechst Fibers Industries.)

Textile Library Elanore Kennedy of DuPont Fibers discusses available fabrics printed on Dacron and Quiana with many designers and manufacturers. Specific types of fabrics and prints are displayed on large panels to assist designers.

INFORMATION ON FABRIC SOURCES

Fabric Libraries

At the beginning of the season, a designer may find it helpful to get an overview of the fabric market. Some excellent sources are the fabric libraries compiled each season by large fiber companies. If a designer requests a specific type of fabric, they can help find it. Most companies have market representatives who interpret the general color and fashion trends in each apparel area. The fiber companies recommend that every converter and mill using their fibers send them *types* (swatches large enough to feel) to include in the library. Seeing the fabrics in a library is advantageous because the designer is not pressured to buy a fabric and may compare in one place the products and prices of many converters.

The large companies that maintain fabric libraries are listed below. Most have offices in Los Angeles and New York.

Natural fibers:
    Wool Bureau
    Cotton, Incorporated

Synthetic fibers:
    DuPont (E. I. du Pont de Nemours and Company)
    Monsanto
    Celanese
    Hoechst Fibers
    American Cyanamid
    American Enka
    Eastman
    FMC Fibers

Textile Directories

The major markets have associations for textile firms and salespeople. The associations work to bring the textile firm and the manufacturer closer together. Their major publication is a textile directory listing textile firms alphabetically and by category. Also included are many manufacturers' names and sources for trims, linings, and other findings. The associations will assist a manufacturer trying to locate a specific kind of fabric.

Textile Publications

Several excellent publications devoted to textile products are available. The foremost periodical in this area is *American Fabrics and Fashion* (*AFF*). The major publications include *American Fabrics and Fashion* and *Knitting Times*, which is a weekly magazine. *Knitting Times* also puts out an annual directory called *National Knitted Outerwear Association*.

Textile Trade Shows

The major textile trade show is held twice annually in Frankfurt, Germany, and is called Interstoff. Most important European textile companies show their lines at this show. American manufacturers and mill representatives also attend.

The New York textile associations present a biannual textile show called Texpo, intended primarily for domestic mills and manufacturers. Various foreign textile associations, like Texitalia, present periodic shows in New York so designers can review fabrics and order from foreign mills.

Color Services

Color services predict what seasonal color trends will be 18 months before the customer sees the merchandise in the stores. Most services divide their information into colors for men's wear and ladies and children's apparel. These color services are used by fiber producers, textile converters and print stylists, manufacturers, and retailers. They are sold on a private subscription basis twice a year. Pat Tunskey produces *The Color Projections* and Jane Resnick edits *The Color Box*. Promostyl is a French color-predicting service available in the United States. In addition, the fashion reporting services discussed in Chapter 6 all produce color projections for the coming seasons as well as style and silhouette information.

FABRICATION

Fabrication means selecting or creating a style for a fabric. Which fabric is suitable for a specific style depends on the characteristics of the fabric.

1. Surface interest. Color, aesthetics, pattern, texture.
2. Weight. Correct weight for wear requirements, season, and construction details.
3. Texture or hand. Correct stiffness for silhouette; fabric feels pleasant and drapes well.
4. Fiber. Suited to the season, good performance and easy care, allergic reactions rare.

These four elements form the character of the fabric. They also dictate many of the limits on styling. The designer should be familiar with all types of fab-

NEW BRIGHTS IN COMBINATION

COLOR:

Darkened or washed brights in unexpected mixes for an exciting approach to stripings, prints and patterns.

FORMULA:

The Prospectors + The Settlers or The Adventurers = NEW BRIGHTS in combination.

MOOD:

● Lively contrasts offer a strong basis for important autumn/winter prints and patterns.

● The color mix is essential to achieve print coordination and pattern "blocking" in layered looks.

PRAIRIE GREEN

TIMBER

CLARET

CRYSTAL BLUE

PRINT & PATTERN IDEA

Oriental scenics and figuratives as all-overs and borders.

THE EASY TUNIC DRESS FOR JUNIORS

Textile Trade Information Subscription fashion reports have many fabrication suggestions. This *IM* page gives the designer a swatch of each fabric, information on its source, and styling suggestions. (Courtesy of *IM International.*)

ric, just as a potter is familiar with the properties of many types of clay. The designer is a fabric sculptor and the human body is the frame of reference.

The experienced designer can look at a piece of fabric or feel it and envision the type of garment it can be made into. This ability is developed by experimenting with many different fabrics and a great variety of styles. Usually, the designer has a working knowledge of basic textile construction, dyeing, and finishing. She or he should also be familiar with natural and synthetic fibers. This basic knowledge should be expanded constantly by listening to textile salespeople and reading textile magazines and trade papers. Innovations in the textile industry are constant, and the fabric mills are eager to keep manufacturers and designers up to date on developments. Many textile and fiber firms will attempt to solve construction problems that arise with a new fiber or method of construction.

The designer must evaluate the performance of a piece of fabric as well as the aesthetic aspects before electing to use it in the line. A shrinking test under the pressing buck of the Hoffman press is the first step. Cut a 12- by 12-inch piece of fabric and a corresponding piece of paper. Press the fabric and line it up with the paper pattern standard. If steam, heat, and pressure have made the fabric shrink more than a ½ inch in a 12-inch span, problems will occur when the garment is pressed. The average length of a jacket is 26 inches. A fabric that shrinks a ½ inch on the pressing buck will shorten the jacket by 1 inch. Interfacing and lining will not usually shrink, so the jacket would be very difficult to construct in this fabric.

Some designers wash or dry-clean a fabric once it has been made into a sample to see how it performs. Trims should also be tested to make sure they can withstand the same care instructions as the base goods fabrics. The designer may elect to send questionable fabrics to a professional testing laboratory that will run tests for color fastness, washability, and abrasion. These professional tests are especially important for garments that must stand up to the rigid quality control inspections of mass merchandisers like Sears, J. C. Penney's, and Montgomery Ward.

Working with fabrics is an excellent background for a beginning designer. Many times, a design student can sell fabrics over the counter, and this exposure to a variety of fabrics is good training. Home sewing is another good way to learn about fabrics. Experimentation and observation are the keys to developing a sense of fabrication.

Surface Interest

The way a fabric looks is the most important factor in choosing it for a style. In most firms, decision making in fabrication is the designer's exclusive domain. Selection of colors and prints should be based on research and observation of the latest fashion trends. But the designer with taste and personal discrimination should rely on instinct, as well as background information, when searching for a new fashion direction.

Technical considerations are even more important when choosing a print. The repeat of the print must be suitable for the garment. The repeat is the amount of material taken for a pattern to duplicate itself. A very large repeat is unsuitable for trims or children's garments. Fabrics with large repeats work best in styles with few seams.

The scale of the pattern must complement the garment. When a very small pattern is used, such as a classic houndstooth or herringbone, the scale of the pattern is less important than when the pattern is large and bold. The pattern should complement the silhouette and style. A bold pattern on a small, delicate garment will detract from the style. A medium stripe on a large woman will make her look larger because the eye will compare the pattern size with the bulk of the garment.

The designer should recognize a pattern that requires special matching. Matching is designing and cutting a garment so the fabric pattern in each piece matches when the garment is sewed together. This is particularly important with bold plaids, checks, and stripes. The placement of the bold print is also an important consideration. A dark spot placed at the bustline, stomach, or crotch will call undesirable attention to these areas. Sometimes the print is arranged so that there are no flattering possibilities for placement; the experienced designer will avoid these problem prints. Matching and placement problems generally require extra yardage.

One-way prints also present technical problems. A one-way print has all motifs printed in one direction. When these prints are cut, all garment pieces must be facing the same direction, so more yardage is needed. (The same problem occurs with pile fabrics.) A two-way print features a motif that faces in both directions, so the print is simpler and more economical to work with.

The way a fabric is printed will affect the look of the print and the quantities that may be ordered in special colors or exclusive patterns. The three major ways of printing fabric are

1. *Screen printing with wet dyestuffs (wet printing).* Wet dyestuffs are applied directly to the surface of greige goods that are prepared for printing (PFP). Flat-bed screens or rotary screens may be used to apply the dyes. The design is cre-

ated by porous areas left in the otherwise impervious screen or roller that allow the dye to come through in the pattern desired. Flat-bed screen prints are most often used for bathing suit panels because there is a limited area that can be printed without leaving a break line. Each color requires another screen in both printing methods. Rotary screens print a length of fabric without a join line. Dye and discharge is another way of using screens to create a design. This method is excellent for spaced prints that have a colored ground because the fabric is dyed first and printed with a caustic solution that removes dye in certain areas when it is washed. Then the design is printed on the fabric with rotary screens in the areas where the color has been removed. All these methods may be used on natural or synthetic fibers and produce a print that has good dye penetration. Minimum yardage for a special color and a confined print (*confined* means only the originator may use the pattern for the first season) is usually 3000 yards for the pattern and 1000 yards for each color combination.

2. *Engraved roller printing.* In this process, a large metal drum is engraved with the design. The roller is inked and run over the surface of the greige goods. Each color requires a different roller. This method is used for small motifs on a light color ground. It may be used to print both synthetic and natural fabrics. Usually large runs are needed for special colors and minimum yardages. Six thousand yards would be a typical minimum yardage because of the cost of engraving the rollers. Many small cotton prints are roller printed; these are often classical designs that are used for many years.

3. *Heat transfer printing (dry printing).* In this process, the design is printed on a specially treated paper, much like a color magazine. The print can be transferred only to a heat-sensitive fabric like polyester, some nylons, and acrylics. Heat and pressure are applied to the fabric and paper as it passes through hot rollers. This method leaves the dyestuffs on the surface of the fabric, but there is little penetration of the base goods. This is an economical way to print a design with many colors and to achieve a very detailed design. Heat transfer printing is less expensive than wet printing because the machinery is less elaborate. The heat transfer paper is often printed abroad and imported into the United States,

where it is transferred to the PFP fabric. Minimum yardage requirements depend on how much paper the printer will print to change the color and design. Occasionally a minimum of 500 yards is available from a printer that makes its own paper. One thousand yards per color and 3000 yards per pattern are standard minimums for a new design that must be engraved and printed.

Basic prints and surface patterns are foundations of a designer's knowledge. Many prints are developed as novelties and become classics when they are used season after season. To increase your knowledge of fabric patterns, study the pictures and definitions in the textile dictionary.

Weight

The weight of a fabric is an important consideration, especially when a durable garment is being designed. Heavier fabrics suitable for pants, skirts, and jackets are called *bottom weights*. Blouse weights are lighter fabrics, best for bodices and blouses.

The fabric weight should be compatible with the style of the garment and the season for which it is intended. Winter-weight fabrics are usually heavier to add warmth. Spring merchandise requires a medium-weight fabric and colors that are lighter and brighter than fall colors. Summer fabrics have the lightest weight of all.

Tailored garments, such as jackets and coats, must be made in a fabric heavy enough to support the tailored details. If the fabric is too thin, the seams will show through when they are pressed. Also, the pockets will show as ridges in the top fabric and bound buttonholes will be lumpy.

Light, transparent fabrics often require a lining, which makes the garment more expensive. Lightweight fabrics can be bonded to give them greater bulk and substance. *Bonded fabrics* have a thin layer of fabric or foam that is laminated (glued with heat and pressure) to the wrong side. If the bonding process is poorly done or the proper glue is not used, the fabric and the bonding material may separate during cleaning or washing.

Fabric Hand

Hand refers to the feel of a fabric. Hand can be altered greatly by the kind of finish applied to the fabric. A crisp finish may give a fabric enough body so that it can be used as a bottom weight. The same fabric with a dress finish will be soft and more easily draped. Finishes break down when pressed, cleaned, or worn. Generally, less expensive fabrics are finished to create a crisper hand and more body.

A fabric's hand greatly influences the way it can be styled. A fabric that is fluid and soft cannot be used for a crisp, well-tailored garment, such as a blazer. The silhouette will reflect the body shape if a fabric with a soft hand is used. A fabric that drapes will fall gracefully and cling to the figure. More gathering can be used with a soft fabric and the garment will not become bulky or awkward.

A crisp fabric, like linen or sailcloth, can be used for a well-defined, tailored silhouette. Interfacing, a stiff, plain fabric added to a garment's inner construction, is used to further stiffen tailored areas. Most often, interfacing is used in the collar, cuffs, and placket. Interfacing may be used in soft, draped garments, but a very lightweight interfacing is appropriate. This will be compatible with the hand of a soft fabric. *A primary rule of design is to style garments in a fabric that is compatible with the silhouette desired.*

The texture of the fabric is an important aspect to consider when fabricating a line. The customer usually touches a fabric that attracts the eye. If the hand is appealing, the customer will consider the potential purchase more carefully. Most designers have developed their tactile sense and evaluate the visual aspects and the hand of a fabric before sampling it.

Some adjectives used to describe fabric hand and texture are as follows:

Dry. Grainy, resilient texture, typical of linen
Slick, or wet. Slippery texture, typical of acetate surah
Crisp. Characteristic of a sized (starched) fabric, like organdy or silk organza
Boardy. Stiff fabric; derogatory term for a cheap fabric with too much sizing
Gutsy. Fabric with much body
Lofty. Fabric with a high pile or nap, like velvet
Flat. Weave with low surface interest, like poplin
Rough. Heavily textured surface, like raw silk
Smooth. Slick surface, like taffeta
Crepe. Light-textured surface, typical of crepe de chine

Fiber

Traditionally, natural fibers have been considered appropriate for a specific season. Wool is the fall fabric because it is warm and usually has a bulky weave. Linen and cotton are warm weather fabrics because they are cool, absorbent, and easily washed. The widespread use of synthetics and blends has altered the seasonal use of specific fibers. Now hand, bulk, and color are more important than the fiber when a fabric is being selected for a specific season. Cotton woven as a bulky corduroy can be used for a fall line. Cotton and polyester blends are appropriate for spring and summer wear. Wools woven as gauze (light crepes) are used for expensive spring garments.

The choice of fiber is important when the designer considers how the fabric will perform. Wash and wear characteristics are generally built into polyester blends. Easy care is particularly important for garments that will be laundered in a washing machine at high temperatures, like children's wear, work clothes, and uniforms. Lurex blends are delicate and react to pressure and heat. Therefore, these blends are used for garments that can be made with few seams, which eliminates pressing, and garments that will not receive much wear. The designer must understand many other fiber characteristics before she or he is ready to design a line. Through experimentation and observation, the designer will add continually to his or her knowledge of fibers and how they react to styling and sewing.

Frequently, fiber companies offer advertising money to manufacturers who use substantial amounts of their fiber. The fiber company may contribute to an advertisement placed in a trade newspaper or magazine. Fiber money is also given to the manufacturer to be passed on to the retailer who advertises a specific garment to the public. The manufacturer may contribute money to the retailer because the manufacturer will gain if sales improve. These advertisements must carry the names of the fiber company and the manufacturer. Because advertising sells the product directly to the consumer, the advertising allowance is good for all three parties.

REVIEW

Word Finders

Define the following words from the chapter you just read:

1. Base goods
2. Blouse weight
3. Bonded
4. Bottom weight
5. Crepe
6. Converter
7. Croquis
8. Delivery date
9. Dress finish
10. Greige goods
11. Heat transfer printing
12. Interfacing
13. Matching
14. Machine screen
15. Novelty fabric
16. One-way print
17. Piece-dyed
18. Piece goods
19. Roller print
20. Repeat
21. Scale
22. Solution-dyed
23. Strike-off
24. Type
25. Vertical textile mill
26. Wet printing

Discussion Questions

1. What are the four characteristics of a fabric? Define these terms.
2. What are the designer's responsibilities when fabricating a line?
3. What are the salesperson's responsibilities when selling piece goods to a manufacturer?
4. Name and discuss the two main kinds of textile firms.

TEXTILE DICTIONARY

The following textile dictionary identifies and defines basic types of fabrics and prints used frequently by designers. The photographs are arranged in groups according to related prints or surface treatments. The contents lists all photographs alphabetically.

Fabric Groupings

Alphabetical Contents

WOVEN BASE GOODS

1. Alaskine: A blend of silk and wool woven in a variety of weights suitable for dresses and suitings. Slight luster make this a dressy fabric. Wrinkles and is rather fragile. Now also woven in synthetic blends.

2. Chambre: Colored wrap yarns and natural filling yarns are woven to create a heathered look. Usually a shirting weight cotton. A blend of two fabrics can be cross dyed after weaving, with one of the fibers resisting the dye that the other absorbs.

3. Crepe: Crepe yarns are crimped and twisted and then woven in a plain weave. The surface of crepe is pebbly or slightly crinkled. Crepe drapes well and is made from many fibers. Often printed and available with a satin back.

4. Muslin, osnaburg, painter's drill, canvas: Plain-weave cotton or cotton blends made up of waste and low-grade cotton yarns. When unbleached, the natural dark flecks in the yarns give this fabric its typical character. Many slubs are also characteristic. Drill and canvas are heavier weights of the muslin base cloth.

5. Heather: A mixture of a color and several lighter shades of the same color to give the fabric a frosted appearance. This coloration is typical of wool, although it is currently used for many synthetic base cloths also.

6. Lamé: Metallic threads woven into a wide variety of base goods. The metallic glint gives the fabric a shiny, dressy look. Metallic threads are often heat sensitive, making pressing difficult.

7. Moiré: A small-rib-weave fabric that has water mark designs embossed on the surface. Has a luster that gives it a dressy appearance. Woven in a variety of silklike blends.

8. Monk's cloth: Rough, variegated threads are woven like a basket to form this textured base goods. A very soft, limp hand is characteristic of this weave, which is often of cotton and cotton-blended yarns.

9. Indigo denim, prewashed: A durable twill fabric woven with a colored warp over a natural or white filler. Indigo is a traditional dye that gradually fades as it is washed. Denim is washed before manufacturing to break down the crisp hand and soften the color of the fabric. Woven in cotton and blends in a wide variety of weights.

1

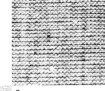

2

3

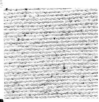

4

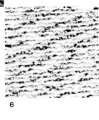

5

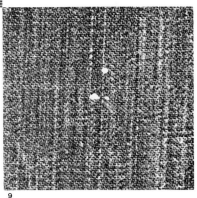

6

7

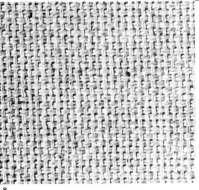

8

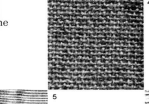

9

10

10. Crinkle cloth: A textured surface created by the tension of some threads woven tighter than others. Often this cloth is woven as a smooth cloth and crinkled in the finishing process. Crinkle can be added to many different weights of fabric.

11. Flannel: A plain or twill weave fabric classically made in wool with a slightly napped surface. Contemporary fabrications include synthetic fibers and blends. This is a classic winter suiting fabric often colored with a heather surface. Cotton flannels are classic winter shirtings.

12. Gabardine: A firm twill fabric, classically made from wool, but currently woven in polyester and blends. The surface is smooth and slick with a low luster unless it has been brushed. This fabric is a suiting base goods.

13. Georgette: Georgettes made in polyester are lightweight shirtings that can be a plain weave or novelties like this crinkle georgette with a leno woven design. This is often a print cloth and is woven in the Orient.

14. Mesh: A woven, open-weave fabric with a fishnet look woven in cotton and blended fibers. Typically a sportswear fabric.

15. Poplin: Firm, plain-weave cloth of a light to medium weight. Fine warp ribs are visible upon close examination because the warp threads are finer than the filling threads. Made of cotton, wool, or synthetic fibers.

16. Reverse twill: The direction of the twills is reversed in a regular pattern to create this base goods with a herringbone effect.

17. Twill: A weave that has a diagonal line or rib because the filling yarns pass over the warp yarn and under two warp yarns. This is the strongest weave. Twills can be woven in cotton, wool, and blended fibers.

18. Wrinkled sheeting: Sheeting is a lightweight, plain-weave cotton that has been permanently wrinkled in the finishing process to give it a casual sportswear look.

11

12

13

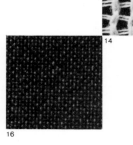

14

15

16

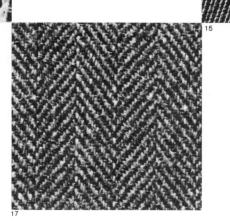

17

18

DOTS AND SPOTS

1. Dotted Swiss, clipped dot: A traditional fabric usually in cotton and cotton blends, with a separate thread woven into the face of the fabric and then clipped to form a small thread dot. Contrast dots or all one color.

2. Dotted Swiss: flock dot: A voile or lawn ground is printed with a bonding agent in dots (patterns are also possible). Flock is then secured to the surface of the fabric with bonding (glue) agent. Colored flock may be used, and the ground can also be colored. Often printed as well.

3. Duco dot, painted dot: The dots are printed on base goods with a paintlike surface. Dots are slightly stiff, so this process is most successful for a small dot. May be printed in colors or white on a wide variety of base goods.

4. Aspirin dot, white ground: A polka dot about the size of an aspirin, which can be printed on a large variety of base goods in many color combinations. The dark dot on a white ground has the most impact of any polka dot color combination.

5. Pin dot, dark ground: Small dots are spaced at regular intervals for an all-over effect. These patterns are easy to use because no matching or special engineering is necessary. These classical dots may be printed or woven into any base goods.

6. Novelty woven graduated dot: The graduated dot is a novelty fabrication that is appropriate for both woven and printed patterns on many base cloths and fibers. Also used for knits. Numerous variations possible.

7. Coin dot: An arrangement of large dots that are about the size of a nickel. This example is on a dark ground, but many color combinations are possible. May be printed on a wide variety of base goods.

8. Confetti dot: Random placement of dots gives a confetti look to the print. The concentration of dots forms a stripe banding called a *biadier.*

9. Foulard: A print typical of men's ties and linings and popular as an accessory for blouses. Often printed on a surah or silk-type fabric. Available in many pattern variations on a range of base cloths.

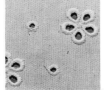

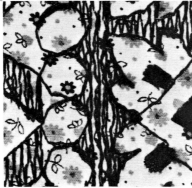

EMBROIDERED-STITCHED SURFACES

1. Schiffli embroidery: Embroidery done by a Schiffli machine, which is capable of embroidering a limitless variety of novelty patterns in multicolored threads. May be embroidered on many base goods, but most typically done on cotton and cotton blends. The pattern design is governed by a punchcard system similar to that used on a Jacquard loom.

2. Eyelet: Schiffli embroidery that covers the entire ground. Holes are often punched out of the base goods and reembroidered to give the fabric a lacelike effect. Most often done on a white or natural cotton or cotton blend. May be dyed and overprinted. Border patterns are also available. A typical summer fabrication.

3. Novelty quilt: Quilt formed by stitching a base goods (usually a thin cotton base goods) to a backing with a thin polyester fiber filler to give a puffy appearance to the unstitched areas. Quilting makes a lightweight fabric warm. Many varieties of quilting are available.

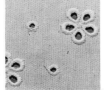

ETHNIC PRINTS

1. Paisley: Printed patterns derived from East Indian shawls first imported to Europe during the early nineteenth century. Typically including a stylized pine cone or tree of life motif. Printed on a wide variety of base goods in many pattern variations.

2. French provincial: Small stylized floral prints often surrounded by a spot of color that contrasts with the ground. Frequently printed in primary colors. Typical of country prints on cotton and cotton blends from the southern part of France.

3. Patchwork pattern: Combinations of prints in compatible color and size ranges. Often a fabric company will team patchworks with pull-out patterns from the individual patches. Many variations, from random patches to typical Americana patterns, are designed.

4. Block print: Rustic-looking print that has unclear borders and surfaces which are typical of a hand-printed block (usually made of wood and metal)— that is used to print ethnic patterns. Often done on cotton base goods, but also available on many other cloths.

5. Tie dye: Circular designs formed by knotted areas of fabric that resist dye. Gradations and random taking of the dye are typical of this hand-dyeing technique. May be done on a variety of base cloths. Typical ethnic dyeing method used by many cultures.

6. American Indian pattern: Indian rug, basket, and fabric patterns have inspired many contemporary fabric prints. Geometrics and stripes are most typical, with many variations possible.

5

6

7

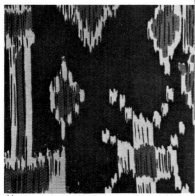

8

9

10

11

12

7. Liberty print: English print firm that specializes in florals and intricately printed fine cottons and silks. Prints are so typical that small florals printed by other firms are often called liberty-type prints.

8. Austrian provincial print (Lanz): Typically a small print, with many variations possible. Most often printed on cotton and cotton-type base goods with small folk art motifs. Popularized in the United States by Lanz line of junior clothes. This example is quilted.

9. Bandana print: These prints are adapted from traditional bandana scarf patterns. They are often printed in primary colors on cotton and cotton blends.

10. Batik: An ethnic print usually printed on a plain-weave cotton broadcloth. Many variations on the traditional wax-resistant, hand-printed and dyed technique that originated in Java. The typical batiks often have a softly cracked color that results from the dye partially penetrating the cracked wax surface. Many commercial variations now available.

11. Ikat: An ethnic printing technique that prints the pattern on the warp threads before weaving. When filler is added, the pattern gets a fragmented edge. This technique has been adapted to prints characterized by an irregular print outline. A generic name is "fractured print."

12. Toilé: Traditional French scenic print usually printed as a dark line drawing on natural or white cotton base goods. Often used in home furnishings as well as apparel. Many variations possible.

111

FLORALS

1. Chintz: Chintz technically describes the glazed surface added to plain or printed cotton. The term is also used to describe colorful cotton prints of stylized floral and natural motifs. This fabric is popular as a home furnishings fabric. Many varieties of patterns possible.

2. Art nouveau floral: Floral patterns emphasizing curving, flowing lines and subtle colorations. Developed from patterns popular during the art nouveau period of the first quarter of the twentieth century. Many variations possible.

3. Calico: Small florals printed on basic cotton-type base goods and other base goods. Many prints fall into this category. Calico prints were used in early American garments and quilts.

4. Pointillist floral: The pattern is formed by a concentration of dots. Can be done in several colors or one color and white. May be done in many variations on any base cloth.

5. Stylized floral (two-way design): An abstract floral pattern that has a stylized image of a floral. A two-way print because the motifs face both directions in a random placement. Many variations are available because this is a basic textile design pattern. Two-way prints are economical to cut because they do not need special matching or pattern placement.

6. Challis: Challis may be solid or printed and was once woven of fine wool. Now it is available in many fibers. Challis is a soft dress- and blouse-weight fabric with a slightly napped surface. Typical prints are paisleys and small, stylized florals.

7. Realistic (naturalistic) floral: Print based on a realistic rendering of a flower. Many variations possible; can be printed on numerous base cloths.

8. Wallpaper floral stripe: A string of flowers separated by a decorative stripe typical of Victorian wallpaper patterns. Often printed on cotton-type fabrics, but may be used on other base goods. Many variations and sizes popular.

KNIT BASE GOODS

1. Lisle: A lightweight, single-knit, fine-gauge fabric, traditionally made in cotton. Now available in synthetics that have a soft hand and a slight sheen to the surface. Also fabricated in a 1 by 1 rib, which has a slightly ribbed effect created by a knit one, pearl one pattern.

2. Knit brocade: Knits often have a novelty face that has a design formed by raised portions of the knit to add dimension to the fabric. Many design variations possible. Frequently done in polyester.

3. Novelty knit, seven cut: Cut refers to the number of stitches per inch (horizontal) that comprise the fabric. Vast variations of ribs and patterns are possible, with vertical stripings being a favorite design theme. Other weights, from very bulky knits (3 cut), to jersey-weight 22-cut knits, are available.

4. Metallic knit, lurex: Metallic threads may be combined with many yarns to form numerous knitted patterns. The shiny addition of the lurex tends to make the fabric dressy.

5. Bouclé: A woven or knitted fabric that uses a looped yarn to create a looped or knotted appearance.

6. Double-knit, quilt effect: A double knit using a basic surface stitch and a catch stitch to the underlayer in a pattern that simulates quilting.

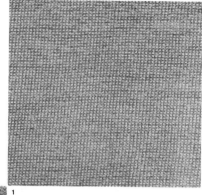

1

2

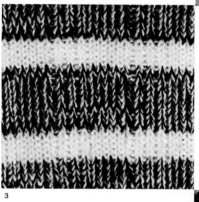

3

5

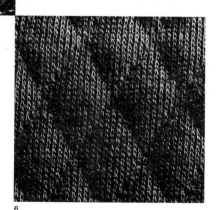

4

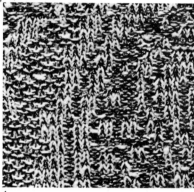

6

7

8

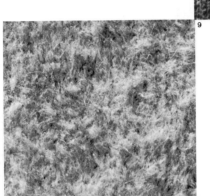

9

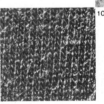

10

11

12

13

7. Double-knit tweed: A blending of basic and novelty yarns in a stitch pattern that resembles woven tweed suitings. Many color and pattern variations are possible.

8. Jacquard: Double- or single-knit fabrics with the designs in multicolored yarns worked directly into the weft knitting. Used in sportswear and dresses.

9. Jersey: A plain-knit rib fabric that is very stretchy. May be knitted in cotton, wool, or blended fibers. Used for soft garments like dresses and blouses. May have a slightly napped surface when knitted in spun yarns.

10. Mock suede: A warp-knit fabric sheered and brushed to look like suede. Available in several weights, this fabric is used as a dress and sportswear fabrication.

11. Ponte de Roma double knit: A basic double-knit stitch used for sportswear and dresses in wool, blends, and synthetic fibers. Sportswear weights are usually 10 ounces in weight and above.

12. Raschel knit: A rigid knit typically used to make lace, nettings, power net, and elaborate sweater-knit fabrics made of novelty yarns in innovative stitches.

13. Tricot, warp knit: Synthetic knit on a warp knitting system available in many patterns and finishes. Classic tricot knits are often used for lingerie and have a smooth, silky surface.

LINEAR PATTERNS

1. Bedford cord: A small vertical cord that is formed by using a two-ply warp to create the ridges. Usually woven in cotton and cotton blends and often printed and brushed (also called sanded or napped.)

2. Bengaline: Horizontal small ribs woven in a lustrous fiber. The surface resembles grosgrain ribbon and has a dressy look.

3. Baby wale corduroy: This example is 14 wales per inch, which usually runs 7 ounces per yard. This ribbed pile fabric is woven by cutting an extra surface filler and brushing it to form the wale. Most often woven in cotton and blends.

4. Medium wale corduroy: A 7 wale per inch corduroy is a medium wale that is also called a thick set. Often used for printed corduroys.

5. Wide wale corduroy: This example is 5 wales per inch, which generally ranges from 10 to 14 ounces per yard. The wider wales are suitable as bottom weights and for jackets and coats. This corduroy is woven in the same manner as the narrower wales, with wider floats that, when cut, form fatter wales.

6. Ribless corduroy: A shallow-wale corduroy that is finished to look like a sueded cord. There are no defined ribs. Often printed.

7. Thick and thin corduroy: A novelty corduroy that is woven with wales of various widths and spacings. Great variety is possible. Most often woven in cotton and cotton blends.

8. Printed corduroy: Many patterns may be printed on all weights and wales of corduroy. The smaller wales are more popular for prints because they are less expensive and more readily available.

9. Awning stripe: Bold, wide stripes named after the canvas used for window awnings. Most typical when woven in cotton base goods. Particularly effective when woven or printed in bold primary colors.

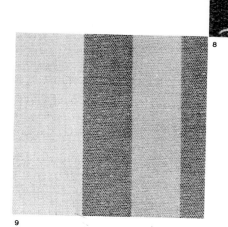

LINEAR PATTERNS *(Continued)*

10. Leno: A woven pattern created by spacing threads to achieve an open look. Most typical of cottons and cotton blends, but also woven into other base goods.

11. Ottoman: A heavy woven ribbed fabric with a wide crosswise rib created by a heavy warp at spaced intervals. Often woven from cotton, wool, silk, and synthetic fibers.

12. Pinstripe, gangster stripe, men's wear stripe: A finely woven or printed stripe on a wide variety of base goods. Typically used in tailored clothing, both for men and women, and shirtings.

13. Satin stripe: Plain-weave stripes are combined with a satin-weave stripe, which is best when woven in a combination of dull or textured yarns and shiny contrasting satin-weave yarns.

14. Ticking stripe: Originally used as a covering for pillows and mattresses. Real ticking is so densely woven that feathers cannot poke through it. First woven in black and natural or navy and natural, but now many novelty variations, often printed instead of woven, in a wide variety of colors. A typical summer fabrication.

15. Rib piqué: Heavier yarns are added to the warp at regular intervals at the back and secured with filling yarns. Ribs may be in a contrast or the same as the background. Typically woven from cotton and cotton blends.

16. French knot: A light- to medium-weight cotton or cotton blend that has a woven novelty bouclé (looped) pinstripe. This fabric is often overprinted.

PLAIDS AND CHECKS

1. Bias plaid: For a novelty effect plaid pattern may be printed or knitted on a 90-degree angle to the selvages. Typical of an argyle plaid pattern. A bias-printed plaid avoids the problem of bowing (bowing is when the straight lines in a pattern are printed off grain, which makes construction difficult).

2. Geometric print: Many printed geometric patterns are possible, and the geometric elements may be printed on the diagonal, a motif not possible with many plain-woven geometrics. Many combinations of regular motifs are classical components of fabric design.

3. Glen plaid: A traditional woven plaid pattern originally done in wool or wool blends. Now available as a woven and a print in either a color and white or beige or several colors. Suitable for many base goods.

4. Woven geometric plaid: Formed by different colored threads arranged into a geometric pattern within the weave. Numerous patterns and combinations are available. May be woven from most fibers.

5. Gingham, ⅛-inch check: A classical plaid formed by the crossing of two colors of thread in the warp and filler and even intervals. Classic colorations are white and color. Woven in tiny checks (1/32 inch) to squares of several inches. Also may be a printed version that can be printed on the straight or the bias. Typical of cotton and cotton blends.

6. Gingham, ¼-inch check: This version shows the very popular ¼-inch check.

7

7. Gingham, 1-inch check: This typical gingham is woven in 1-inch checks and larger, although these larger checks are usually less popular than the smaller ones.

8. Herringbone: Stripes of reverse twills in alternating colors. Traditionally woven in wool, although now available in many fabrications and as a print.

9. Houndstooth: A traditional woven pattern for wool. Often done in white with a strong color contrast check. Typical shape of the pattern is now interpreted as a woven in many fibers and frequently printed on many base goods. May be done in two or three colors.

10. Shepherd's check: A woven wool plaid that resembles cotton gingham. Now also duplicated in synthetics with a wool-like surface and hand.

11. Tartan plaid (quilted example): Woven and printed plaids derived from the traditional Scottish clan plaids are printed on numerous base goods. Originally the tartan plaids were woven in wools. Modern interpretations include color and scale changes.

12. Windowpane plaid: Widely spaced plaid that resembles a windowpane. May be printed or woven on numerous base goods.

13. End-on-end shirting: Yarn-dyed plaid woven into a vast variety of plaids typically used for men's shirtings.

8

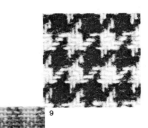

9

10

11

12

13

PILED, LOOPED, AND NAPPED SURFACES

1. Lofty surface: Thick, furry, or napped surface used to describe both knits and wovens with a brushed face. Descriptive term for many lofty base goods.

2. Felt: Nonwoven fabric created by applying heat, pressure, and a bonding agent (glue) to different fibers. This fabric will not ravel and takes dye vividly. Because the fibers are not woven together, this fabric is fragile and thus used for special garments.

3. Camel's hair: A coat- or dress-weight fabric usually made from a blend of camel hair and wool because pure camel's hair fabric is very expensive. Very lightweight, warm, and naturally water repellent. The fabric is usually softly napped and has a characteristic light tan color.

4. Cotton outing flannel: pilou (French): A twill or plain-weave, lightweight, cotton or cotton blend fabric that has a napped, sanded, and brushed surface. Both sides may be brushed. Often printed. This traditional sleepwear fabric may be flameproofed. After washing and wearing, the napped surface has a tendency to pill.

5. Panne velvet: A finish is applied to the pile of a napped fabric. This lays the pile in one direction. Can be applied to knitted or woven pile fabrics in many fibers.

6. Suede cloth: A sueded surface may be found on knitted, woven, and nonwoven fabrics. Sueded surfaces vary greatly in character. Price range is from expensive to inexpensive. Various weights and hands are available, depending on the fiber and construction method used.

7. Terry cloth: Uncut loops, on one or both sides of this fabric, make terry cloth very absorbent. Practical for towels and casual wear, especially in water-related sports clothing. Many print, woven, and knit variations, including stretch terry knits. Most often woven or knit from cotton or cotton blends.

8. Velour: Knit with a pile face that may be printed or embellished with woven stripes. Often knitted in cottons and blends. Soft, drapable hand.

119

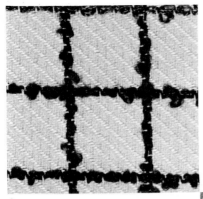

1

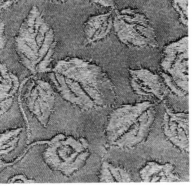

2

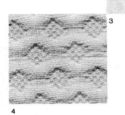

3

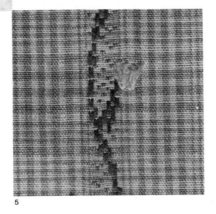

4

5

WOVEN PATTERNS

1. Bouclé linen: Loopy yarns woven into a windowpane plaid. The bouclé yarns can be a blend of several fibers and can be woven into many base goods and novelties. Also used in knits.

2. Damask, satin type: The design is woven on a Jacquard loom on both sides of the fabric. Raised surface is created by a combination of satin and twill stitches. Woven in numerous fibers.

3. Bird's eye piqué: A classic fabrication woven in cotton and cotton blends. Made in the typical piqué method of a large filler yarn that is held with a larger filler to make the standard pattern. Can be printed and dyed, although white is the traditional color. A knit stitch emulates the surface texture of this woven fabric.

4. Waffle piqué: A cotton or cotton blend woven with a dobby look; pattern formed by a heavy stuffer yarn on the back of the cloth that is caught at intervals by a filling thread. Many pattern variations possible. Often overprinted and dyed.

5. Eyelash novelty: A woven plaid shirting in cotton or cotton blends may be woven with a novelty stripe accented with a woven dot that is trimmed to a small fringed spot which resembles an eyelash. Many pattern variations are possible.

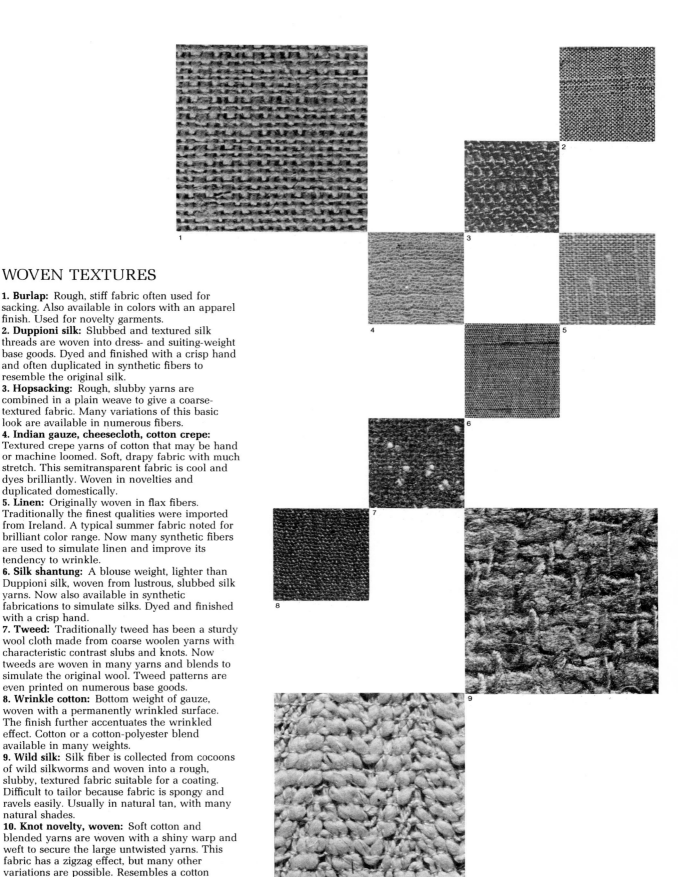

WOVEN TEXTURES

1. Burlap: Rough, stiff fabric often used for sacking. Also available in colors with an apparel finish. Used for novelty garments.

2. Duppioni silk: Slubbed and textured silk threads are woven into dress- and suiting-weight base goods. Dyed and finished with a crisp hand and often duplicated in synthetic fibers to resemble the original silk.

3. Hopsacking: Rough, slubby yarns are combined in a plain weave to give a coarse-textured fabric. Many variations of this basic look are available in numerous fibers.

4. Indian gauze, cheesecloth, cotton crepe: Textured crepe yarns of cotton that may be hand or machine loomed. Soft, drapy fabric with much stretch. This semitransparent fabric is cool and dyes brilliantly. Woven in novelties and duplicated domestically.

5. Linen: Originally woven in flax fibers. Traditionally the finest qualities were imported from Ireland. A typical summer fabric noted for brilliant color range. Now many synthetic fibers are used to simulate linen and improve its tendency to wrinkle.

6. Silk shantung: A blouse weight, lighter than Duppioni silk, woven from lustrous, slubbed silk yarns. Now also available in synthetic fabrications to simulate silks. Dyed and finished with a crisp hand.

7. Tweed: Traditionally tweed has been a sturdy wool cloth made from coarse woolen yarns with characteristic contrast slubs and knots. Now tweeds are woven in many yarns and blends to simulate the original wool. Tweed patterns are even printed on numerous base goods.

8. Wrinkle cotton: Bottom weight of gauze, woven with a permanently wrinkled surface. The finish further accentuates the wrinkled effect. Cotton or a cotton-polyester blend available in many weights.

9. Wild silk: Silk fiber is collected from cocoons of wild silkworms and woven into a rough, slubby, textured fabric suitable for a coating. Difficult to tailor because fabric is spongy and ravels easily. Usually in natural tan, with many natural shades.

10. Knot novelty, woven: Soft cotton and blended yarns are woven with a shiny warp and weft to secure the large untwisted yarns. This fabric has a zigzag effect, but many other variations are possible. Resembles a cotton dishcloth.

121

1

2

3

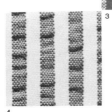

4

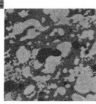

2

1

2

3

4

5

6

PUCKERED SURFACES

1. Matelassé: A blistered-surface fabric that is created from a double warp-faced fabric which has interlaced yarns in the warp and filling. Contrast metallic threads may be used, as in this example. Tends to be dressy in appearance.

2. Plissé: This print simulates the warp-print technique in a floral print. When the traditional technique is used only the warp is printed and the filler is added, giving a fragmented, softened look to the pattern. The base goods is a plissé cotton. The plissé effect is created by printing the base goods with a gum and passing it through a soda bath. The soda crinkles the fabric where the gum is not protecting the surface. Typical summer fabrication.

3. Novelty seersucker: A medium-weight cotton, with alternating smooth stripes and crinkled bands woven with alternating tension to give the crinkled effect. Many patterns and variations are possible.

4. Seersucker: A medium-weight cotton or cotton blend, with a woven crinkled stripe or novelty geometric pattern. The crinkle is created by alternating slack tension in the warp yarns. The stripe is yarn dyed. The classic pattern is usually colored with a white and contrasting color ⅛-inch stripe.

MISCELLANEOUS PRINTS

1. Clay print: A print technique that simulates the ornate endpapers used to finish quality books. Most of these patterns are handmade in France and Italy. Patterns may be printed on many base goods. Usually printed by the heat transfer method because of the many colors and fine quality of printing required.

2. Heat-transfer print, photographic print: The image is printed first on a specially treated paper that can be printed with many colors. The image is transferred from the paper to a suitable base goods by a heat-transfer process. Many colors and designs are possible.

3. Marble print: A print that simulates the veins and colorations of marble. This example is printed on velveteen, but marble print can be printed on numerous base goods.

4. Ombré: A shaded print that graduates from light to dark tones of a color. Available on many base goods.

5. Border print: One edge of the fabric (or both in a double border) has an added design. Borders require careful designing and may take more yardage than an average fabric. Many border print patterns are printed on various base goods.

6. Engineered print: The motif is usually designed to be placed on the garment before the sample is made. Bathing suit prints are designed in this manner. Stock engineered prints include scarf prints, large block designs which must be carefully designed so little fabric is wasted.

5.
kinds of trims and their uses

Trimming means decorating a garment with functional or decorative accessory parts or details. Accessory parts are areas of a garment that are not part of its basic structure, such as buttons, collars, cuffs, or shaped edges. Details are trims added to the basic garment, like appliqué, topstitching, ribbons, pleats, and ruffles. We will not discuss collars and cuffs in this chapter, although they are classified as trims. Collars and cuffs are so varied in design and function that a special chapter is needed: Chapter 14.

When a designer selects a trim for a garment, she must consider many of the same factors as when she chooses a fabric.

1. The trim must enhance the garment or make it unusual, thereby increasing its sales potential.
2. The trim cost must be within the framework of the garment's price.
3. The process of trimming should not delay production.
4. The trim's color and scale should complement the design and enhance the garment's proportion.
5. The trim should have care instructions compatible with the fabric it decorates.

A designer has two options when he is selecting a trim to add to a garment. He can review trim lines and select a ready-made trim, just as he would select a fabric. The second option is to create a trim design and then search for a contractor to make the design. (Actually, most designers use both options.) It is worthwhile to review trim lines, if only to get an idea of available techniques. Generally, a trim contractor will hire designers to invent new applications for its machines' techniques. The contractor will compile a reference library of trim sketches and examples and encourage designers to use the library.

Designers who can create their own trim have an edge on competitors because imaginative trims are increasingly important in the moderate and inexpensive markets. Fabric companies selling popular-priced goods are no longer able to confine prints and fabrics to a single manufacturer. Even special colors require large yardage orders. Therefore, many manufacturers in the same market are limited in their choice of piece goods, and style duplication results. To further complicate the design situation, when a fabric company has hot base goods, other converters in the same price range try to duplicate items that are selling well. Therefore, many fabric firms offer a similar product for the same price. The designer who makes a garment unique by adding an innovative trim will be superior to competitors who may be using the same fabric.

Two design areas that use applied trims frequently are children's wear and lingerie. Children's clothing is often appliquéd. Lace and ribbons on a small girl's dresses are appropriate, as are nonfunctional buttons. Lingerie items, both intimate apparel (garments worn close to the body like bras, girdles, slips, and panties) and at-home garments, use a wealth of special machine edgings, lace insets, and appliqués. Often, so many special edgings are used that a lingerie factory will have its own edging machines with interchangeable attachments.

A third kind of trim is produced by a fabric converter who embroiders designs on base goods and then sells the goods by the yard. This converter develops a line and shows it in the same way a regular piece goods firm would. Usually these converter firms are flexible enough to adapt the designer's ideas and combine or invent special motifs. Often the patterns can be embroidered on a variety of base goods. These firms maintain reference libraries of samples to stimulate new ideas and combinations.

A manufacturer usually works with one or two contractors who supply all buttons and belts. It is advantageous to have an ongoing relationship with these suppliers so that they can adjust their production standards to the manufacturer's specifications. The salespeople for these contractors can service an account individually and make up samples quickly because they can count on a large order.

Most garments shown in this chapter illustrate classical applications of trims. Because fashion changes so rapidly, the design student should recognize traditional trims and traditional uses. Then, armed with good taste, the classical methods of trimming, and knowledge of available trims, a designer can create unique trims that are in step with current fashion.

Classifying trims by kind and the method of application is handy for a person trying to organize information, but this organization is not particularly useful to the working designer. Some trims fall into several categories. For example, buttons and zippers can be functional or decorative. They can be carefully hidden or boldly displayed. In practice, the merit of a trim is determined by this question: "Does this trim make the garment more attractive and salable?"

BELTS

A belt can be a big help in selling a garment. For example, if the waist is slightly too large, the belt will pull the fabric to the body and make the garment look better. Or if a dress with a full silhouette has a belt, the customer can belt the dress or let it fall loosely.

Defining the waist with a belt goes in and out of fashion. During the 1940s and 1950s, a small waist was very fashionable. From childhood through adulthood, women wore waist-cinching undergarments and belts. The average waist measurement for a size 10 was 24 inches. During the early 1960s, the chemise (a loose dress with no waist definition) and the overblouse dominated the fashion scene. These shapes were unfitted at the waist and women abandoned their corsets and tight belts. When belts reappeared after an 8-year absence, manufacturers found that women's waistlines were larger. A size 10 now had a 26-inch waistline. Women were not larger overall, but the waist returned to its natural dimensions when it was unconfined.

There are three main shapes for belts:

1. Straight. Worn at the waist or above; a long, straight strip of fabric that can be stiffened with interfacing.
2. Contour. Shaped in a long curve to conform to the hipline or give shape to the waist. This kind of belt is almost always stiffened with interfacing.
3. Tie. There are several varieties:
   a. Spaghetti. Long, narrow cords covered with the garment fabric or made of leather or plastic. The ends can be finished with a knot or a novelty finish.
   b. Straight. Usually a tie belt that is cut on the straight grain (cut parallel to the selvage); cannot be too wide unless the fabric is very soft. This belt may have a light interfacing. It makes a crisp knot when tied.
   c. Bias. This belt, cut on the most flexible grain of the fabric, can be wider than a straight belt. It will have a soft bow, rather like a scarf. Because of its ability to drape, a bias belt can be wrapped around the waist several times for a dramatic effect.

As with any trim the designer selects, the belt must be compatible with the garment's price. Therefore, more expensive belt fabrications must be avoided in moderate- and low-priced garments. Generally, this cost restriction eliminates leather as a material (unless the belt is narrow). Leather has been copied in an inexpensive plastic material. In fact, almost all expensive belts can be knocked off in less expensive fabrics.

Many belts must be made outside the manufacturer's factory. Two methods are used. In the first meth-

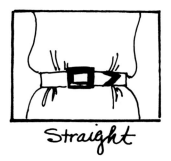

Straight

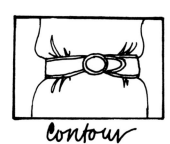

Contour

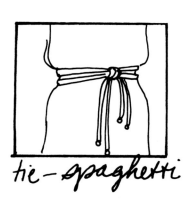

tie—spaghetti

tie—straight

tie—bias

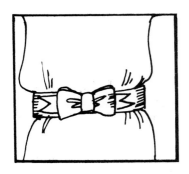

Pretie—rigid and proper
looking.

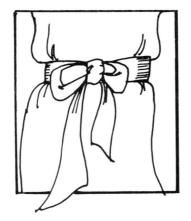

Self-tie—has to be tied each time.
Softer looking, more flexible than
pretie.

od, the backing and the belt material are glued to a
stiff interfacing, producing a smooth, elegant belt.
Unfortunately, prolonged exposure to pressure and
body heat may cause the backing to separate from
the core of the belt. In the second method, the belt
material, interfacing, and backing are sewed together
on a sewing machine. This type of belt will have
stitching around the edge but it is sturdier than a
glued belt.

Several kinds of belts can be made in the factory.
Tie belts are often made in house. If the designer
wants buckles, they can be sampled from the button
supplier. Generally, a belt with a soft core (interfacing) or a belt made of the garment fabric can be constructed in the factory. Belts made in house are more
likely to be ready when the garments are shipped
and are generally less expensive.

A bow with interfacing can be used as an ornament on a belt. The belt will snap shut. Snap belts do
not allow much room for adjustment, as tie and
buckle belts do, but they can look dressier. When a
nonadjustable type of fastening is used, the belt can be
made of stretch braid or garment fabric covering an
elastic core. Either will make the belt more adaptable.

Many times, the designer will have an idea for a
unique belt and will sketch it for the belt contractor
to make up. The belt should be as inexpensive as
possible without losing its distinctive look. If the designer is planning a sophisticated garment but cannot
justifiy the high cost of a leather belt, there are three
alternatives: substitute a plastic fabric that looks like
leather, (2) select a novelty material like chain or
braid, or (3) use a self-fabric belt, which will match
the garment fabric exactly and give the customer a
belt that cannot be duplicated. Besides being a fashionable choice, a self-fabric belt is usually less expensive than novelty selections.

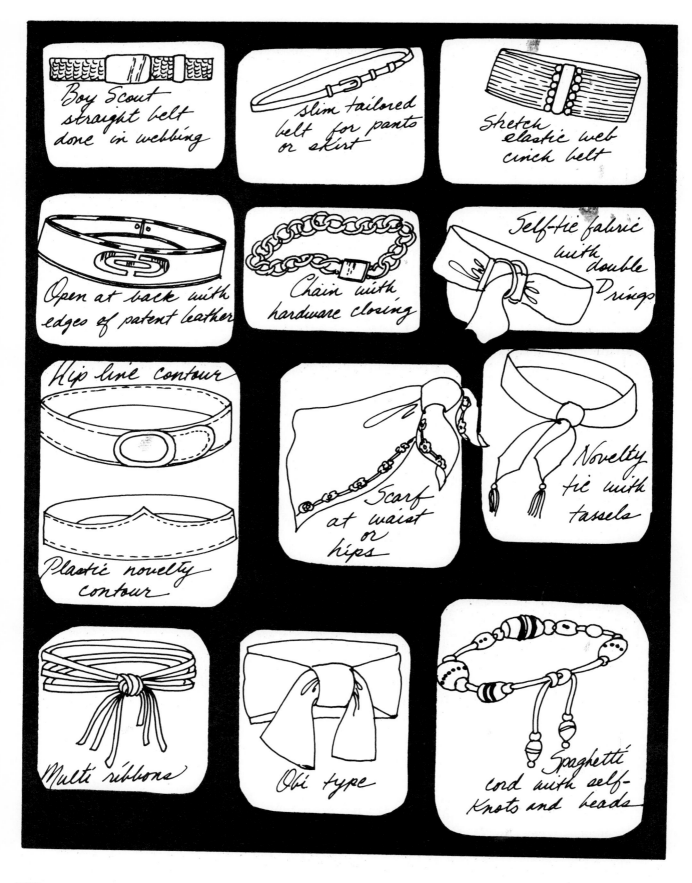

Boy Scout straight belt done in webbing

slim tailored belt for pants or skirt

Sketch elastic web cinch belt

Open at back with edges of patent leather

Chain with hardware closing

Self-tie fabric with double D rings

Hip line contour

Plastic novelty contour

Scarf at waist or hips

Novelty tie with tassels

Multi ribbons

Obi type

Spaghetti cord with self-knots and beads

POCKETS

Pockets are the most important trim for functional clothing. Frequently, sportswear has pockets because people wear this clothing for everyday life and they like to carry things or have a place to put their hands. Well-designed pockets will enhance many other kinds of garments. When using pockets on a garment, follow these guidelines:

1. Make the pocket reflect the shape of the garment's details. If a soft, rounded collar is used, geometric pockets will destroy the unity of the design.
2. Pockets that require precise geometric shapes should not be designed for a garment made of a soft fabric that drapes, because the pockets will sag.
3. Place the pockets where they are both functional and attractive. Consider the normal reach of the arm and a comfortable resting place for the hand.

Left: Square pockets with round collar creates an ununified look. *Right:* Compatible pockets.

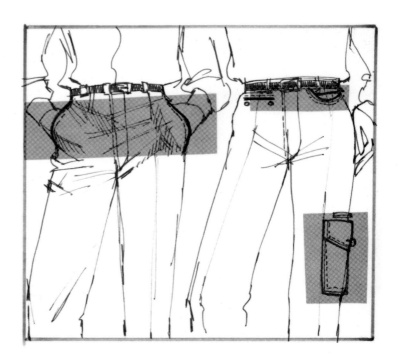

Left: Functional pockets.
Right: Nonfunctional pockets.

4. Pockets used in pairs should have a related shape and be carefully placed. Avoid contrast pockets at the bustline or hipline because they will call attention to these areas and make the design look spotty. Buttons on pocket flaps will look awkward if the buttons are placed over the bust.

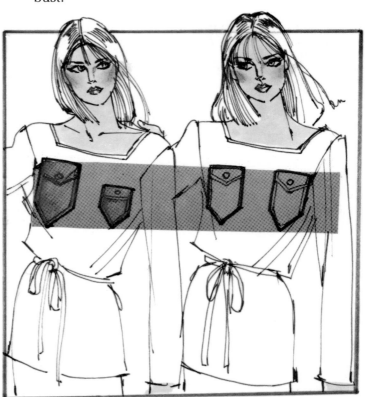

Left: Spotty pockets. *Right:* Related pockets.

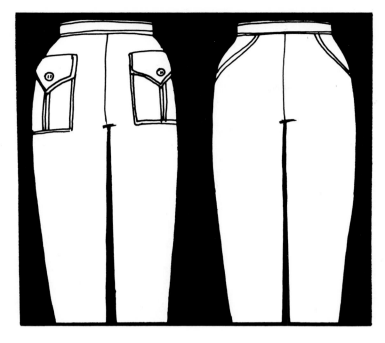

Left: Exaggerates hip width. *Right:* Slims hipline.

5. Remember that, visually, pockets add bulk. When designing for a person with heavy hips or a large bust, placing pockets over these areas will emphasize the figure problem, especially if the garment is fitted.

6. Scale the size of the pocket to the garment it will be used on. A small pocket on a large woman emphasizes her size by contrasting the large expanse of fabric with the small pocket size. The reverse happens if a large pocket is used on a small garment. A pocket at the hipline should be large enough to contain a hand. Pockets on the upper part of the garment can be smaller.

The best way to experiment with shape and placement of pockets is to drape muslin on a dress form. Cut out several potential pocket designs in various sizes and shapes. Pin these samples on the garment. Step back and consider the garment from a distance. Look at the garment in a mirror. The mirror gives you a different perspective on the style because the image is reversed. In fact, this method is excellent for judging your drape when it is completed. When you work steadily on a muslin, your eye tends to adjust to unbalanced lines and awkward proportions. Looking at the reverse image helps you to see what corrections the drape requires.

Pockets tend to be used in pairs. Two equally spaced pockets give the garment a symmetrical design; that is, the design is the same on both sides of the center front line. Symmetrical designs are appro-

Asymmetrical Arrangement

Symmetrical Arrangement

priate for the human body because, ideally, it is equal on both sides. The eye readily accepts a balanced or symmetrical design. When only one pocket is used, the design is asymmetrical and it emphasizes one side of the garment. Asymmetrical designs are used in more expensive garments, probably because the design requires a more subtle balance to succeed.

There are three major kinds of pockets, with many possible variations on each kind:

1. Patch pocket. A pocket applied to the outside of the garment. A great variety of shapes and details is possible. It may have a flap closing.

2. Slashed pocket. This pocket's functional pouch is hidden inside the garment. A decorative finish is used on the opening.
   a. Welt or buttonhole pocket. May have a variety of shapes and is also called a bound or slot pocket.
   b. Upright flap. Characteristic of men's suits. The flap may have novelty shapes.
   c. Flap. When the flap is secured with a button, the pocket is practical because its contents are secure.
3. Pockets may be hidden in a seam. These pockets can be sewed into a side seam, a princess seam, or a yokeline seam. A tremendous variety of pocket stylings can be achieved by combining kinds of pockets, using several pockets on top of each other, or adding various trims.

FASTENINGS

Buttons

Buttons were invented in the late thirteenth century. People who wore buttons were considered morally loose because they could undress more rapidly than people who wore clothing that was laced or sewed closed. Soon buttons became the fashion rage. During the fourteenth century, buttons were used both ornamentally and functionally, just as they are today.

A designer usually selects buttons before a style is made up. He may sample a range of buttons and have them ready for the garment when it is finished. Many times, the designer will have to order new buttons and have them dyed to match the fabric, or he may find a novelty or antique button and ask the supplier to copy it. The relationship between the button supplier and the designer is constant. Because a designer requires continuous service, he will use one or two button companies regularly. The button supplier is more likely to give good service when asked for samples if he is reasonably sure of receiving a stock order. For the supplier, making up samples is time-consuming and unprofitable, but it is necessary if he is bidding for a large quantity order.

The designer must consider the following things when selecting buttons:

1. Price. As always, price is a primary consideration. The unit price of a single button must be extended (multiplied) by the number of buttons

Pockets

Zippered Pocket

quilting

Detail!

Pin Tucks

Inset - self-braid

Watch Pocket

Smile Pocket with contrast lining

yoke detail

134

on the entire garment. The cost may be less if buttons are ordered in quantity for stock production.

2. Aesthetics. A button can be a simple fastening or a major ornament.
   a. Shape. Should reflect the garment's styling and the fabric. Several kinds of surfaces are available (including shiny or matte), depending on the material and method of producing the button.
   b. Color. Buttons will stand out if a contrasting color is chosen. The most subtle and inconspicuous button is self-covered. Beware of too many contrasting spots on a garment.

3. Weight. On a light, delicate fabric, a heavy button causes the placket to droop and look unattractive. A small, lightweight button on a bulky fabric will not secure the placket.

4. Durability. A sturdy button should be used if the garment will be washed often. Many buttons must be cut off before a garment is dry-cleaned and then resewed. On an inexpensive garment, a fragile button that requires expensive special handling is inappropriate. Beware of buttons with jeweled insets because the jewels often fall out.

5. Size. The size of the button should be appropriate to the function of the garment and the visual effect of the total design. Frequently, the same button in several sizes will be used on the same garment. For example, the front placket of a shirt requires a larger button than the cuff. Buttons are measured by "lines" across their diameter. Forty lines equal 1 inch. Check the line chart to identify some familiar sizes.

WHAT ARE BUTTONS MADE OF?

1. Mother-of-pearl (or other shells, like abalone). This is a classic material for buttons on men's shirts. These buttons are made in novelty sizes as well as small sizes for shirts and children's wear. Real shell buttons are fragile, especially when subjected to heat during washing or ironing. These buttons are expensive and they are not always available in a range of styles.

2. Plastic. Plastic is the most versatile of all button materials. It has been used to copy the classic pearl button. Any surface can be produced, from matte (dull) to shiny, and plastic can be dyed any color. Also, it can be clear or opaque. Prices may be high or low, depending on the styling.

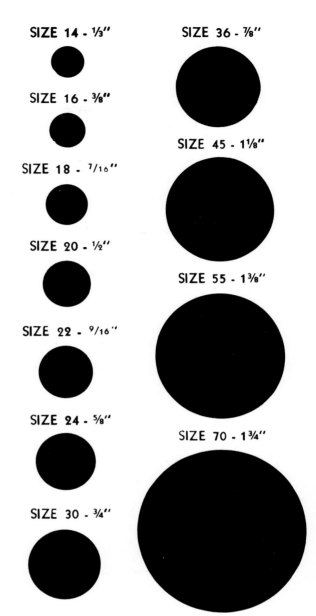

SIZE 14 - ⅓"
SIZE 16 - ⅜"
SIZE 18 - ⁷⁄₁₆"
SIZE 20 - ½"
SIZE 22 - ⁹⁄₁₆"
SIZE 24 - ⅝"
SIZE 30 - ¾"
SIZE 36 - ⅞"
SIZE 45 - 1⅛"
SIZE 55 - 1⅜"
SIZE 70 - 1¾"

Button Line Chart This convenient chart shows the line size of a range of buttons and the equivalent size in fractions of an inch. (Courtesy of *Lidz Brothers, Inc.*)

Buttons

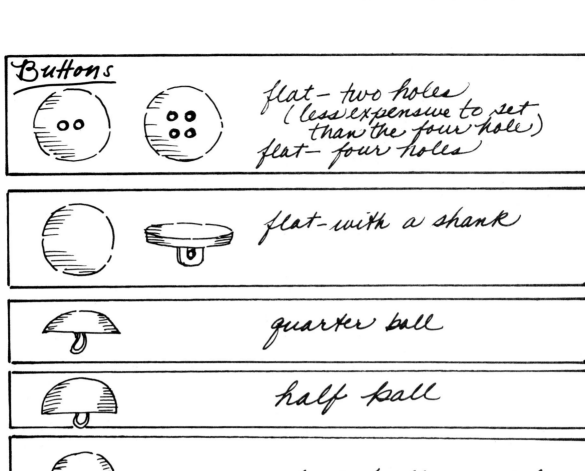

flat– two holes
(less expensive to set
than the four hole)
flat– four holes

flat– with a shank

quarter ball

half ball

full ball – metal shank

full ball – built-in shank

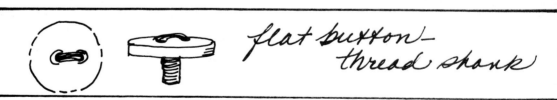

flat button –
thread shank

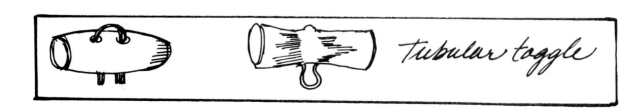

tubular toggle

3. Wood (or pressed wood). This type of button is generally used for casual or sporty clothing. It can have many different shapes and be stained, painted, or have a natural finish. Generally, this button will have holes or a metal shank (a loop through which thread is passed to attach the button to the fabric). Usually, wood is more expensive than plastic.

4. Cloth. Self-covered buttons can be made in many styles and shapes. They can be subtle, yet elegant, but an extra should be included because they are hard to replace. Price depends on style and fabric cost but they are usually inexpensive.

5. Metal. Casting metal is used for many metal buttons. They can be solid or hollow, dull, antiqued (a darker metal), or very shiny. Gold, brass, and silver are the usual finishes, and medals and coins are popular designs. Metal may be enameled to match a fabric color. Prices vary.

6. Leather. Good for a sporty look. Often tied in a knot (a style that has been copied in plastic).

7. Jeweled. Rhinestones, jet, or any other stone can be set in plastic or metal for a dressy look. Stones often fall out. Usually more expensive than plastic.

8. Bone and horn. Rarely used because the materials are expensive and can be duplicated in plastic. Bone and horn are hard to get domestically because of ecological restriction, but they can sometimes be found as imports.

BUTTONHOLES

The most common kind of buttonholes are worked on one side of the placket. By tradition, women's garments button right side over left, so the buttonholes are made in the right side of the placket. The buttonholes are placed so the buttons will fall on the exact center front of the garment (unless it is an asymmetrical closing or the garment is double breasted). An extension remains between the end of the buttonhole and the leading edge of the placket. The size of the extension depends on the size of the button and the weight of the fabric. Usually, a larger button or a heavier fabric requires a bigger extension. The extension can be ½ to 2 inches beyond the center front line. It should be large enough to balance visually the size of the button.

Three kinds of buttonholes may be used on a garment. The most widely used is the machine-made buttonhole because it is inexpensive and suitable for

Machine Made

Bound Buttonhole

Slot Buttonhole

almost every fabric. Machines automatically space, make, and cut the buttonholes.

The second most popular buttonhole is the bound type, which is used on well-tailored garments, particularly coats and suits. There is a machine that makes this bound or corded buttonhole. A bound buttonhole is more expensive than a machine-made one because the back facing must be sewed by hand to the back of the finished buttonhole. Any area requiring hand sewing adds considerably to the cost of the garment.

The third kind of buttonhole is used rarely. It resembles the bound buttonhole and is often used in conjunction with it. When a yoke seam crosses the front placket, a space large enough for a buttonhole is left in the seam and the facing. The ends of this opening are secured and the sides are slip stitched together to form a buttonhole.

LOOP FASTENINGS

Loops that extend from the leading edge (the outside placket edge that is not stitched to the garment front) may also be used to secure the front of the garment. Loops must be spaced more closely than buttons and the placket size differs from a buttonhole placket. A half- or full-ball button is usually used with a loop fastening so the loop will fit over the button more easily. This type of fastening is popular for bridal and evening styling. The loops are more difficult to button so they are not used regularly in day wear.

PLACEMENT OF BUTTONS AND BUTTONHOLES

Buttons should be functional. When buttons and buttonholes are decorative, costs increase because a functional opening must be constructed too. Also, a front-opening collar is used for dresses with buttons down the front, and dividing the collar at the center back for the functional opening spoils the collar's drape. Many times, a beginner will design a dress that buttons down the front to the waistline but will forget to carry the placket into the skirt, which makes it impossible to get the dress on or off.

Self Spaghetti

Braided Tape

Rope loop for sporty toggle

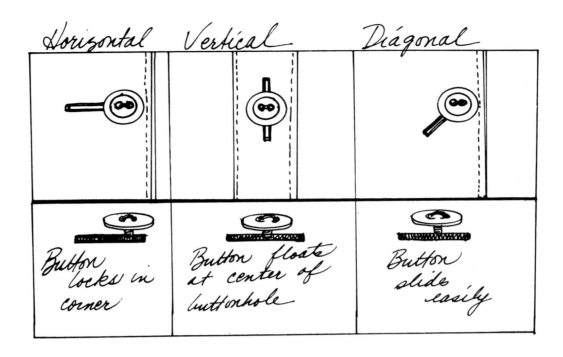

Horizontal   Vertical   Diagonal

Button locks in corner

Button floats at center of buttonhole

Button slides easily

Bust (holds roll of collar)

Waist

Hips

Buttonholes should be placed horizontal to the leading edge. In this way, the button is held on the center front line by the reinforced end of the buttonhole. A vertical buttonhole may be used if the stress on it will be light, as in a loosely fitted shirt. Vertical buttonholes are also used on a narrow placket. For a novelty effect, buttonholes can be placed on the diagonal, but the button is not secured at the end of the hole so the garment cannot withstand much stress on the placket.

Buttons should be placed where they can control the stress on the garment. Stress areas on a jacket or bodice are as follows:

1. Top of the neck. To hold the neck of the garment closed or to establish the roll of the collar.
2. Bust. Place a button parallel to the bust apex point.
3. Waistline. Secure at the waist.
4. Hipline. Placement may vary, depending on the length and fit of the garment.

The other buttons should be equally spaced between the buttons at the stress points.

Button companies sell other accessories—for example, ornamental pins and buckles.

Zippers

Zippers can be used decoratively or functionally. Heavy-duty industrial closings with contrasting tape and novelty pulls are used for casual wear, loungewear, and children's garments. Zippers are available in almost every length and color, and they can be dyed to match an odd shade. Furthermore, zippers can be used to accent design lines or pocket areas. Frequently a zipper is hidden in a seam so that a lower panel can be zipped off to give the garment an optional shorter length. Other novelty effects are possible with hidden or decorative zippers.

Snaps

Two kinds of snaps are commonly used, most often on Western wear and work clothes. The decorative snap looks like a button and is attached to the fabric with a pointed gripper. The head of the snap has a mother-of-pearl inset or another kind of decorative element. The second type of snap is functional and is sewed to the garment through holes at its edge. In expensive garments, if this snap is exposed, the designer will cover the snap with a piece of lining fabric.

Hardware

Various kinds of hardware are used for garment closings. Perhaps the most inventive designer using hardware for fasteners is Bonnie Cashin. Her clothes have anything from a dog-leash clip to a hardware snap. Hardware closings are particularly appropriate for outerwear that is made of bulky fabrics with enough weight to support the metal fastenings. Hardware closings are also used on belts in place of buckles.

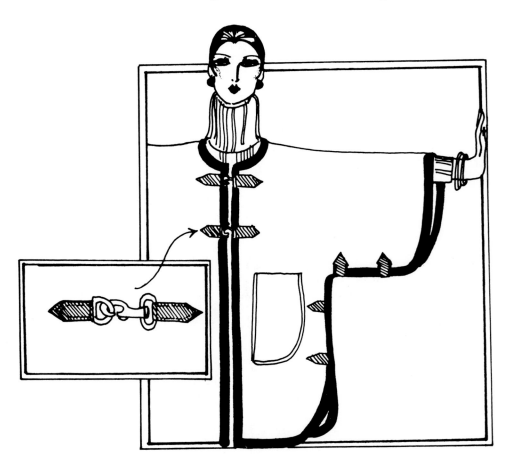

Lacings

Lacings are another novelty fastening. The laces can be threaded through metal eyelets set into each side of a placket. Fabric loops are an alternative to eyelets.

Ties

Ties, either in the garment fabric or in contrasting novelty braids, are used to secure garments. They are adaptable to both casual and dressy styles. Ties are particularly popular on ethnic garments.

LINEAR TRIMS

Linear trims accent seamlines and garment edges. The simplest kinds (which are usually least expensive) are stitched trims. They include the following:

1. Slot seam. A good tailored look.
2. Welt seam. Particularly good for suiting.
3. Multineedle topstitch. Can be used with novelty threads and colors.
4. Corded edge. Outlines and defines a shape.
5. Corded seam.
6. "Hand" picked trim. Really a machine trim that simulates hand-stitched detailing.

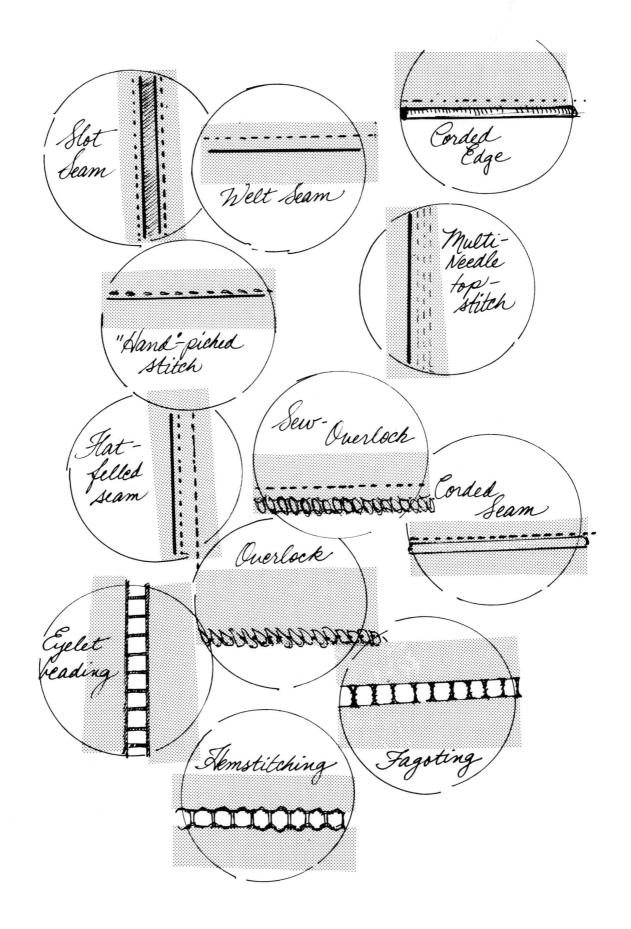

Slot Seam

Welt Seam

Corded Edge

Multi-Needle top-stitch

"Hand"-piched stitch

Flat-felled seam

Sew-Overlock

Corded Seam

Overlock

Eyelet beading

Fagoting

Hemstitching

144

7. Flat-felled seam. The classic seam for jeans; appropriate for shirts and sporty clothes.
8. Fagoting. Openwork (linear), most effective for straight lines.
9. Hem stitching.
10. Eyelet beading. An inset of open lace.
11. Sew-overlock seam. Mostly an internal seam finish.
12. Overlock. Can be used as a hem, to decorate a seam, or as an internal seam finish.

These stitched trims can be varied by using contrasting threads or by alternating colors. Many linear trims are completed on special machines by specialty contractors.

Elastic Multineedle Techniques

Multineedle techniques are frequently used with elastic yarns. This style of trim is most successful when it is used on lightweight fabrics that drape well. Several rows of elastic linear trim are usually used to form an area trim. The elastic yarn causes the fabric to conform to the body shape without the use of darts or seams.

Elastic Multineedle Machine This machine is sewing elastic threads in eight parallel rows on a precut strip of fabric. This shirred fabric will cling to the body without the use of darts or gores when it is stitched into a tube. (Courtesy of Mr. Pleat.)

145

Ray Matsunaga of Chic Lingerie inspects trims he has designed for robes. All trims can be made in house because Chic, like most lingerie firms, maintains many special trim machines.

Shaped Edges

Shaped edges were fashionable during the fourteenth century and for several hundred years thereafter. Shaped edges are still used today, but sparingly. They are expensive and pose some technical problems. For example, decorative effects on skirt and pant hemlines prevent alterations. If the hem is raised or lowered, part of the design impact is lost. Shaped edges are most successful when the garment will not have to be shortened or lengthened. Some examples of shaped edges are

1. Scallops
2. Fagoting
3. Lettuce edge (marrow edge)
4. Bias cording
5. Crochet edging
6. Wired edge
7. Picot edge—one of the many edges used for lingerie and intimate apparel

Ruffles

Ruffles are shaped in two ways: as a straight piece of fabric gathered along one edge or as a circular shape (or a complete circle resembling the shape of a doughnut). Ruffles must be set into a seam, bound at one edge, or gathered in the center to control their fullness. Both circular and straight ruffles can be used at a hem, on the edge of a garment, or as an area trim.

STRAIGHT RUFFLE VARIATIONS

The following are seven basic variations of the straight ruffle:

1. Simple straight ruffle
2. Bias ruffle
3. Pleated ruffle
4. Centrally gathered ruffle
5. Edge finished with a ruffle
6. Lace ruffle
7. Area ruffle

Cascade

Ruffle
set into
a
seam

Shaped
Hem

Circular
ruffle
with
wired
edge

Large
ruffles
at hem

1830s

CIRCULAR RUFFLES

The closer the curved shape of the ruffle resembles a complete doughnut shape, the fuller the ruffle will be. The curved edge of the ruffle limits the kinds of edge finishing that can be used. The ruffle can be made double if the fabric is fine. Otherwise, it can be hemmed with an overlock stitch or edged with a fancy finishing stitch. A circular ruffle usually has a smooth, ungathered edge attached to the seam, and the ruffle makes a graceful, curved edge. The four most common circular ruffles are

1. Large ruffle at hem
2. Cascade
3. Ruffle set into a seam
4. Circular ruffle with wired edge

Passementerie, Braids, Ribbons, Ricrac

Passementerie trim is a broad term for most kinds of braided and corded trim. Ribbons and braids are available in a wide variety of colors, styles, and prices. They range from elaborate and sometimes very wide metallic fancies (usually imported from France and Switzerland) to the inexpensive and classic narrow soutache braid. An important characteris-

tic to consider when choosing a ribbon or braid trim is its flexibility. A braid or ribbon woven on the straight grain must be sewed to the garment in a straight line. A straight trim may be used on a square neckline if the corners of the trim are mitered (matched at a 45-degree angle).

Straight Trims

The following are general types; many novelties are available:

1. Grosgrain ribbons (available in narrow and wide widths)
2. Satin ribbons
3. Novelty wovens

Flexible Trims

Flexible trims are easy to sew around curved edges. Often they are woven on the bias or knitted. Sometimes these trims are flexible because they are narrow. To determine if a trim is flexible, lay it on a flat surface and try to shape it into a curve. If it forms a smooth curve with no gathers in the edges of the trim, it is flexible. Flexible trims can be sewed in a

Flexible Trims

straight line. The accompanying illustration shows four kinds of flexible trims. Note that many of these examples have ethnic origins. Generally, ethnic costumes are basic in cut but elaborately embellished with distinctive handwork.

AREA TRIMS

Area trims cover a larger expanse than linear or spot trims. Many times the area trim can be applied to the yardage before the garment is cut out. An area trim is usually added to inexpensive piece goods because the trim greatly increases the cost of the yardage. The actual price depends on the number of stitches and the time required to apply the trim to a yard of fabric. Area trims can also be applied to a garment section after the section has been cut out. There are three major area trims:

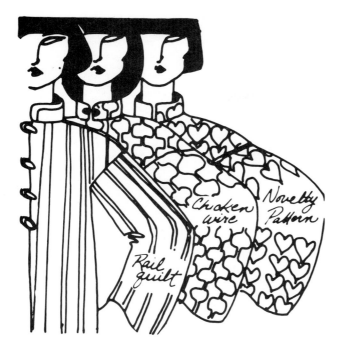

1. Quilting. Fabric can be quilted with filler (a light stuffing) or without.
   a. Rail quilt.
   b. Chicken wire.
   c. Novelty patterns.
2. Trapunto. A stitched design in one area of the garment that is padded for added dimension.
3. Tucking.
   a. Pin tucking.
   b. Vertical
   c. Diagonal.
   d. Horizontal.
   e. Heat.
   f. Side.

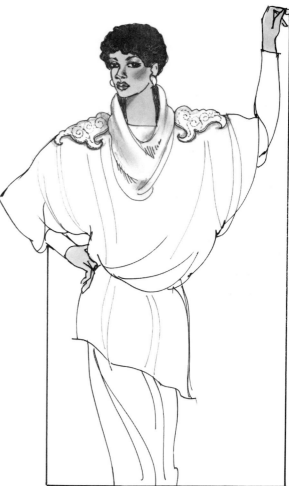

Heat Tucking The fabric is run through a heated element that sets small tucks. A windowpane effect, like the dark fabric to the right of the operator, is also possible with this machine. (Courtesy of Mr. Pleat.)

Contrast Fabric Trim

Combining several fabrics in a single garment is another effective method of trimming. The contrasting color or print can be used as a lining or facing. The contrast will show the customer the possible combinations he or she can make with the garment. When combining prints is popular, fabric converters often design twin prints. These prints are intended for use together, and they feature a common design motif or color theme. Two main problems may arise when several patterns are combined in one style. First, stock yardage must match the original sample. Sometimes dye lots in stock yardage are different, so the stock yardage cannot be matched to the sample goods. Second, all fabrics used in one garment must have similar delivery schedules so the cutting will not be delayed if one pattern arrives later. A separate marker must be made for each print or pattern used. Therefore, the cost of cutting a garment that uses several fabrics is higher.

Embroidery

Embroidery may be added to uncut yardage or to a garment piece after it is cut. Each of the three types of embroidery comes from a different source. The embroidered yardage is available by the yard from converters. A specialty contractor adds the spot em-

Dressy
fabric group
of black velvet
with black
satin trim

broidery trim to the garment piece after the manufacturer has purchased the fabric and cut it. Three important kinds of embroidery are

1. Schiffli. A versatile embroidery technique that can cover the whole fabric or be confined to a border or edging. The process is named for the Swiss manufacturer who invented the embroidery machines for the technique. Elaborate patterns are possible. The cost is based on the stitch count and time needed to embroider a yard of fabric.
2. Gross. A spot embroidery technique that is less expensive than Schiffli if the pattern is confined to a small space. In one design, several colors and a variety of yarns and threads may be used. The process is named after the machines that do the work.
3. Eyelet. An overall pattern (a border is optional) that is embroidered on a Schiffli machine with the following added characteristics (see the textile dictionary in Chapter 14 for an example):
   a. The classic look features white thread on white cotton base goods (or a cotton blend).
   b. Some areas of the design may be stamped out and then the holes embroidered around the edge to give a lace effect.
   c. Eyelet is almost always purchased as yardage. Because eyelet is a classic type of embroidery, comes in one color, and has set patterns, it is the most inexpensive fabric with allover embroidery. Typically this fabric is used in the spring and summer.

Appliqués and Patches

Appliqués are pieces of fabric in decorative shapes that are sewed to a garment with an ornamental finishing stitch. The most effective appliqués are simple, graphic shapes scaled to complement the garment to which they are applied. Appliqués can be made three-dimensional by stuffing tiny "pillows" and stitching them to the garment. This type of trim is particularly suitable for children's wear, but it is used in many other kinds of garments. Patches of embroidery can also be sewed on garments.

Pleating

Fabric is pleated by putting a garment piece into a manilla paper pattern that has been scored with the

Geometric appliqués

Decorative appliqués

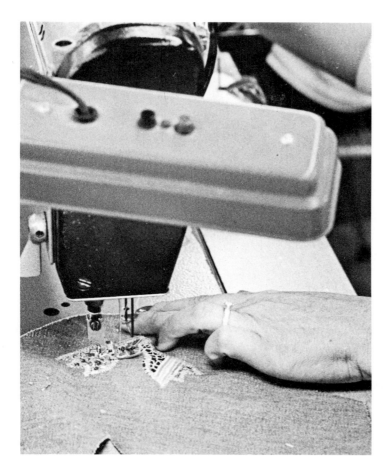

Appliqué Decorative calico flowers have been stamped out with a die (a metal stamp in the shape of the design). Then the design is stitched onto the precut garment piece with an edging stitch that prevents raveling. (Courtesy of Mr. Pleat.)

desired pleat dimensions. The paper pattern is folded tightly along the guidelines and securely tied. Then the bundle is baked in an oven. Almost any fabric can be pleated, but unless there is some heat-sensitive fiber in the fabric, the pleats will come out when the garment is cleaned or washed. Almost always an outside contractor is used for pleating. Because pleats are most frequently employed for skirts, there is a complete discussion of pleat types in Chapter 10.

Pleating The pleated piece is taken from the paper pattern after being baked in an oven that sets the pleats. While the pattern is open, another unpleated piece of fabric, cut to the desired shape, is put on the pattern. It is wrapped to be baked in the oven. (Courtesy of Mr. Pleat.)

Studding

Studding was first used by Levi Strauss as a means of reinforcing the seams on work pants designed for miners in the California gold fields. Strauss patented the process in the nineteenth century, but when the patent ran out, many other manufacturers used the riveting process. These early rivets fastened pockets securely and reinforced stress points, making the early denim pants very durable. Today studding is decorative as well as functional. Types of studs include rivetlike nailheads and rhinestones. Depending on the type of stud, the garment can be sporty or dressy.

Openwork

Openwork is a design cut out of the fabric and edged with an overlock stitch or a corded detail. Sometimes lace insets or transparent fabrics replace the opaque top fabric.

156

Airbrush and Hand Painting

Airbrush designs are painted freehand or stenciled on a garment. The paint or dye is sprayed on by air pressure to achieve a subtle effect or a more commercial look. Depending on the design and technique, the garments can be dressy or very casual. Hand-painted garments are usually quite expensive. Some manufacturers have turned to the Orient for cheaper hand-painted fabric. Quality is high and the price is lower because wages are lower.

Heat-Transfer Prints

Heat-transfer prints are a more commercial method for putting an image on a garment. Many colors may be used. The fabric that prints most successfully with this system is polyester. First the image is printed on a specially treated paper. Then it is transferred to the fabric by a machine that applies heat to the paper and fabric. This inexpensive method is often added to T-shirts.

REVIEW

Word Finders

Define the following words from the chapter you just read:

1. Bias belt
2. Bound buttonholes
3. Chemise
4. Contour belt
5. Extension
6. Flap pocket
7. Full-ball button
8. Hardware
9. Intimate apparel
10. Lacing
11. Leading edge
12. Line
13. Loop button fastening
14. Mitered
15. Mother-of-pearl
16. Passementerie
17. Patch pockets
18. Placket
19. Schiffli embroidery
20. Shank
21. Slashed pockets
22. Soutache braid
23. Spaghetti
24. Twin print
25. Welt pocket

Discussion Questions

1. What factors must a designer consider when selecting a trim?
2. What are the three belt shapes? What materials can be used to make a belt?
3. Name and sketch 10 pocket details.
4. What materials can buttons be made from?
5. What stress points on a jacket require a button?

6.
sources of
inspiration

Paris couture and European prêt-à-porter (ready-to-wear) are the traditional sources for fashion trends. Each year at show time, buyers, fashion editors, and manufacturers flock to Paris, London, and Milan to review the new styles. Manufacturers of missy and designer apparel tend to watch couture shows with the greatest interest. The manufacturers of junior and young contemporary clothes avidly follow the prêt-à-porter styles because they are more trendy and can be produced more easily for the young customer.

Before the shows begin, American publications preview the openings with articles on fabric trends, rough sketches or style predictions, and interviews with designers. As soon as the shows are over, fashion editors select the styles they feel are prophetic and send photos, sketches, and stories to the United States for publication in consumer and trade fashi-

portant to remember that all European collections we see in domestic publications have been edited by American journalists. In fact, many potentially important ideas may never reach American designers unless they attend the shows or read European fashion magazines.

A fashion trend born in Europe is not necessarily destined to succeed in the United States because some ideas are too advanced or impractical for an American life-style. Generally, though, the influence of Paris will be felt eventually as it filters into the fashion mainstream and is reinterpreted by SA (for Seventh Avenue in New York, where most established garment manufacturers have offices and where American ready-to-wear manufacturing is centered). Because American fashion retailers, fashion editors, and manufacturers watch European design carefully, it is a source of common inspiration that is usually translated into apparel for the American consumer.

While reading about the European sources of fashion trends, you may have thought that many American designers create similar garments because they are inspired by a common source. This is indeed a frequent occurrence, but many American designers are wary of this tendency toward uniformity. To avoid duplicate styling, some American designers use Paris fashion trends only as a frame of reference and do not copy the styles exactly. Although these designers are influenced by colors, silhouettes, and details, they reinterpret the foreign trends so that the garments they produce are uniquely suited to their customers and their firms' production limitations.

Other designers follow the fashion trends for amusement but find their inspiration elsewhere. Specific markets, such as swimwear, develop completely different sources of inspiration. Generally the most exceptional styling comes from designers with unusual sources. The designer who creates a trend and develops a unique product will have a loyal following of retailers and customers.

TIMING

Timing is an important aspect of successful styling. Most designers try to fit their garments into the general fashion climate. *Climate* is a combination of new trends in fashion, the general economic condition of the country, current technological developments, and current retail trends. If current fashion tends toward the loosely fitted garment with a crisp shape in a rigid fabric, the designer working with soft knits that are cut to reveal the body shape will be out of the fashion mainstream. However, this soft styling will appeal to a small segment of the market. In time, this particular styling may become the predominant fashion trend, and then the crisp silhouette of the loosely fitted garment will be passé.

Fashions tend to evolve, and any item will have several phases to its fashion life.

Start of a Fashion

A new style or silhouette is shown. The style may catch on slowly or even fail at first. Often, but not always, the innovative style appears first in a high-priced garment. Some fashions start "in the streets" (that is, they are created by nonprofessionals for their own wear). Finally, the new style begins "checking" with the more fashion-conscious retailers. During this phase, the style will be covered in trade and consumer fashion publications.

The Fashion Evolves into a Staple

The style has become a hot item for the original manufacturer and has checked with several retailers. Other manufacturers *knock off* (copy) the original, often at a lower price. Many manufacturers design versions of the successful style. Generally department stores across the country sell the item at several prices in a variety of fabrics. At this point chain store manufacturers reinterpret the strong trends, knock them off, and offer them at even lower prices. Retail stores will advertise the style heavily in newspapers.

Staple Becomes Chain Store Merchandise

Manufacturers who sell to chain store catalogs must design their lines more than a year before the selling date. For this reason, styling is usually conservative and emphasizes proved items. If the style is successful in the catalog, it may be repeated for several issues. When sales decline, the item is dropped.

Closeout and Demise

The style is knocked off in very inexpensive fabrics for the lowest possible prices. Now all kinds of people wear the style. The cheapest versions have lost the original subtlety and good fit. Finally, the style is

closed out at all price levels. But 10 or 20 years from now the style may be rediscovered in a wave of nostalgia and reinterpreted in the context of that period.

Timing has another meaning for the designer of ready-to-wear. The designer works long before the season, usually 6 to 8 months before the garment is finally sold to the consumer. A designer must anticipate the weather across the country during the *selling period of the garment*, rather than the weather when the customer will wear the garment. Retail seasons differ considerably from actual seasons. For example, spring merchandise is shipped to the stores during January and February, generally the coldest months of the year. The garments emphasize pastel colors, but they are neither too lightweight nor too bare because the selling season precedes the actual wearing season. The customer wants to buy the latest style now, although he or she will not wear it until the weather warms. The designer must understand and anticipate weather probabilities, general fashion trends, and retailers' schedules.

Study the timetable on pp. 164–165 and follow a season's merchandise through these processes: designing, selling to the retailer, manufacturing, shipping, and selling to the customer. This cycle takes about 8 months. Note that chain store manufacturers often add 6 to 8 months to the design phase.

PRINTED SOURCES OF INSPIRATION

Successful designers must motivate themselves when they begin designing for a new season. If no fresh ideas occur spontaneously, they must do some research. Published sources of fashion trends should be basic to a designer's weekly reading. In addition to the domestic fashion reports, which most designers read, there are many foreign magazines that report on specialty markets or present an in-depth look at European couture and prêt-à-porter. Foreign publications are valuable because they are free from the bias of an American editor. The more widely a designer reads, the more imaginative his or her ideas will be.

Trade Newspapers

Women's Wear Daily (WWD). Fairchild Publications, 7 East 12th Street, New York, NY 10003. This is the most important trade publication for

	January	February	March	April	May	June
The Designer	Style early fall →	Shop for fall fabrics / Sample, design, and construct	Duplicate sample line →	First of month, early fall goes into showroom		Shop and research spring cruise
		Refabricate summer promotions ←	Research late fall and holiday colors and fabrics	Style late fall and holiday	Duplicate samples	Late fall and holiday, breaks late May or early June
		Paris couture shows, spring		European prêt-à-porter shows, fall	Interstoff, international fabric show, Germany	
The Manufacturer	Summer line goes into showroom right after New Year →			Sell early fall / Sell summer promotions and reorders →		Sell late fall and holiday / Order fall fabric
	Order summer stock fabric	Manufacturer and ship summer →			Manufacture summer promotions and reorders	
	Ship and produce spring clothes (reorders) →				Manufacture early fall and ship—	
The Department Store	Receive spring/cruise / Sell spring / Stores have new color story →		First spring markdowns		Major spring — markdowns ←	
		Rainwear important in coat department		Early summer—sell summer →		Summer promotions
	After-Christmas sales of holiday and late fall garments			Easter promotions for children's wear / Swimwear opens	Graduation dresses / Wedding promotions →	

July	August	September	October	November	December
Style spring	Duplicate spring →	Early October, spring goes into showroom			Research early fall colors and fabrics
	Refabricate and do fall promotions	Research summer colors and trends— sample fabric for summer	Style summer →		Duplicate samples
	Paris couture shows, fall		European prêt-a-porter shows, spring	Interstoff, international fabric show, Germany	
Sell reorders and promotions →		Sell spring cruise →			→
Manufacture and ship fall		Order spring stock fabric	Manufacture cruise and spring. Ship late November–early December		
Order late fall and holiday fabrics			Set Christmas catalog merchandise	Ship Christmas catalog merchandise	
		Manufacture and ship late fall and holiday →			
Early fall —	selling →	Fall opens Sell fall →		→	First fall markdowns
	Coats important now				Children's party clothes
	Furs open				
Summer clearance		Early fall markdowns →		Christmas catalog goes to customers mid-month →	Christmas promotions sells →
	Back to school for young apparel →		Holiday merchandise arrives ——— sells →		
					Mark down glittery-dressy after Christmas
→	Swimwear sales				

EARLY FALL

The KNIT BIT...

Bronson does a 100 per cent acrylic hooded sweater in black, with rust, white and cream detailing for Fall. The sweater is teamed with a European texturized spun poly gab pant.

Jantzen takes 100 per cent wool and works up a jacket-weight sweater. The tweedy-hand knit sweater is colored in grey with rust animal treatment and features looped wool on the arms and body.

Sebastian does a three-piece wool outfit for Fall. Shown, the ribbed crew teamed with the basic pant and topped by the scalloped wrap tie jacket. The crew and pant are colored in brown; the jacket is in cream, mustard and brown horizontal stripes.

Wine and cloud are the colors—100 per cent bright Creslan is the fabric for this V-neck sweater from **Kingston Knits.** The top criss-crosses in front, ties in back, is side vented and paired with a basic pull-on pant.

Marbella Knits creates a drop shouldered button-down tunic in 70 acetate/30 poly. The tie-belted tunic features ribbing at the hem and belt and is colored in black and white. The tunic is shown with Marbella's black pull-on pant.

Sketches by Fernando R. Flores

Trade Newspapers *California Apparel News,* a weekly publication, covers local manufacturers and fashion trends. (Courtesy of *California Apparel News* and Fernando R. Flores.)

Knitwear was an important part of the pret-a-porter show and is an equally important part of the Early Fall knitwear market as shown locally.

Silhouettes include two- and three-piece dress looks, dresses with lots of detailing and layered looks. Necklines include big cowls, bateau and square necks. Shoulders are dropped and frequently buttoned. Short tops, jackets, tunics, tabards are slipped over cowls and turtles and worn with split skirts, six- to eight-gore skirts, basic pull-on pants.

Drawstrings have hit the knits — at the waistline, creating blouson looks, and at the cuffs. Multicolored jacquards are important at the yoke, sleeve and hem.

Sweaters look new with Nordic jacquards and Russian dancer figurines, fringe, hoods, big cowls, stripes and ethnic border designs.

Silhouettes include wrap sweaters over cowls; tunics and short jackets over pants and culottes; looped yarn jacket-weight sweaters.

Colors — black and white, especially in stripings; brights used as accents over black grounds, grey, taupe, brown, navy, rust, berry and wine shades. Winter white has forest and camel accents.

Fabrications include lots of wool — important in flannel knit — along with blends of poly and wool, acrylic and wool, acrylic and poly, acetate and poly, acrylic/mohair/nylon, in addition to acrylic, poly and cashmere.

Dea Eldorado

167

women's apparel. *WWD*, a daily newspaper published in New York, covers women's and children's apparel in the United States. Reports from abroad are published after the couture and prêt-à-porter shows. Known as "the Bible of the women's apparel industry," *WWD* includes retailing activities and want ads. Fairchild also publishes the *Daily News Record* (*DNR*), the *Men's Wear Magazine*, and the twice-monthly *Sportsdial*, which covers active sportswear.

California Apparel News. California Fashion Publications, 945 South Wall Street, Los Angeles, CA 90015. A trade publication that covers the West Coast market. It is published weekly and includes want ads.

Fashion Showcase. 1145 Empire Central Place, Suite 100, Dallas, TX 75247. Focuses on commercial fashion in Texas and the midwestern states.

American Fabrics and Fashion. Doric Publishing, 24 East 38th Street, New York, NY 10016. Published quarterly, this magazine covers fabric and fabric design innovation.

Apparel Industry Magazine. 6226 Vineland Avenue, North Hollywood, CA 91606. Covers technical manufacturing news.

Fabric News to the Trade (commonly called *Trade*). 21 East 40th Street, New York, NY 10016. A directory to New York textile firms and industry news.

Stores. 100 West 31st Street, New York, NY 10001. A trade magazine for retail stores.

Daily or Weekly Consumer Newspapers

Local newspapers. Daily newspapers for each city carry current fashion information for the local manufacturer and retailer. The advertisements throughout are as valuable as the fashion pages. Manufacturers can subscribe to *A Digest* or Mittlemark *Retail Ad Report*, both of which compile the best local department store advertisements and publish them according to category.

New York Times Sunday Magazine. The magazine is particularly important to the fashion trade because many retailers and manufacturers advertise in it. Occasional fashion supplements are published.

W. A weekly newspaper with some color printing, put out by the publishers of *Women's Wear Daily.* It carries reprints of "soft" news (interviews with personalities, fashion reports, society news, and so on) featured during the week in *WWD.* Included are manufacturers' and retailers' advertisements that have not been carried in the daily paper.

Consumer Domestic Magazines (Glossies)

Children's and young girl's wear. *Ladies Home Journal*—occasional articles on children's wear; *Seventeen*—the publication that most influences children's and teen's wear in the United States.

Young women. *Glamour* and *Mademoiselle*—magazines that appeal to high school and college students and young businesswomen; both magazines stress contests and articles that promote audience involvement.

General and high fashion. *Vogue* and *Harper's Bazaar*—coverage of American and foreign fashion scenes, aimed at the fashion-conscious mature woman.

Magazines with some fashion articles. *Town and Country*—appeals to the very wealthy; *Red Book* and *Cosmopolitan*—both are for career women and young married women; *Woman's Day, Ladies Home Journal,* and *Family Circle*—mainly for homemakers.

Men's fashions. *Gentleman's Quarterly*—now published monthly, this magazine is the most influential men's wear fashion publication. *Playboy* and *Esquire* also feature men's fashions.

Patternmaker Publications, Pattern Books

The home sewing market is well covered by monthly publications from the three largest pattern companies: Vogue, Butterick, and Simplicity. In addition to these monthly publications, which are available on the newsstand or by subscription, large, comprehensive pattern books can be purchased from yardage stores when the books are out of date. Pattern books are valuable reference materials for designers and students.

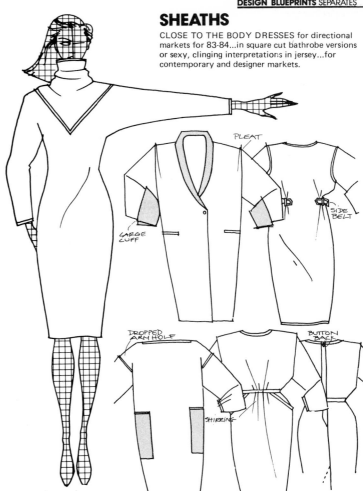

SHEATHS

CLOSE TO THE BODY DRESSES for directional markets for 83-84...in square cut bathrobe versions or sexy, clinging interpretations in jersey...for contemporary and designer markets.

Design Reports *IM* is a subscription fashion report frequently used by retailers and manufacturers. Concise reports on foreign fashion markets with specific styling sketches and information are provided. There are no advertisements in design reports, so the information has no commercial bias. (Courtesy of *IM International.*)

Design and Retailing Reports

These reports require an annual subscription because they do not rely on advertising for support.

IM, Nigel French, Here and There, Faces, Report West, Design Intelligence, and *Design Direction.* Published in England, France, and the United States. These expensive reports, intended for the American industry, feature detailed fashion and fabric information from European couture and *prêt-à-porter*

The Color Projections (by Pat Tunskey), *The Color Box* (by Jane Resnick), and *Promostyl.* Color services that predict color trends for various markets 18 months before the merchandise is shipped to retailers.

Tobé. A retailer report that features analysis of national retailing trends, reports on hot manufacturers, and details on growing consumer trends. Available to retailers, but not manufacturers, on a subscription basis.

JUMPERS

JUMPERS and OVERALLS, the NEWEST APPROACH
TO DRESSES for the junior market. Note WIDE CUT
BIB FRONTS and the true workmen's overall approach
to shoulder straps.

Buying office reports. Buying offices compile for
member stores specialized information on
fashions and vendors.

Video Fashions, Inc. Video fashions of European
prêt-à-porter collections. Most designers make
videotapes of their fashion shows for the use of
the press and retail stores.

Foreign Trade and Fashion Publications

Belezza. Aldo Palazzi Editore, Via Zuretti 37, Milan, Italy. Italian high fashion.

Bimbi Eleganti. Editrice Viscontea, Via Palladio
5, 20135 Milan, Italy. Elegant children's wear.

Brigitte. Postfach 30-20-40, 2000 Hamburg 36,
West Germany.

Calze Moda Maglie. Calze Moda Maglia, SES,
Co. S1, Magenta 32, Milan, Italy. European
knitwear, especially Italian.

Chic. Ross Verlag, Spinchernstr. 12, 5 Cologne,
West Germany. German fashions.

Depeché. Mode, 3 rue de Teheran, 75008 Paris, France.

Elegance. Gartenstrasse 14, Postfach CH 8039, Zurich, Switzerland. Available on the newsstand only.

Eleganza. CIMS Vianelli, Eleganza, Via Verdi 10/1, Venice, Italy.

Elle. 6 rue Ancello, 92521 Neuille, France. Published weekly. This is one of the most influencial junior life-style publications.

Flair. IPC Magazines, Ltd., Tower House, Southampton Street, London WC2, England.

Grazia. Published by Arnoldo Mondadori, Editore, 20090 Segrate, Milan, Italy. Trendy junior designs.

Fashion Magazines Many foreign and domestic fashion magazines are available. The designer should be familiar with domestic magazines because they cover current developments in American fashion. Foreign magazines tend to have more avant-garde fashion information.

Harper's and Queen. Chestergate House, Vauxhall Bridge Road, London SW1, England. British version of *Harper's Bazaar.*

Harper's Bazaar (Italia). Corso di Porta Nuova, 46 Milan, Italy. Italian edition of *Harper's Bazaar.*

Linea Italiana. Mondadori Publishing, 437 Madison Avenue, New York, NY 10022. High-fashion women's wear. Also publishes *Linea Italiana Uomo* for men's wear.

Marie Claire and *100 Idees.* 11 bis, rue Boissyd' Anglas, 75008 Paris, France. Influential magazines covering junior fashions and life-styles.

Mode. Friedrica Ebert Str. 76–78, 701 Leipzig, East Germany.

Officiel de la Couture et de la Mode de Paris. Officiel de la Couture SA, 226 Rue du Faubourg St. Honoré, Paris 8e, France. Most important couture publication, published quarterly.

Officiel du Prêt-à-Porter. Societé Europeane d'Edition et de Publicité, 265 Avenue Louise, 1050 Brussels, Belgium.

Publicaciones Herrerias. SA, Morelos 16–3er Piso, Mexico 1, DF, Mexico.

Sposa. Edizioni Moderne Internazionali, Via Builamiacci 11, 20135 Milan, Italy. Italian bridal magazine.

Style. 481 University Avenue, Toronto, Ontario M5W1A7, Canada. Fashions in Canada.

Ultima Moda. Mexican report on domestic and foreign high fashion.

Vogue. Published in France, England, Italy, and Australia. Each edition covers domestic fashion for that country plus foreign styles. Special editions cover men's wear and active sports that influence fashions, like *Uomo Vogue* and *Vogue Mare* in Italy and *Vogue Homme* in France.

Domestic Trade and Special Interest Publications

Apparel Executive. Apparel Institute, 77 Maple Drive, Great Neck, NY 11021. Journal for top-level management.

Apparel Manufacturer. Forge Associate Publications, Inc., Riverside, CT.

Body Fashions. Harcourt Jovanovich, Inc., 757 Third Avenue, New York, NY 10017.

Retail Week. 380 Madison Avenue, New York, NY 10017.

Color Predictions Fiber companies and fabric converters publish color predictions before the season to give manufacturers and retailers fashion direction. Color reports are also presented by some fashion publications.

Modern Bride. Ziff Davis Publishing, 1 Park Avenue, New York, NY 10016.

Western Apparel Industry. 112 West 9th Street, Los Angeles, CA 90015. Trade developments and innovations with a West Coast perspective.

Historical Publications

For historical research, the following publications are available in many research libraries across the country.

Bazaar. Late 1860s to present (began in 1866, but early copies were sometimes lost).
Godey's Lady's Book. 1830s to late 1890s.
Ladies Home Journal. 1883 to present.
Le Bon Ton. 1912 to mid-1920s.
Sears' Catalogs. Old editions reprinted at periodic intervals.
Vogue (USA). 1893 to present.

GOOD WORK HABITS

Besides printed fashion information, color trends from fiber companies, and fabric information from textile firms, the alert designer has other sources of inspiration. The way the designer uses these sources makes the difference between innovative designing that has a unique personality and styling that simply repeats market trends. It is probably most important for the designer to be aware of current life-styles and trends. Designers should develop a sensitivity to objects and ideas. In many instances, painters, sculptors, and other fine artists develop trends long before the general public picks them up as commercial fashion. Constant exposure to museums, art galleries, and popular events is important for every designer.

Another asset is the designer's intuition. Learn to respond to the demands of your own life. Perhaps to solve a clothing problem you have will create a new style. Claire McCardell's innovation in the late 1940s stemmed from a personal style problem. She felt that women should have casual garments for everyday life. Designed for Townley, her uncomplicated and easy-to-wear dresses and pants were the basis for American sportswear. One of McCardell's clever garments was an inexpensive wrap dress that gave women an alternative to the dowdy housedress. In 1973, Anne Kline designed a simple cotton dress in a variety of fresh prints. This dress was designed to meet the modern woman's need for a simple garment that would be stylish, easy to care for, well made, but moderately priced.

Scrap

To benefit the most from constant exposure to fashion information, designers must develop two good working habits. First, cut out any picture that appeals to you, triggers your imagination, or has a detail you like. Keep these clippings ("scrap") in a folder and refer to the folder often, adding clippings constantly. Scrap can suggest styling possibilities, details, trends, and color combinations that you may not have thought of. But the scrap folder should be a source of inspiration, not a substitute for it. Copying published styles has little merit unless the designer greatly modifies the styles. Scrap should be used as a pin to prick the imagination and stimulate creativity.

Sketch or Croquis Book

The second important tool is a sketch or croquis book (*croquis* is the French word for a drawing of a style or pattern). Select a handy-sized book with plain un-

Sketchbook   A designer's sketchbook should be a handy size so it is easy to carry on shopping expeditions. The designer should develop the habit of sketching garments and innovative ideas. These can be quick sketches, even sketches of half the garment, as long as the style's essence is recorded for later development.

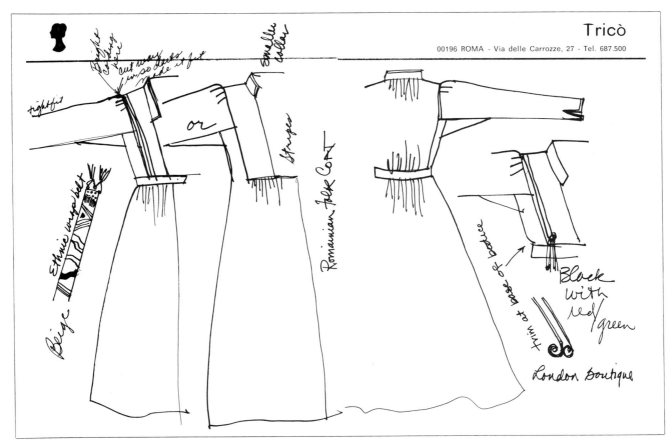

Tricò

00196 ROMA · Via delle Carrozze, 27 · Tel. 687.500

lined pages. Cover the book with fabric or paper so it will be a pleasure to carry without being conspicuous. Keep your sketchbook with you at all times, and fill it with quick informative sketches, impressions, and color and fabric swatches. The sketches can be rough because they are for your reference only. Make as many notes as necessary to clarify your visual ideas. Use your sketchbook to record memorable garments you see in stores or to sketch details and styles you find while doing period research. To develop the habit of sketching, set aside some time each day for working on your sketchbook. While riding on the bus or visiting a store, add at least ten sketches or ideas to your book. If you are consistent, you will find that sketching your ideas is an effective way of recording impressions for future use. As you finish them, keep your sketchbooks for reference.

Draping and Patternmaking

Designers who are able to drape and make their own patterns frequently find that the design they have imagined is altered as they drape it because working with fabric on the human form suggests added de-

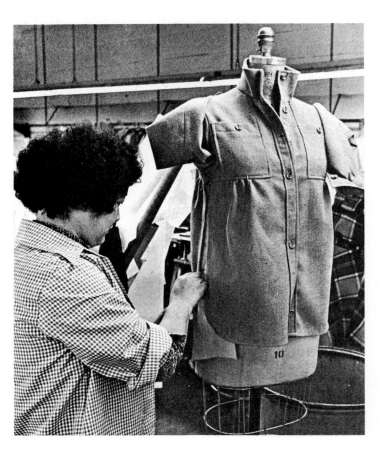

Sample Fittings The designer and patternmakers must fit and refine the original idea until an attractive, well-fitted first sample evolves.

sign dimensions. Many designers are excellent dressmakers, and they can anticipate in early stages of design what the final product will look like and what construction problems may develop. They can suggest to the sample maker details that will enhance the total design and sewing techniques that will save time and trouble.

The designer must have constant contact with the garment as it is constructed—even if the pattern is made by an assistant patternmaker. Fitting the garment correctly is an essential part of the designer's work. The image on paper or the idea in the designer's head is unimportant compared with the actual garment. Furthermore, characteristics and construction details can be a fertile source for design inspiration.

Other Sources of Inspiration

RAGBAG

A rag or swatch bag holds a collection of fabric swatches. The swatches will be more valuable if they are labeled with fiber content, source, price, and date. Touch each swatch and develop your tactile sense. Imagine the garments a fabric could be fashioned into. Invent new combinations of colors and patterns.

COLLECTING TRIMS

Period trims, buttons, and ribbons are a rich source of inspiration. Often they can be copied for modern production. Antique stores and sales are an excellent source for antique trims.

COLLECTING GARMENTS

Collect both historical and contemporary garments that appeal to you. Wear other designer's clothes so you can experience firsthand a new silhouette, fabric, or concept. Be aware of fashion trends and details in other areas of clothing—for example, men's wear, active sportswear, uniforms, and children's wear. Garments from the twentieth century are widely available in secondhand clothing stores and are a tremendous source of design inspiration.

MUSEUMS AND FINE ARTS

Numerous museums have fine collections of period and contemporary garments, particularly the Metropolitan Museum in New York, the Smithsonian Institute in Washington, DC, and the Los Angeles County Museum of Art. Also, many museums maintain excellent libraries of fashion books and periodicals.

Two outstanding collections of historical apparel are housed in Paris and London. In Paris, Le Centre du Documentation de la Mode Parisienne has collections of twentieth century couture design. Both garments and sketches are available for viewing by special request. The Victoria and Albert Museum in London has a vast collection of costumes and periodicals, which the museum displays in occasional shows.

Do not confine yourself to the costume departments in museums; visit all sections. Pay particular attention to special exhibits because they may reflect a trend in public interest and they usually contain the best examples of a particular type of work.

Contemporary fine arts and commercial graphics are an important influence on color combinations and general fashion trends. On many occasions these areas have started a trend that becomes the commercial fashion several years later.

HISTORICAL AND ETHNIC COSTUMES

Garments from the past are invaluable for design inspiration. A designer can use old magazines, reference books, period movies, and actual garments. Most cities preserve garments in public and private collections. Most libraries have periodicals of historical interest.

Ethnic costumes—that is, costumes worn by the people of a specific area—are a rich source of inspiration. Beware of accepting a modern designer's interpretation of an ethnic costume. If fashions of a particular culture are becoming a trend, do original research on the culture and costumes rather than relying on secondhand information.

FILMS

Costumes designed for the movies used to provide many commercial fashion trends. Several decades ago, movie stars were always expensively and elaborately costumed. The trend toward more realistic movies has altered movies' fashion impact, but occasionally a movie will still influence contemporary fashion, as did *Bonnie and Clyde*. The costumes generated a wave of 1930s fashions that emphasized the unconstructed dress, the braless look, and longer skirts. Sometimes a studio will promote a film's cos-

inspiration

FROM ANCIENT EGYPT

prints, colours, silhouettes, accessories

FROM THE LIFE HEREAFTER...for evening

Marvellous body kilts, developed from the simple loincloths worn by the fellaheen who worked by the Nile, into sophisticated spring versions... lettuce-leaf edged, pleated or fine ribbed single-knits.

Historical Costume Inspiration   The English fashion report *IM* develops a fashion theme based on the styles, prints, and colors of ancient Egyptian costumes. (Courtesy of *IM International*.)

tumes as a commercial fashion trend, but these attempts to influence fashion directly are rarely effective. Truly original and timely film costumes will catch on without being promoted.

LIFE-STYLES

Designers should attend popular events that appeal to the typical customer. They should observe life around them and investigate how people in different situations live and dress. They should observe people at beaches, sporting events, and underground cultural events. For example, the bathing suit designer should be an expert on beaches from Southern California to St. Tropez. Tennis clothes designers should play the game and attend tennis events in all parts of the country.

Fashion from the streets (that is, created by non-professionals) is a potential influence on all levels of ready-to-wear. Crafts and hobbies currently in vogue will also influence design, as will travel.

Observe, record, and experience the events that shape current life-styles.

HOME FURNISHING TRENDS

Many trends that influence fashion originate in home furnishings. Usually the way people style their homes influences the way they style their clothes, and vice versa. Observe the trends published in such interior design magazines as *Better Homes and Gardens, House Beautiful, House and Gardens,* and *Architectural Digest.* Color trends in wall coverings, linens, fabrics, and paints may influence apparel colors. Upholstery fabrics are frequently modified for use as apparel fabrics. In general, real upholstery fabrics are unsuccessful as apparel fabrics because they are too expensive and the finishes are inappropriate for garments. Reinterpreted upholstery patterns and weaves, however, make excellent apparel fabrics.

Shopping Retail Stores

Manufacturers and designers should constantly shop department and specialty stores. In this way manufacturers and designers can look at their own garments in comparison with garments from other sources. But what should you, as a designer, look for? First, you should get an overall impression of current fashion and consider the total look. Then, you should consider the following points.

YOUR MANUFACTURER'S GARMENTS

1. Determine how the manufacturer's garments fit into the price structure of the particular department where they are sold.
2. Talk to salespeople and check customer reaction to the garments. Check the fit of the garments.
3. Check the sales records with the buyer or assistant buyer.
4. Check the markdown rack for your mistakes.
5. Observe how your garments fit customers with less than perfect figures. This is the ultimate test of your product.

OTHER MANUFACTURERS' GARMENTS

1. Check higher-priced garments and original designs for fashion trends. Many manufacturers

Shopping Retail Stores The designer should be aware of merchandise in retail stores. Shopping should be done continuously and should not be limited to a specific area or store.

buy garments they feel will sell well and then knock them off. All fashion is public domain (that is, not copyrighted) once it is for sale in a store.

2. Check general trends in colors, promotions, and silhouettes. Observe which items are checking in your own fashion area and in other merchandising areas.

3. Compare similarly priced garments with your garments. Do yours look like a good buy?

4. In your price range, look for hot items and items that are checking.

5. Know the vendors, especially the larger ones, and the innovative stylers. Know vendors in your price category and in more expensive categories.

FABRICS

1. Many times, the prints and fabrics used in a line are duplicated. It is to the manufacturer's advantage to have a fabric used in garments that are more expensive than those of its line. The same print used in lower-priced garments is a disadvantage and may signal the need to change the print.

2. Check new merchandise for fabric trends. Particularly important here is European ready-to-wear.

3. Some fabrics do not stand up under handling. Note fabrics that retain their hanger appeal and do not look shopworn.

4. Check fabric trends and colors in other areas: higher-priced, more advanced styling, junior, sportswear, and designer. Check the color trends in accessories, shoes, and handbags.

5. Avant-garde fashion stores (those that are original and trend-setting) often feature prophetic colors and fashions.

6. Check the fabrics you had difficulty working with to see how other manufacturers solved construction problems. Be aware of shortcut finishings and new detail methods.

ORGANIZING YOUR STORE INFORMATION

1. Many stores do not like a person to sketch or make notes while on the floor (in the store). Develop your memory, and always carry your sketchbook to record important styles. Then you can sketch after you have left the store.

2. Analyze the new things you see. Project wearable modifications into high-style trends if you are designing for the mass market.

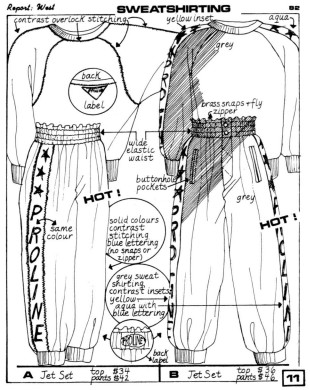

contrast overlock stitching   yellow inset   aqua

grey

back label

brass snaps + fly zipper

wide elastic waist

buttonhole pockets

HOT!

PRO LINE

same colour

solid colours contrast stitching blue lettering (no snaps or zipper)

grey sweat shirting contrast insets yellow aqua with blue lettering

grey

HOT!

PROLINE

PROLINE

back label

| **A** Jet Set | top $34 pants $42 | **B** Jet Set | top $36 pants $46 | 11 |

Shopping Stores *Report West* by Bill Glazer focuses on current trendy stores and illustrates the importance of keeping abreast of current retail trends. Elaborate sketches of the clothes seen are not necessary. The illustrations should show the silhouette and the details of the clothes. (Courtesy of *Report West*.)

3. Note advertised merchandise and items featured in department displays and store windows. The retailer thought these items were better than the general stock and wanted to call them to the consumer's attention.

4. Notice overall fashion trends. See how a trend can be duplicated in different categories of merchandise. Decide if a trend is on the ascent or if it has peaked.

5. Try on garments that seem to be the coming style. Especially try on new silhouettes and proportions, then analyze them. The style need not be flattering for you, but trying on the garment is the best way to judge proportion.

6. Check garments for any construction and finishing details you can incorporate into your line. Do not be intimidated by better stores or designer departments. Look at as much merchandise as possible in higher price ranges. *Hint:* if you dress like the store's average customer, you will not feel like an intruder.

7. Go to the stores several times a week, if possible. Visit different kinds of stores in many areas because a fair sampling of stores is essential. Include small boutiques and custom shops as well as large department stores.

8. Buy and wear as many commercial garments as you can afford. Try to analyze them in terms of comfort and clever design. Your own experience in clothing will add to your designing creativity. Observe the selling patterns of new merchandise in department stores. Try to attend trunk shows and import shows. Trunk shows feature a manufacturer's new line that has not yet been shipped to the store. Look for the newest trends in styling and apply them to your merchandise.

9. Department stores are constantly trying to increase their sensitivity to consumer demand. Be aware of department organization, merchandising policies, and new techniques in display. Watch imaginative small stores for new selling methods. Often merchandising changes will influence styling and buyer demands. By analyzing what you see, carefully reading trade papers, and talking to knowledgeable sources, you can be on top of these changes. Then, by altering your design projections, you can keep up with the changes or keep ahead of them.

Note the four Rs of shopping: *remember, record,* and *respond to all you see in fashion merchandising Return frequently to the stores.*

REVIEW

Word Finders

Define the following words and phrases from the chapter you just read:

1. Avant-garde
2. Consumer publications
3. Croquis book
4. Ethnic costume
5. Fashion from the streets
6. Fine arts
7. Glossy magazine
8. Prophetic
9. Ragbag
10. SA (Seventh Avenue)
11. Scrap
12. Staple
13. Trade publication
14. Timing
15. WWD

Shopping Workbook

Visit department stores and specialty shops to complete the following shopping worksheets. Try to collect many impressions of the stores and merchandise. Do not think in terms of buying garments for yourself. Rather, determine how the things you see would appeal to the general buying public. Men should shop with women to benefit from the trying-on phase of this exercise.

SHOPPING WORKBOOK

Purpose: Compare junior sportswear with missy sportswear. Shop in a department where garments are moderately priced.

Source: A large suburban or downtown department store. Try to compare similar merchandise.

Criteria	Missy	Junior
1. Try on a pair of pants in the size you usually wear.	Size tried on _____ Your usual size __	Size tried on _____
2. Measure the leg length and width for each pair of pants.	Inseam length Width at cuff	
3. How are the seams finished?		
4. Compare the fit of the two pairs of pants.		
5. What is the price of each pair? (Try to pick pants that are comparable.)		

Criteria	Missy	Junior

6. Compare and contrast the fabric choices on the basis of fashionability and durability.

7. Try on a top in each department. Compare fit, especially bust size, length, and sleeve length.

8. Compare finishing details. Check seam allowances, cuffs, and hem finishes.

9. Compare merchandise selection in general and the variety of colors available. Which department showed more fashion innovation?

SHOPPING WORKBOOK

Purpose: To note and sketch a fashion trend you think is prophetic.

Area: Fashionable misses or designer garments, either sportswear or dresses.

Source: Large department store or better specialty store.

Criteria	Comments and Observations

1. Describe the garment you feel is innovative. Consider silhouette, details, and unusual elements.

2. Who made the garment?

3. What store and department is the garment sold in?

4. What is the price?

5. Comment on any similar merchandise you see in other departments.

6. Describe the fabric and color.

7. Sketch the garment, noting all important details.

SHOPPING WORKBOOK

Purpose: Compare a moderate missy dress with a better or designer dress. The moderate dress should be under $95, the better or designer dress should be over $100. Compare street dresses.

Source: Shop two different departments of a large store.

| | OBSERVATIONS | |
Criteria	Moderate	Better-Designer
1. What is the price of each garment?		
2. What fabric is used in each?		
3. Compare the fit of the two garments (select the same size and general silhouette).		
4. Compare the finishing techniques on each garment.		
5. What type of lining is used in each garment?		
6. What size of hem is used?		
7. How large are the seam allowances?		
8. Does the dress carry the manufacturer's label or the store's label?		
9. What do you conclude about each department, based on your shopping experience?		

Fall Outlook

"Strolling"

186

7.
principles and elements of design

Fashion can be defined as the ideal of beauty currently accepted by a given segment of the population. Fashionable apparel is a group of garments that are more or less new and are accepted by a group of people as desirable and beautiful. The aesthetics of garment design are difficult to define specifically. Fashion is constantly changing, and as a new fashion becomes popular, a new standard of beauty becomes desirable. Often a new fashion begins when the proportion of a garment is altered; for example, a silhouette is changed in width or a skirt is lengthened. Usually, when a truly innovative fashion begins, it takes a long time for the general public to retrain its eye and develop an appreciation for the new look. People tend to emulate trend setters and fashion leaders, so more and more people will accept and wear the new style. As more people wear the item and interpret it in many different ways, the mass of people find it easier to accept the fashion as beautiful. Conversely, as a fashion saturates the marketplace and is interpreted in many inexpensive versions, the fashion leaders tire of it and reject the style as passé. Then the leaders experiment with a new style. Because of this constant cycle, the criteria for a beautiful garment are constantly changing.

The human body comes in many shapes and sizes. Design principles should be interpreted for each figure. When a person deviates from what is decreed beautiful by current fashion, she tries to minimize the difference between her appearance and the ideal by clothing her body to resemble the ideal. The current ideal is a tall, slender, youthful woman. Most women wish to emulate the fashion models they see in magazines and movies and on television. Today most successful clothing uses visual devices to make the wearer seem taller and more slender than she actually is. Yet a woman who is very tall may wish to diminish her height so she will look more like an average person. The short, overweight woman will approach the ideal as closely as possible, given her figure. Clothing can greatly alter a person's appearance and compensate for discrepancies between an average body and the current fashion ideal.

DESIGNING A SUCCESSFUL GARMENT

Successful garments stimulate purchases because these clothes will serve a consumer in four specific ways:

1. Image. The garment should be suitable for the image, occasion, and life-style of the person who is purchasing it. Price is a major consideration. Consumers evaluate the cost of a garment with the use and pleasure they anticipate receiving by wearing it and what they can afford to pay for this gratification.
2. Function. The garment must be suitable for the activity the customer will wear it for. The care instructions should be appropriate for the use the garment is being put to.
3. Structure. The design of the garment should enhance the face and figure of the person purchasing it. The garment should be appropriate for the customer's need to be in fashion.
4. Decoration. The color and fabrication should be appropriate to the occasion the garment will be used for and should enhance the person wearing the garment. The pattern in a print fabric should be appropriate to the size of the customer and the use the garment will be put to.

These four factors govern the aesthetic appeal of a particular garment and are the constant concern of

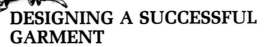

Dramatic silhouettes are best worn by a tall, slender person

188

designers and the retailers who select garments to sell to the ultimate consumer. Components of the goals include psychological and visual guidelines that lead to the creation of a successful garment.

Image is dictated by taste factors that are largely psychological. Function involves the appropriate use of fabric and construction techniques to make a garment that is appropriate for a specific end use. Structure involves the three-dimensional rules of construction that govern clothing design: silhouette modification, proportion, line, balance, unity, rhythm, and emphasis. Decoration is the use of fabric color, value, texture, and pattern. These are the elements and principles of design. The principles of design are the rules that govern how the elements are combined. If you were baking a cake, the principles would be the directions of the recipe, and the elements would be the ingredients. The elements are the raw materials that must be combined successfully. These rules are flexible and should be interpreted within the context of current fashion or the particular problem the designer is solving. The designer making costumes for a movie or play may use the principles in a way exactly opposite from the ready-to-wear designer, who wishes to dress the person in the most becoming current fashion.

Principles	*Elements*
Proportion	Line
Balance	Silhouette (shape)
Rhythm or repetition	Color
Emphasis	Value
Unity	Texture or fabric

IMAGE

The clothes people wear communicate what others will think of them when meeting them for the first time. Clothing is a cue to identifying occupation, status in the community, and self-image. In Western society, there is a strong cultural pressure toward modifying a person's appearance to conform to an acceptable image. This acceptable image may differ depending on occupation and area of the country. A working person living in a large, commercial Eastern city would be expected to dress conservatively in business-like suits or dresses. The same person working in a rural setting could often wear more informal clothing and be appropriately dressed for his or her occupation.

People are subtly conditioned as they grow up to recognize what is appropriate dress among their peers. Developing a taste level begins as a toddler. Concepts of what to wear to gain acceptance come first from the family setting. Here, children learn what colors are appropriate to wear together, standards of cleanliness, and when to dress up. These early guidelines are often rejected when a child becomes a teenager and moves away from the dominant influence of the family and into a wider group of relationships. Teenagers often dress to shock older people with the difference of their dress—in actuality, they are conforming to rigid dress codes set down by members of their own group. Often the unorthodox or experimental clothing is a symbol of the rejection of their parents' values as well as a fashion statement that proclaims: "I belong, I am accepted by my friends."

Young adults usually relax their rebellious stance as they realize clothing will help them be accepted in the world of commerce. Many fashion publications focus on showing young adults what kinds of fashions should be worn for working and social events. The taste level of an individual continues to expand as fashion awareness begins. Usually the fashion focus is on enhancing the attractiveness of the wearer. Often this begins when the young adult is exposed to "ideal" women, movie stars, or models the media promotes as beautiful and successful. Often a person's taste level will increase along with the ability to recognize and purchase quality apparel.

Young clothing tends to be inexpensive to moderate in cost. Leisure clothes are often less expensive than tailored suits and business apparel. Clothing from the Sun Belt states, where life is more informal and relaxed, is designed with casual fabrics, brighter colors, and more fashion experimentation. A consumer developing greater fashion awareness should shop for many different kinds of apparel and experiment with fashions that reflect the message he or she wants people to "read" from appearance. This varies depending on a person's life-style and geographic location. Investment clothing worn during the business day to proclaim a person's seriousness and worth should reflect a tasteful, current image, yet not detract from the personality of the wearer. A woman's skills and attributes should be framed, not eclipsed, by the clothing she wears. Individualism can be expressed in color combinations, subtle mixes of fabrics and textures, and fashionably detailed tailored clothing. Leisure clothes offer the fashion innovator a chance to experiment with novel cuts and styles. Fewer, quality garments are usually preferable to many less expensive garments for working women on a clothing budget, because quality is a more profound expression of worth than a variety of mediocre clothing.

Emulating the media ideals stimulates the consumer to style her hair and makeup in a specific way, to diet and dress like the model. Gradually, the person gains more self-confidence and begins to realize that clothing and makeup camouflage faults of figure and face and should not overwhelm the individual's personality. Clothes should be selected because they are flattering and focus attention on the best features of the individual, not because they are so flamboyant the person is noticed for what is being worn. As the person enters the work force, the reality of conforming to a standard that proclaims him or her to be a valid and accepted member of the larger business community should be reflected in the working wardrobe. Conformity is a part of the reason for selecting working apparel, but the wise, upwardly mobile person often dresses slightly ahead of the current professional station as a signal that he or she anticipates advancing up the business ladder.

Manufacturers and retailers constantly try to adapt their merchandise to the price and quality range their customers want. Economic considerations often affect the merchandise mix consumers purchase. During recessionary periods, very inexpensive clothes seem logical to sell in great volume, because people have less money to spend on clothing. Often expensive clothes sell well during a recession because the customer purchases fewer items and expects to wear them longer. Usually these clothes are conservatively styled, so they are not quickly dated. Many retailers focus on one economic level and gather merchandise from all catagories of apparel that will satisfy a particular customer's desire for quality and fashion at a specific price. Retailers and manufacturers focus on a particular customer because they realize they cannot be all things to all people.

FUNCTION

The quality of the fabric and construction are the two main factors in evaluating the way a garment will wear. Fabrication depends on the use desired of the garment. Temperature dictates the kind of fiber and weave that will be most comfortable.

Outerwear is typically bulky.

	Fiber	Construction
Warm or hot climates	Cotton Linen Rayon	Lightweight wovens and knits; gauze and open weaves; puckered surfaces that allow for greater air circulation near the body; smooth finishes. White and light colors reflect the heat and are psychologically cool.
Temperate climates	Acetate Rayon Cotton Linen Polyester Nylon Silk Acrylic Lightweight leather Lightweight wools	Midweight weaves and knits in a wide range of colors that may be modified by wearing layers of clothing to adapt to temperature variations.
Cold climates	Wool Nylon Acrylic Furs Heavy leathers Hairblends like camel vicuña, and alpaca Heavyweight polyesters and cottons	Heavyweight knits and wovens. Tightly woven fabrics to stop the wind. Fiber- or down-filled inner layers quilted to add warmth. Psychologically warm colors are red, orange, bright yellow, and black.

The quality of the fabric will greatly affect the wear that can be expected from a garment. Evaluate the care instructions given for a particular fabrication with the end use of the garment. Realize that a dry-clean label will require a continuous investment in the garment over its lifetime. This would be appropriate for a fine silk blouse, but unacceptable for a jumpsuit or children's wear.

Garment use also dictates the fabric it should be made of. For example, garments used for active wear are more comfortable if they are constructed with the stretch factor provided for by lycra or a spandex fiber in combination with cotton or a synthetic. Luxury fabrics can add a feeling of quality to classical styling.

Construction details are a guide to the durability of a garment. Carefully evaluate the mode of construction. Seams should be sewn with small, even stitches. Sturdy garments should have reinforced seams. Flat-felled seams or double-stitched seams are the most durable. Inspect the inside of a tailored garment to see if the interfacings and construction details are well made and carefully finished. Hems should be closely stitched with a blind stitch, preferably in a colored thread to match the garment instead of the clear thread that often pulls out. Buttons and fastenings should be firmly sewn to the garment with no telltale end of thread exposed, as this can easily pull out. A spare button sewn into the inner seams of the garment is always a welcome addition.

STRUCTURE

An apparel designer is a sculptor who uses the basic human body as an armature (form) for a soft fabric sculpture that enhances the figure. Apparel is three-dimensional, which means it is perceived in the round. The designer usually begins sketching a garment in two dimensions, visualizing the back and sides as the details are drawn. Flat fabric is seamed and structured to have a three-dimensional shape. The size and shape of the garment are first perceived by the silhouette or outline of the garment. Then the eye of the viewer moves to the subdivisions created by seams and other design elements to capture a total impression. The other elements that influence three-dimensional structure are the proportion of the spaces, the use of line, the balance and unity of the design devices, and the rhythm and emphasis of the details within the garment.

The Silhouette

The silhouette is the most dominant visual element of a garment and dictates a great deal of the other styling elements that comprise the design. Fashion cycles often focus on a specific silhouette, but because of the diversity of modern life, many kinds of apparel are used concurrently and a person usually has a great variety of silhouettes in a wardrobe at any one time. Silhouettes are modified by adding fabric and padding to various parts of the body to create a specific illusion. The shape of the silhouette usually complements the shape of the body, but exaggeration is often used to create a special effect or balance and emphasize a part of the body that is a current focus of fashion.

Aesthetically the *natural body silhouette* is best worn by an active, physically fit figure. The comfort and functional advantages of stretch body suits and leotards are desired by all figure types. One device to make this silhouette more wearable is to use the body-hugging attire on the parts of the body that are

Natural Body Silhouette

Typical garments: Very active sportswear and exercise suits, bathing suits, and dance costumes.

Function: Freedom of movement is most important. Knits are often preferred, and their naturally stretchy structure is enhanced by using lycra and spandex fibers to increase stretch.

Structure: Stretch fabrics make construction lines less important for fit. Tight fit emphasizes the body's curves with little chance to camouflage figure problems.

Decoration: The most important aspect of active wear. Dark colors like black, navy, and brown will minimize figure curves best. Diagonal stripes will slim the figure. Bathing suits are often styled with prints that focus on one area of the figure and create a two-dimensional style impact.

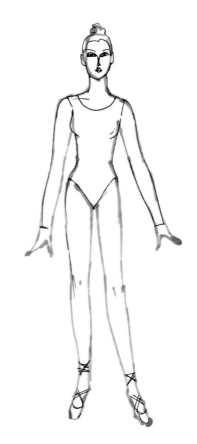

the shapeliest and to use dark colors where the figure is less desirable. For example, large thighs can be minimized with dark tights and a small wrap skirt added to the leotard. A large waist can be camouflaged by teaming a dark body suit with a tonal leg covering, or adding a vest or sweatshirt to the body suit to balance the larger area.

Bathing suits are made for various kinds of figures from matronly to youthful. The difference is often found in the underconstruction of the suit as well as the cut of the outer shell. Fuller figures require a defined bustline and have a hard bra cup that is preformed in durable interlining fabric to provide support. Suits for a mature figure are often designed with a small skirt added to the suit to hide the hipline. Slim legs can be made to look longer if the leg line on the suit is cut up slightly. Conversely, a straight line at the crotch will make the thighs seem wider. The "boy leg" style is flattering to a heavy thigh.

Color and pattern are very important for styling active wear. Color is often engineered to give a special effect to the bathing suit. Dark colors tend to recede, making an area seem smaller. They are used at the bust and hipline to reduce the width of these

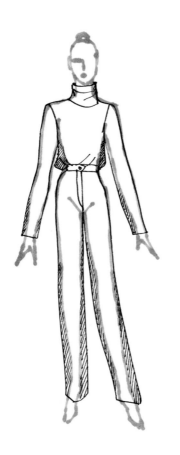

Slim Line Silhouette, Pants

Typical garments: Snugly fitted jeans or pants made from knit fabrics with a slim leg (typically called a straight or boot leg).

Function: Freedom of movement is impaired unless stretch wovens or knits are used as the bottom weight.

Structure: Darts and seams must be used for woven fabrics to achieve a fit this close to the body. This is a good silhouette for knits. When a contrast top is used, the person will emphasize the length of legs.

Decoration: Darker pants will tend to make the legs look longer and the hips smaller because dark colors recede visually.

areas. Diagonal patterns and stripes are also effective slimming devices. Colors are important in styling bathing suits because so much skin is exposed. Dark, rich colors and bright colors tend to enhance a tan and are therefore desirable. White is an excellent contrast to a tanned skin but is difficult to make opaque when wet, so it must be used with care in the area of the crotch and bust.

The *slim line silhouette* hugs the body with very little air space between the garment and the body. This is the classic tailored silhouette. The tailored silhouette for women is very acceptable for business apparel because it is similar to the man's business suit. Pants must fit well to enhance a figure. There are two kinds of pants: the snug jean fit and the looser straight leg trouser.

The trouser is often styled with darts or release pleats to compensate for the *drop*, the difference in measurement between the waist and the hips, which is usually 10 inches or more. The trouser should fit smoothly over the top of the hips and fall in a straight sweep of fabric from the fullest part of the upper hip to the cuff. Pants that cling to the thighs or fit too snugly through the seat will emphasize the width of the hips and accentuate the fullest part of

A higher hairdo increases height

A V neck and bodice verticals both heighten and slim

A raised waistband visually adds to the length of the pants and makes bodice seem smaller

Creases, ironed in or stitched, are verticals to dramatize the length of pants

One color, or subtle tones enhance height

Slightly wider pant leg will emphasize the fall of pant leg

No cuff to accent horizontals

Shoes with platforms or high heels can add up to six inches to height

195

Slim Line Silhouette, Skirts

Typical garments: Slim suits and clinging dresses fitted with darts and seams if cut in woven fabrics. This is the equivalent of the man's business suit and is called a tailored silhouette.
Function: Movement is impaired by the slim skirt unless slits or pleats are added to help leg movement. Fitted jacket limits exaggerated arm movement.
Structure: Vertical lines, slim lapels, and small details will make a person seem taller and slimmer. Slightly padded shoulders balance a wide hipline. Good way to camouflage a thick waist, as the silhouette is basically rectangular.
Decoration: Similar colors in the jacket and skirt emphasize height. Darker skirts will shorten the figure but tend to make the hips seem smaller.

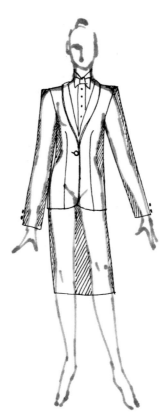

A white blouse worn with a dark suit focuses on the face and makes person seem taller

Shirtdresses are classic tailored garments

Vertical style lines add to slim silhouette

the figure. This pant is more often tailored in wool and blends of cotton and synthetics because the loose fit does not overstress the fabric.

A jean is made in sturdy, heavyweight denim. The typical jean fabric is an 11½ ounce denim, which is durable enough to support the figure. Jeans should fit snugly. The durable fabric, flat-felled seams, and a heavyweight zipper are designed to have direct contact with the figure from the thighs up. Jeans are too tight if they are uncomfortable at the crotch area, wrinkle through the thighs, are uncomfortable to sit in, or force extra flesh above the pant at the waist area.

The illusion of height is easily created with pants and a slim-fitted blouse. Pants automatically make a person look taller because the torso from the waist down is covered with a single expanse of fabric. Artificial devices like high-heeled and platform shoes add physical height. The shoes can be covered with the pant leg and will not be visible. Upswept hairstyles and a slight flare in the pant leg will also increase the illusion of height.

The slim line skirt silhouette is very flattering for most figures. A straight, tailored skirt slims visually because no bulk is added to the figure at waist and hips. When worn with a tailored jacket, padding and construction techniques fill in and balance a figure that is narrow in the shoulders or has a small bust-line. Tailored garments are made of heavy fabrics that are seamed and padded so the jacket has a firm structure that can camouflage many figure problems. The length of the jacket depends on the height of the wearer and the kind of bottom it will be worn with.

A jacket should cover the crotch if worn with pants or hit the figure high on the hip so that the jacket hemline does not lead the eye to the wrinkled crotch area. A jacket that is too long on a short person will reduce the length of the skirt and appear to make the person shorter. The length of the jacket also depends on the color of the bottom. A contrast jacket should be carefully balanced for length because the hem and the colored area will stand out against the skirt. A one-colored suit will have a less distinct body division and there is more leeway for the length of the jacket. A short dressmaker jacket is most flattering worn with a skirt that is slightly eased or gathered at the waistline. A short jacket will make a short person look taller because of the visual contrast between the shortness of the bodice and the longer expanse of the skirt or pant. Fashion dictates that hem length and the length of the jacket should relate to skirt length.

The tailored silhouette is also appropriate for dresses. The classic shirtdress has a slim silhouette. This is a very flattering style for many figure types because the vertical line the placket makes carries the eye the length of the dress and tends to slim and elongate the figure. A jacket worn over a shirtdress is also an appropriate, conservative business outfit.

Soft dressing describes garments styled with more ease and a fuller fit. Softer, thinner fabrics are usually used for this silhouette. Details like structured collars and pocket flaps typically used in tailored garments are usually inappropriate for this kind of styling because the fabric is too light. Ease, shirring, tucking details, and other decorative means of controlling ease are the styling devices used to create soft garments. These clothes are particularly appropriate for warm weather because of their loose fit and thinner fabrics, which allow air to circulate near the body. This kind of styling tends to look dressier than tailored garments and is often used for special-occasion and after-five dresses.

Soft pants are usually styled in lightweight fabrics. Pleats and gathers are used to control the drop. Fullness in the hip area will visually enlarge the lower torso. This style is very appropriately worn to balance a slender hip with a heavy bust. A figure with a large

Moderate Silhouette Modification, Pants

Typical garments: Softly pleated pants and trousers styled with a straight, flared, or slightly ballooned leg. A soft shirt would be a typical top. This is a typical silhouette for cold-weather active sports.

Function: Movement is easier and shoulders may move unimpaired. Knits and wovens may be used in this silhouette successfully.

Structure: Less need for seam and dart lines. Ease or gathers are used to fit the garments at waist and bust. Knits are often styled with rib banding instead of structured waistbands. The silhouette can be used to camouflage many figure problems, creating basically a wide, rectangular silhouette.

Decoration: Appropriate for bolder prints. Same rules of color to emphasize height and diminish width apply.

hipline and a small bust and shoulder can balance these two elements with the use of fuller sleeves, shoulder pleats, or a ruffle at the neckline combined with a softer pant. A slender, well-balanced figure can also wear this kind of silhouette well. Mobility is very good in this kind of styling, making the soft pant an appropriate exercise garment for cold weather. Sweatshirt fabrics are made into pants with a drawstring waist and pant legs finished with a knitted rib banding so they do not flap when used for jogging.

Soft dressing in skirt silhouettes include full dirndls and gathered skirts. When this silhouette is made in lightweight fabrics, the effect softens and dresses the heavier figure with an illusion of fabric, adding bulk to the figure instead of flesh. Soft bows, ruffles, tucking, and pleating details are typical for this feminine style. The moderate skirt silhouette is basically rectangular and adapts itself to camouflaging the figure that is thick through the waistline and hips. A dress that is one color will lengthen the figure. Darker and neutral tones will seem to recede, making the figure seem more streamlined. The shift or float version of this silhouette is flattering for heavier, shorter figures because the waistline is not defined, and this gives the person a longer line to accentuate stature. The important elements of this

Sweat suit styling is designed for good mobility

Fuller Pants make hips look wider

Moderate Silhouette Modification, Skirts

Typical garments: Dirndls and fuller blouse silhouettes. This silhouette is typically called soft styling.

Function: Movement is easier, and legs and torso are unimpaired. More bulk is surrounding the hips.

Structure: Gathering and ease is the primary styling element. Yokes to control the shirred areas are popular styling devices. This rectangular silhouette may be used to emphasize a small waistline by contrasting the two larger areas of the bodice and skirt with a bright belt.

Decoration: Appropriate silhouette for larger prints as well as small and soft textures.

silhouette are fabric and color when styling a dress to flatter the smaller, bulky figure.

Gathered fabric tends to lead the eye to the source of the gathers. This can be used effectively to highlight a heavy person's face, neck, and shoulders, often their best features. Gathers coming from the snug cuff of a full sleeve will focus attention on small, attractive hands, often a good feature for the larger woman who also wishes to cover fleshy elbows and arms. Conversely, a softly gathered blouse in an elegant fabric will cover bony elbows and overly thin arms and add femininity for an angular, thin person.

The soft silhouette can be contrasted with fitted garments. This will accentuate parts of the body. For example, a person with full hips can wear a soft dirndl contrasted with a belt to accent a slim waist and a fitted top. This will focus attention on the slim parts of the figure and diminish the size of the hips by hiding them with the soft gathers of the dirndl.

The *shoulder wedge* uses padding or fullness in the sleeve area to increase the visual width of the bodice at the shoulders. This gives the figure a masculine look. Width at the shoulders tends to make the hip area look narrower by comparison, and usually the bottom is slim to contrast with the shoulder width. This silhouette also makes a person seem tall-

Shifts have the most rectangular shape

Contrasting fitted garments with soft, full garments makes the fitted area look smaller

Extreme Silhouette Modification, Shoulder Wedge

Typical garments: Shoulder pads or other style devices like leg-o-mutton sleeves and shoulder ruffles are used to create the wedge shape. Width at the shoulder is most effective when contrasted with a slim bottom.
Function: This fashion is often popular during times when independent women are valued by society.
Structure: Padding is essential for achieving this look in a tailored garment. Larger lapels that reflect the wedge shape enhance the illusion. Hips seem smaller with this shaped top.
Decoration: Details like epaulettes on a wide shoulder will accentuate the wedge shape. Lighter tops over dark bottoms increase the illusion.

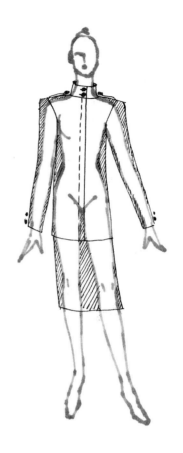

Dark Jacket emphasizes shoulder width

Ruffles and puffed sleeves create a wedge shoulder illusion

er. The effect is easily achieved in a tailored suit, where shoulder pads are hidden by heavy fabric. The lapels of a jacket can be slightly enlarged to increase the illusion of width. Extreme shoulder extension tends to overpower a small figure. Slight padding or sleeve extension can effectively balance any figure, and squaring the line of the shoulders makes a person seem taller and more youthful.

Shoulder pads support the garment and make it look more attractive on the hanger, adding to its initial appeal in a store. Shoulder pads may also be added to soft garments, though they are usually smaller and should be covered in self-fabric so they are not obvious. To duplicate the wedge effect in evening gowns, crisp fabrics like taffeta or silk organza may be used. A great deal of volume can be added with sleeves in a leg-o-mutton style, contrasted with a slim skirt. Ruffles at the shoulder line also create a wedge silhouette.

Batwing, dolman, and raglan sleeves cut with a great deal of fabric under the arm will create a wedge silhouette. This silhouette is a style variation that tends to be popular when more masculine values are attributed to women. Shoulder pads were very popular in tailored suits during World War II,

Extreme Silhouette Modification, the Hourglass

Typical garments: Flared skirts teamed with tops that have full sleeves and a very fitted waist create this illusion. This silhouette is very feminine because the width of the hips and bust are subtly increased by contrast with a small waist.

Function: Movement may be impaired, especially when the waist is tightly bound and when full, long skirts are worn.

Structure: Fitting and padding are used to define the shoulder line and the waist. Contrast colors at the waist effectively direct attention to the tight portion of the garment. Flared skirts and peplums add to the illusion.

Decoration: Emphasis at the widest part of the wedge, either at the hem or the neckline, will exaggerate the illusion.

when women were encouraged to join the work force.

The *hourglass* is a feminine silhouette because it contrasts a full bust with wide hips. The narrow waist is the accent that provides contrast between wider areas of the figure. This has been a dominant theme throughout fashion history because it emphasizes typical feminine figure characteristics. In the past, waist cinchers were used to pull in the waist. Sometimes these cruel efforts to make the flexible waist area smaller were so harsh that women fainted from being corseted. Corseting would begin early for girls, and often several of the lower ribs would be broken by constant compression. This practice made women's waistlines consistently smaller. During the 1960s there was a turn toward shift dresses, and for the first time in many years women stopped trying to compress their waistlines. When belts returned to fashion almost a decade later, clothing manufacturers found that women's waistlines had increased over an inch per size.

The visual illusion of a small waistline is still possible through techniques similar to those used in the past but without severe corseting. A contrasting belt worn with a flared shirt to define the waistline and a

Raglan sleeves give an hourglass silhouette to this jacket

Decoration at the fullest part of the flare emphasizes the width

201

Extreme Silhouette Modification, Figure Volume, Skirts

Typical garments: Layering several bulky garments over each other creates extreme figure volume. This silhouette is particularly appropriate for cold weather dressing and is often found in outerwear.

Function: Warmth is the most obvious function of the full silhouette, but when the style is fashionable it will be adapted to warm weather by draping voluminous layers of lightweight fabric on the body.

Structure: Styling devices are full cuts and bulky fabrics. Quilting, fur, and heavy leathers are often used for warmth. Layers of clothing create this effect.

Decoration: Ethnic clothing is often popular during periods when volume silhouettes are fashionable because costumes like caftans are full and figure-enveloping. Pattern mixes are popular, and large prints accent the volume of the clothes.

A short, full fur adds weight

Exaggerated Volume typifies outerwear

Layers add Bulk

romantic blouse with a full sleeve can create the hourglass silhouette. This effect is enhanced when skirts are longer than the knee. The sweep of a long, flared skirt makes the waist seem even smaller. The fitted waistline and a slightly fuller sleeve with a very full skirt has been a successful evening and wedding gown formula for many years because of its femininity. The hourglass silhouette should be carefully worn by very small women. Petite women may wear the silhouette, but the proportion and volume of the skirt should be modified so the person does not seem overwhelmed. A bulky torso and large waistline is better concealed by another silhouette.

Extreme *volume* is sometimes a popular fashion silhouette. To achieve this look, several layers are usually worn at one time. The figure is minimized, and the draping and design of the fabric becomes most important. Often a mix of prints and textures is popular because the figure is less visible, and decorative elements of fabric and design take over.

The extreme volume silhouette is a classic and acceptable theme for outerwear even when slim silhouettes are fashionable for other clothes. Bulk implies psychological warmth as well as physically providing it. Long-haired furs, heavy wools, bulky quilts often filled with down or fiber, and heavy leathers are

Extreme Silhouette Modification, Figure Volume, Pants

Typical garments: Layering several bulky tops over full pants creates this effect. More popular is wearing bulky garments over the torso contrasted with a slim trouser.

Function: Warmth is the primary goal. This silhouette is often adapted to active winter sports, where mobility of the legs is important and warmth is necessary.

Structure: Tailored garments as well as draped shawls and capes over pants are popular. Wide-leg pants and versions of the jodhpur and harem pants are typical of this silhouette. The torso appears bulky and large. Fabrics are light in warm climates, and a great deal of ease is added to increase the volume of the garment.

Decoration: Large prints and bold colors are used effectively for this silhouette.

typical cold weather fabrics. Bulky sweater knits worn over wool shirts and long skirts are popular during the winter. Coats are often voluminous enough to cover suits and dresses. Capes and large shawls are popular additional accessories during cold weather.

These full garments successfully camouflage many figure problems, and large women have a wide variety of wardrobe choices when fashion decrees fullness is beautiful. The very petite woman will have to balance the size of her clothes and accessories with the size of her figure to achieve the look of volume without being overwhelmed by her clothing. One way to do this is to wear slightly shorter skirts and keep the colors of all the components of an outfit in one tone. Wear smaller prints. Keep handbags and scarves smaller than those worn by large people. To appear taller, wear one-color boots or stockings and shoes that match the skirt. This silhouette is very effective and dramatic on a tall woman. It will successfully camouflage angular body lines if worn by the tall, slender woman.

The extreme volume silhouette is difficult for most figures to wear when fashion decrees pants should also be very full. This silhouette emphasizes the width of the hips and legs and makes a person seem

Long tunics and straight leg pants camouflage many figure problems

Capes and stoles add bulk to the figure

Bulk above the waist is a good cold weather silhouette

shorter, so only a tall, slender person can effectively wear the full pant. The most successful way for a great variety of figures to wear the extremely full silhouette is to keep the volume above the hipline and contrast it with a slim leg line. Dark pants will make the person seem taller, even though he or she wears bulky tops. This modified silhouette is the typical cold-weather active-wear garment. A parka or bulky sweater is worn over slim pants, often made of stretch material for added mobility.

People with large figures will sometimes wear bulky pants in the hope that the fabric volume will hide their figure problems. Usually the total silhouette is overwhelming. A large person may choose to modify this effect by wearing a loose tunic that covers the thighs and a straight leg pant all in one color. This will lengthen the torso and avoid focusing on the waistline. The continuous line of the pants will make the very large person seem taller, yet the hips will be covered—usually a problem area for the large woman. Caftans are also popular with extremely large women because they offer a long, continuous line and cover the figure without attempting to fit any area snugly. These garments are more attractive when worn for casual events at home. They are not appropriate for street or business wear.

When fashion decrees volume is important, summer clothing is often made from lightweight cottons gathered at the waist and worn loose enough to allow air circulation near the body to keep it cool. Often the outline of the body is visible through the sheer fabric, and even though the garments are full, the illusion is of a slender body.

A great diversity of silhouettes is usually contained in an individual's wardrobe because of the great many different occasions people dress for. Wardrobe diversity also reflects changes in fashion that continually modify the stylish silhouette. Most people do not purchase an entirely new wardrobe when a style changes. They often use older components with newer garments to create fashionable outfits. Diversity is the rule rather than the exception. In addition, people with figure problems often dress in conservative silhouettes that flatter their figures and ignore radical fashion changes.

Proportion

After silhouette modification, the proportions of the various parts of the garment affect design structure the most. *Proportion* is the relationship of the sizes of the different parts and divisions of a garment and the volume of the garment as it relates to the figure wearing it. There are three important guidelines to the proportion of a garment and its parts:

1. Similar horizontal divisions of space shorten and widen the visual length of a garment.
2. The viewer's eye automatically compares the smaller portion of a garment with the larger portion, making an unequally divided garment seem longer because of the expanse of a long skirt or pair of pants.
3. Width above and/or below an area makes the area seem smaller.

The following illustrations demonstrate the extremes of proportion. Generally the designer is concerned with moving a line less than an inch. The designer constantly experiments with subtle variations in proportion, style line placement, length of hem, and size and placement of trim until the combined elements give the desired effect. Use the examples of proportion as your guidelines for styling. Experiment and observe constantly to improve your awareness of proportion.

Abstract Proportion Problems

The two rectangles represent a human body in garments of two different lengths. The first rectangle has the same proportions as an average body wearing a dress that comes to the middle of the knee. The second rectangle represents an average body wearing a garment that covers an average body from shoulder to ankle. These rectangles will be used in many abstract examples of apparel design.

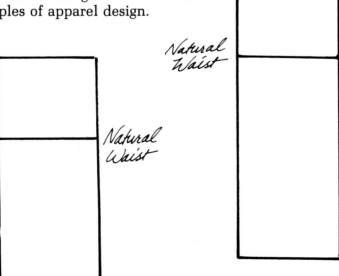

Which rectangle looks the longest?

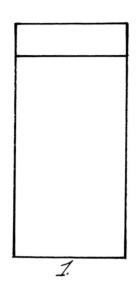

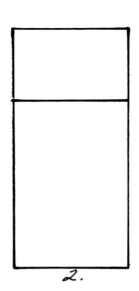

1.

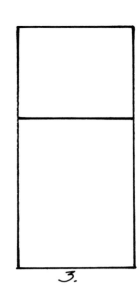

2.

3.

The greater the difference between the size of the bodice and the skirt, the taller the figure will look. The eye automatically compares the two areas and concludes that the longer skirt indicates a taller figure. Also, a high waist and small bodice look youthful. The high-waisted bodice is used in children's wear. It is also used in maternity clothes to camouflage the fuller stomach and emphasize height.

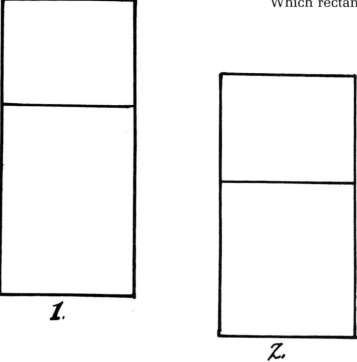

Which rectangle looks the thinnest?

1.

2.

Evenly divided spaces emphasize the squareness of a shape. Uneven horizontal divisions make the whole shape seem thinner.

207

Which rectangle looks the longest?

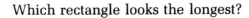

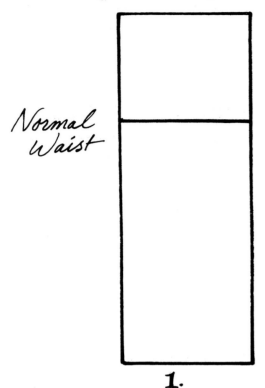

Normal Waist

1.

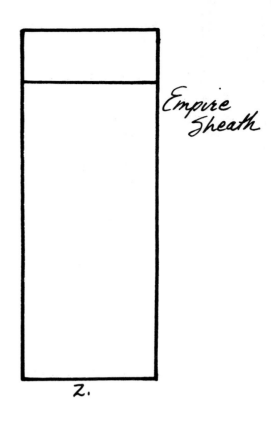

Empire Sheath

2.

Empire Sheath worn during Napoleonic Period

Long dress with normal waistline

Modern wedding dress with high waistline

Exaggerated Proportions   The more exaggerated the difference between the bodice and the skirt, the taller and more slender the figure will seem. Thus the long dress with a raised waistline is popular for brides. The floor-length gown can also conceal high-heeled shoes, which add to a person's height. This proportion was very popular after the French Revolution and retains the name *empire*, after the court Napoleon established. The empire is a good proportion for an overweight, small woman if her bust is not too large.

208

Which shape looks younger?

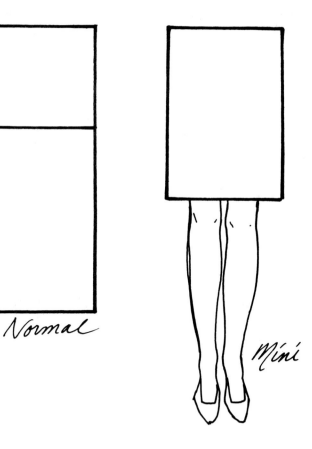

Normal

Mini

Exaggerated Proportions The miniskirt (very short, several inches above the knee) can make a person look taller. So much leg is exposed that the legs become a major factor in the proportion of the entire garment. The waistline is often raised to accentuate the youthful look. Note that accessories, such as tall boots, stockings the same color as the shoes, and high hairstyles, enhance the whole image of height.

209

Which rectangle looks the longest?

Exaggerated Proportions Unequal proportions, even when they are reversed and the emphasis is placed on the thighs, enhance the illusion of height. The second rectangle looks the shortest because the proportion is almost the same. But elongating the torso presents some problems because many women have hips that are larger than their busts. If a fitted garment is designed, a low torso will overemphasize the bulges in the hip area.

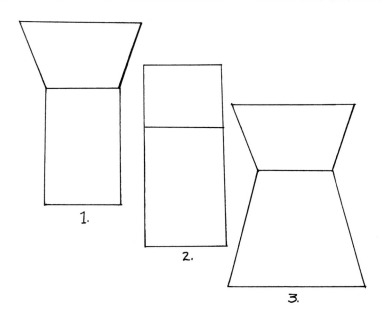

1.

2.

3.

Note how width at the shoulder and hemline affects the visual size of the waistline and the size of the silhouette.

In the example at the right, the wedge silhouette makes the hips seem slender. The normal silhouette does not camouflage a large waist or hips. The third silhouette at the left makes the waist seem very small in comparison to the wide sleeves and full skirt. Darkening or contrasting the waistline with a belt adds to the illusion by focusing the viewer's attention on the smallest space in the silhouette.

Line

Line refers to the edge or the outline of a garment and the style lines that divide the space within a garment. Line can create visual illusions, such as height, which can lengthen or shorten the figure, and width, which can make a figure seem thinner or heavier. Because the eye follows a line, the line can attract the eye to particular areas and draw it away from less desirable areas. Straight, diagonal, and curved lines are all used in garment design. Study the illustrations to see how line can visually deceive the eye.

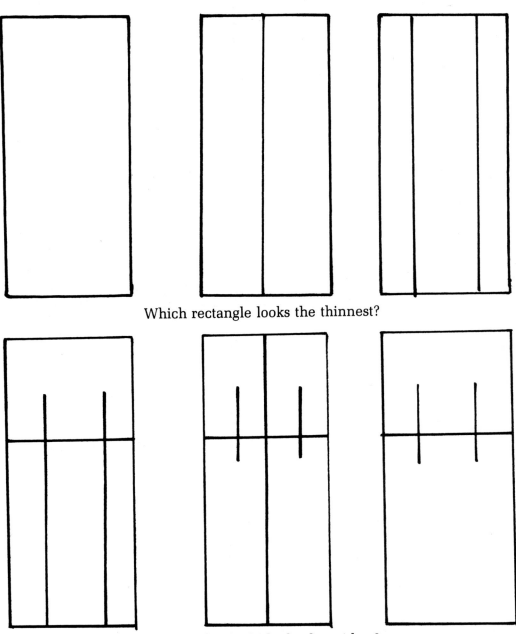

Which rectangle looks the thinnest?

Which rectangle looks the widest?

Examples 2 and 3 appear more slender than example 1 because the added vertical lines divide the space, and the eye interprets this division as a smaller whole. The uninterrupted vertical lines quickly draw the eye upward and make the rectangles seem longer and slimmer. Vertical divisions in garments are called gores. Because gores form an unbroken line from end to end, they are more slimming than darts.

The second and third rectangles look thinner than the first one because the vertical lines are interrupted less frequently. Notice how the darts, which look like short lines, do not carry the eye through the whole composition. this adds width to the rectangle and the garment.

Which rectangle looks the most slender?

Which rectangle looks the most slender? Which rectangle looks the tallest?

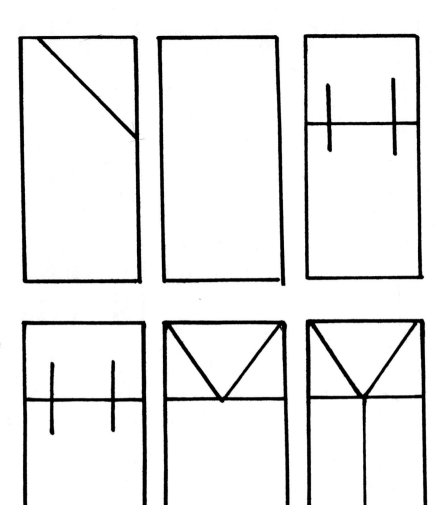

Line leads the eye and can be used in apparel design to reinforce the theme of a garment. The characteristics of line are its path and length. A horizontal line will direct the viewer across the garment, emphasizing its width at that point. Off-the-shoulder, square, and boat necklines will shorten a long face and make the shoulders seem broader. If worn by a short person, they will make the person seem shorter. A band or seam at the hipline will make the hips seem wider.

A straight vertical line gives a heightening effect and divides the body, making it seem thinner. A gentle curve is feminine and passive. The more exaggerated a curved line becomes, the more time it takes to view the contour and so it will seem fussy, as in a circular ruffle that decorates a scooped neckline and exaggerates femininity. A diagonal line will slim the

214

Diagonal Lines Diagonal lines in a garment tend to slenderize the whole more than abrupt vertical lines. A diagonal line usually creates an asymmetrical design.

Diagonal lines combined with vertical lines, as in the bottom part of the illustration, is the most slenderizing effect and makes the figure seem the tallest. The eye follows the center front seam up through the skirt and the symmetrically divided bodice. This style line emphasizes and enlarges the bust and shoulder areas.

figure if the angle is not too abrupt. The slim V neckline formed by an open shirt or jacket will make the figure seem slimmer and taller. This neckline will also lengthen a round or square face. If the shape is reinforced by contrast when wearing a light-colored blouse under a dark suit, the effect will be even stronger. When a line is thickened and contrasted to the rest of the garment by using a braid or trim, the line becomes stronger. Coco Chanel, the French designer, was famous for suits with braid trim outlining the front edges of the jacket. The jackets were very slenderizing and have become a classic style because they are so flattering.

Which rectangle looks the longest?
Which rectangle looks the broadest?

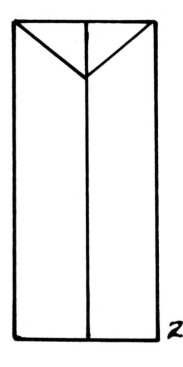

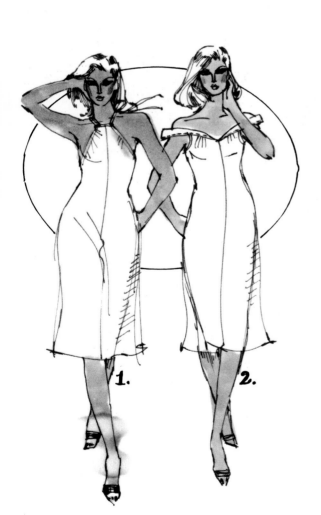

The first dress adds to the illusion of height because it emphasizes the ascending (upward) diagonals. These diagonals focus on a central point, which makes the shoulders seem less broad. Example 2 emphasizes the horizontal quality of the person's shoulders. The horizontal line also stops the eye from moving upward, so the appearance of height is diminished.

Balance

A symmetrical design is the most logical and easily accepted arrangement for the elements of a garment and therefore the most common design for apparel. The average human body is visually symmetrical, which means that the body seems to be the same on each side of a central line. Two arms, two eyes, and two legs are balanced on either side of a central axis. Actually, if a picture of one-half of the face were duplicated and reversed to produce a picture of a whole face, the picture would look quite different from reality. In the same way, the body image is slightly different on each side. The eye corrects minor discrepancies in size and shape, so when an object is close to being symmetrical, the eye sees it as equal on both sides. When a person's body differs noticeably on one side, carefully designed clothes can minimize the difference.

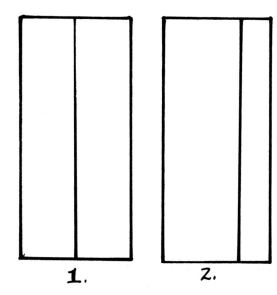

1.   **2.**

Which rectangle looks the thinnest? Which rectangle looks the tallest? The first rectangle tends to make the figure look taller and more slender because the eye does not compare the discrepancy between the large and small sides of the asymmetrical garment. The first dress is symmetrically balanced; that is, the garment is the same on each side of the center front line.

Center Point

Now look at the jacket in the accompanying drawing. Is it a symmetrical design? Actually, the jacket is asymmetrical. If you thought it was symmetrical, your eye probably ignored the one asymmetrical detail and concluded that the design was balanced. The eye follows the buttons up the center front and does not notice that the lap and leading edge actually extend beyond the center line. The design lines, collars, and pockets emphasize the formal balance.

Designing a truly asymmetrical garment requires more thought and experimentation than designing a symmetrical one. Separate pattern pieces must be made for the right and left sides. These pieces cannot be reversed during cutting because they must fasten right over left, as symmetrical garments do. Balance and proportion are more experimental in an asymmetrical garment because there are fewer formulas for the placement of style lines. For these reasons, fewer asymmetrical garments are designed.

Some figure problems can be camouflaged by wearing an asymmetrical garment. Figures that are unequal can be corrected visually by emphasizing one side to balance the discrepancy, as shown in the illustration.

Examples 1 and 2 at the left have a consistently asymmetrical theme. Notice in figure 3 how an asymmetrical closing combined with a center front seam in the skirt creates disharmony. Asymmetrical design should be consistent within the outfit.

Unity

Unity means that all elements of a design work together to produce a successful visual effect. Study the following six examples of simple garments and see if you can find the elements that are not combined successfully.

The following six examples point out basic principles of unity in design.

> *Principle 1.* Style lines should be consistent on every area of the garment and on separate garments that are sold as coordinates.

Solution

> *Principle 2.* All areas of the garment should reflect the same shapes. In the incorrect example, the collar, cuffs, and hem are curved, so the square pockets interrupt the continuity of design. Curved lines are most compatible with the shape of the body. Geometric lines and shapes must be more carefully designed because they are less compatible with body curves.

Solution

Principle 3. Avoid small differences in the hem lengths of sleeves and the garment bottom. A small jog interferes with the horizontal flow of the hemline. This does not mean that all sleeves must be the same length as the jacket. The difference between the sleeves and the jacket should be significant enough to look planned, or the sleeves should be aligned with the jacket hem.

Solution

Principle 4. Stripes and plaids used on the straight grain should match, particularly on sleeves that hang parallel to the bodice. Stripes and plaids cut on the bias can be combined effectively with garment pieces cut on the straight grain, but the pattern on bias pieces must be matched with other bias pieces.

Solution

Principle 5. Seam lines and trim details on sleeves should align with similar lines on the body of the garment. Small jogs are visual interruptions of the horizontal design.

Principle 6. Style lines on all areas of the garment should have compatible angles and complement each other.

Train your eye to analyze garments that are pleasing to you, and recognize how the designer has unified all elements to create a successful garment. When you see an awkward-looking garment, check carefully to see if the elements are in competition rather than in harmony.

Rhythm

Rhythm is the repeated use of lines or shapes to create a pattern. Uniform rhythm is the repetition of the same space, as illustrated in example 1. In progres-

Do any of these dresses look awkward or uninteresting?

1.

2.

3.

sive, or graduated rhythm, the size of the unit increases or decreases as it is repeated, as example 2 shows. Unequal rhythm is an unequal use of space, as example 3 illustrates.

Example 1 in the illustration has the most uninteresting rhythm. The uniform use of space contributes to a chunky, awkward design. Unequal or graduated rhythms are usually the more desirable methods for breaking up horizontal space. As with proportion, careful experimentation is necessary to design a garment that has a pleasing rhythm.

Emphasis

Emphasis creates a center of interest by focusing the viewer's attention on a specific area of the garment. The designer uses the principles of emphasis to direct the eye. Lines that lead to the face are particularly effective because the face is a focal point of beauty in our culture. Contrasting colors and trims can emphasize an area. For example, a black dress with white collar and cuffs will direct the eye to the face and hands. The three illustrations on this page are good examples of how emphasis does and does not work in design.

The placement of dark spots in prints, pockets, and appliqués is an important consideration. Dark spots on a light-colored garment and white spots on a dark background emphasize the body part they are placed over. Avoid the placements shown in illustrations 1 to 3. Generally these parts of the body are not emphasized when designing street wear. A costume designer may reverse this rule of emphasis to create a special effect.

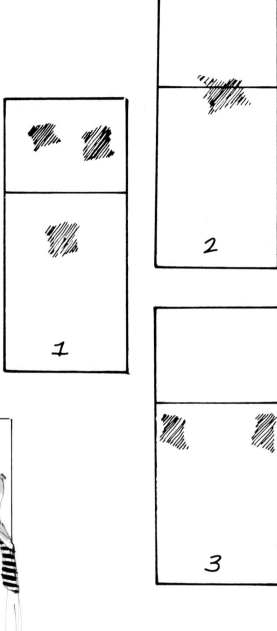

In this illustration, notice how the design devices attract your eye to the bust, stomach, and hips.

DECORATION

The decorative characteristics of a garment are usually what attracts a buyer's attention first. Often, only a sleeve is visible as the garment hangs on a rack. The customer is attracted by a color or pattern and puts out a hand to feel the fabric. If the texture is pleasing, and she or he likes the color, the person may pull out the garment to evaluate the style and decide to try it on. The components of decoration are all present in this primary evaluation of the garment. They are

> Color
> Value
> Pattern
> Texture (or hand)

A designer creates garments for a specific market. Very often a designer of a line will become so caught up in the mechanics of creating the merchandise that he or she will lose sight of the customer. There is no substitute for constant contact with the people who wear the clothes you design. Visit the stores that sell the merchandise and work with the salespeople and customers who have firsthand knowledge of what is selling. This knowledge can be blended with the new offerings that are available in prints, colors, and fabrications so the line offers newness and variety without losing sight of the fact an individual must like the garment enough to purchase it. This is the way a designer develops a good taste level.

Color

Color is an important fashion element that is fairly well controlled by commercial fashion sources and textile converters. Color can be used to create illusions. Some examples follow:

1. A garment in one color (or tones of that color) adds to the illusion of height, especially in a floor-length garment (long skirts, pants, and so forth).
2. Generally, darker colors are more slenderizing than light and bright colors.
3. Darker colors recede visually, and light, bright colors pop out. A woman with a large bust and slender hips can equalize her figure by wearing light-colored pants and a dark top.
4. Light colors are flattering around the face. The eye seeks out light colors when they contrast

with a dark garment. A white collar on a dark dress emphasizes the face.

5. People tend to wear colors compatible with their complexions. People who promote fashion colors often ignore the fact that colors should flatter people.
6. Environment affects the use of color. People who live in warm climates tend to have more pigment in their skin, so they are protected from overexposure to the sun. Warm climates encourage people to wear bright, light colors that complement tanned complexions.

Bold effects are created by using light and bright colors, which make a person seem larger. Enclosing a shape with a dark outline of braid or trim in a contrasting color will emphasize an area of the body. Textured or patterned shapes of advancing colors (some specific examples are red, bright purple, chrome yellow, and hot pink) against a plain background will visually "pop out" the shape. All these uses of color will emphasize and enlarge the figure.

Flattening effects are created by using receding or neutral colors with no bold outlines. Plain, unbroken shapes tend to recede and can be accented with a textured or detailed area to direct the eye to a specific part of the body. Space filled with pattern will seem larger than plain space. Combining a bold treatment with a neutral or flattening color effect will diminish the impact of both. An example would be wearing a bright, boldly patterned blouse with a pair of dark pants. This outfit would focus attention on the bust and torso area and lead the eye to the face, especially if the blouse has a V-shaped neckline.

Value

The contrast between light and dark is used frequently to create effective illusions that disguise figure problems. Contrasts accent different parts of the body and create subtle illusions. Dark areas recede visually, so an area of the body that is disproportionately large can be balanced by covering it with a dark garment. Light colors stand out, which makes light areas seem larger than they are, especially when contrasted with dark areas. Look at the illustrations here and on p. 226 to see the effects of value.

In the illustration on p. 226, garment 3 gives the most slender appearance. The white front panel stands out, and the dark side panels recede, making

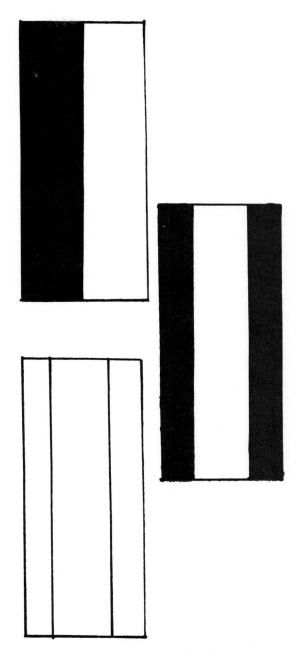

Which rectangle seems the thinnest?

225

the eye less conscious of them. Garment 1 is more slenderizing than garment 2 because the value contrast is sharp. The eye "sees" only half the garment because the dark half is less noticeable.

Now study the illustration on p. 227. When the bodice has a darker value than the skirt or pants, as in the first example, the shoulders and the size of the bust are minimized. The figure will seem shorter than it would in a garment of only one tone. When the darker value is used below the waist, as in the second example, the hips will look smaller. The lighter bodice will make the bust seem larger. Also, this example gives the appearance of height because the dark area below the waist is a heavier visual mass and so does not dominate the light torso, unlike the first example.

These examples are simple illustrations of the principles of value, principles that can be extended to many other kinds of garments.

Pattern

Developing an eye for selecting patterns that appeal to a great many customers is a special talent. It is important to expose yourself to a great variety of fabrics and to try to imagine how a pattern will look made up in a garment. The fabric that carries the pattern is extremely important. A beautiful fabric like silk crepe de chine can carry a rather somber or dull print and look very elegant because of the quali-

ty and luster of the fabric. The same print on a flat, lusterless synthetic will lose a great deal of its beauty and sophistication.

Extremes of pattern will accent extremes of the figure. A very large print on a small woman will tend to dwarf her. A moderately-sized pattern or a small motif would be more appropriate. A huge print on a very large woman will accent the size of her figure, especially if the patterns are widely spaced, because the eye unconsciously counts the number of patterns needed to span her girth. Widely spaced, huge prints tend to fall unpredictably on the figure and may land on the bust, tummy, or derrière and accent these areas. Tall, slender women can best carry bold designs. Small prints and florals tend to be dainty and feminine.

Directional patterns emphasize the figure because the eye follows the direction in which they flow. A vertical stripe will carry the eye from the hem of the garment to the wearer's face in a quick, uninterrupted glance that makes a person seem more slender. Plaids on the bias are flattering because they create a diagonal and lead the eye to the face. Geometrics are more versatile than specific images.

A good rule of thumb is to use simple styles for complicated prints because the print has a lot of intrinsic interest. This lets the fabric carry the style of the dress without diminishing the impact of the print with small structural details. Select a variety of sizes and ground colors when selecting a print group. Include one bold print, one geometric or dot, and a third print that is currently fashionable. Trends in print size and styling have cycles like fashion silhouettes and are often closely linked to them. When full silhouettes are popular, many large prints will be offered. When feminine styling is popular, look for florals and tiny prints. Conversational prints have an amusing motif and are often popular in the junior market.

Texture

Texture means the hand—that is, the way the fabric feels. Texture also means the appearance of the fabric. Hand and appearance dictate the silhouette and the kind of garment that can be made. A soft fabric that drapes cannot be made into a stiff, structured garment without using interlinings or a stiff lining. A thin organza is not appropriate for a coat, nor is a thick wool appropriate for a clinging evening gown. These are exaggerated examples of inappropriate fabrications. The professional designer must consider the subtle differences between fabrics and then style them accordingly.

Every person has experienced the texture of garments since birth. The designer develops this vague awareness of how fabric feels (the tactile sense) into a conscious knowledge of the appropriate texture for specific garments. A designer uses tactile evaluation of fabric just as a sculptor or potter experiences the basic stone or clay with hands as well as eyes.

The design student should begin to develop a tactile sense by sewing and draping fabric. Observation is a valuable tool. Look at fabrics and feel textures. Experiment with fabrics to see how they cover the body. Notice that shiny fabrics reflect light, making the body seem larger, especially in a tightly fitted garment. Shiny surfaces also look dressier than matte (dull) surfaces. Feel matte fabrics. Decide which fabrics look appropriate for casual wear. Relate the fabric's hand to the season. Feel a soft, spongy, thick fabric with your hand and decide in which climate a garment made of this fabric would be worn. Sense why a thin, crisp, absorbent, plain weave is appropriate for a warm climate. You have experienced these sensations subconsciously many times. Now you must begin to develop on a conscious level your understanding of fabric uses.

Feel, look, and experiment. Developing these skills will expand your ability to judge what a fabric can be made into and when a fabric can be worn.

REVIEW

Word Finders

Define the following words from the chapter you just read:

1. Asymmetrical
2. Balance
3. Body Suit
4. Design
5. Diagonal style lines
6. Elements
7. Emphasis
8. Fashion
9. Hourglass
10. Line
11. Man-tailored
12. Proportion
13. Principles
14. Progressive rhythm
15. Rhythm
16. Symmetrical
17. Silhouette
18. Tactile
19. Texture
20. Unity
21. Uniform rhythm
22. Value

Figure Problems

Using the principles from the chapter, design garments for the following situations and figure problems.

1. Design an evening gown and a garment for spectator sports that will make a small woman with large hips and a small bust seem tall and slender.
2. Design a day dress for a very tall woman who wants to minimize her height.
3. Imagine you are a costume designer dressing an actress who is average in height and has an average size 10 figure. Her part calls for a mature person, 20 pounds overweight. The actress needs two costumes, one for daytime wear and the other for an evening occasion.
4. A short woman with a very large bust and narrow hips will be having dinner at a restaurant. Design a garment that will make her look as tall as possible.

8.
drawing
a working
sketch

A designer must be able to draw a working sketch or croquis of the garment planned. This working sketch may be shown to the manufacturer during a discussion about which garments to make up. The working sketch is given to the assistant as a guide in making the pattern and shows the placement of construction lines. The silhouette or shape of the garment is important because it tells the patternmaker how much fullness should be in a skirt, sleeve, or bodice. A working sketch is placed as identification on each pattern. It is also used on the cost sheet.

A working sketch differs from an illustration. A fashion illustration is a finished, carefully rendered drawing that glamorizes a garment. A designer who is fond of drawing may prepare a more elaborate sketch for use outside the workroom, but will also draw a working sketch to guide the patternmaker in constructing the garment. A designer does not have to know how to illustrate, but must know how to draw a working sketch.

To begin sketching, the designer must understand basic body proportions. Fashion figures are elongated and stylized versions of the typical figure. The minimum fashion figure is 8 times the length of the head. Many designers and illustrators further elon-

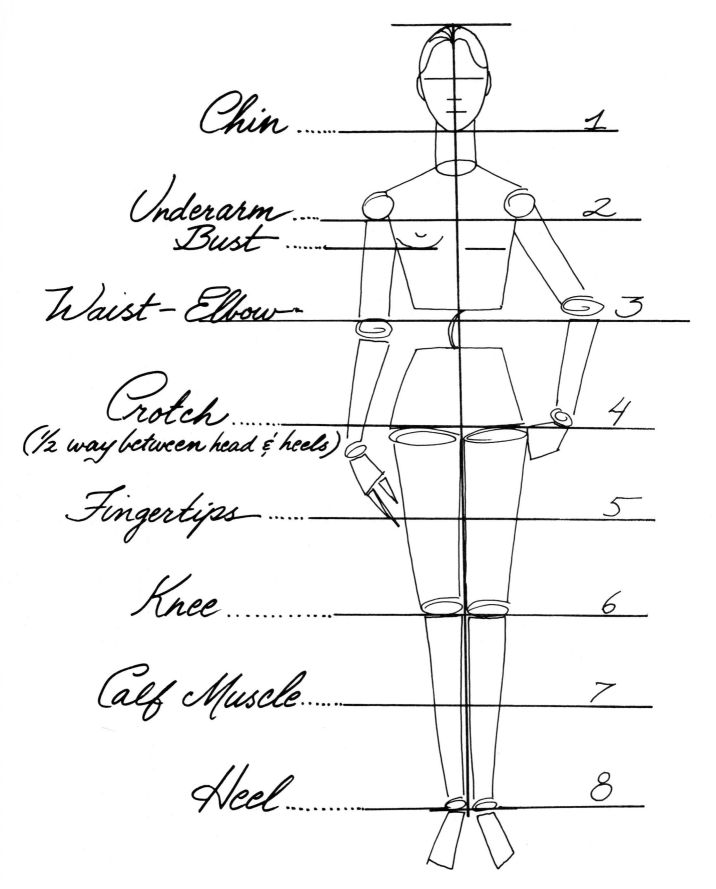

Chin 1

Underarm 2
Bust ....

Waist - Elbow 3

Crotch 4
(½ way between head & heels)

Fingertips 5

Knee 6

Calf Muscle 7

Heel 8

232

gate the figure to dramatize the garment. The beginner should practice on the 8-head figure, elongating it later as sketching ability develops. To start, use a #2 soft lead pencil (we will discuss other media in a later section).

Sketching is a tool for recording and developing ideas. Working sketches should be done quickly, but proportion, silhouette, and construction details must be accurate. Sketching is very much like handwriting: a person who sketches a great deal will develop her or his own style. Detailed hands and feet are not important in a working sketch, so many designers draw only the garment without a body in it. This is adequate if the garment's proportions are accurate.

BASIC PROPORTION

The accompanying drawing shows proportions for a fashion figure based on 8 heads. In other words, the size of the head multiplied 8 times equals the height of the figure from the top of the head to the heels.

Practice sketching the basic figure many times. Notice the following things as you draw:

1. The circles indicate very flexible joints where most movement occurs (the waist is also very flexible).
2. The width of the shoulders equals about 1½ heads.
3. The width of the waist equals about 1 head.
4. The elbow is parallel to the waist. The elbow moves upward from the waist in a slight arc as it is bent away from the body.
5. The neck is slightly longer than normal to give the figure a graceful look.
6. The crotch is the halfway measurement of the body. The legs must be equal to or longer than the distance from the top of the head to the crotch.
7. The legs can move only at the hip socket, knee, and ankle. The other areas are inflexible bone.
8. When the arm bends, double check its length by comparing it to the body.
9. The feet must look large enough to support the figure.

FLESHING OUT THE FIGURE

Practice drawing the basic figure, and then take the drawing one step further. Add flesh to the basic

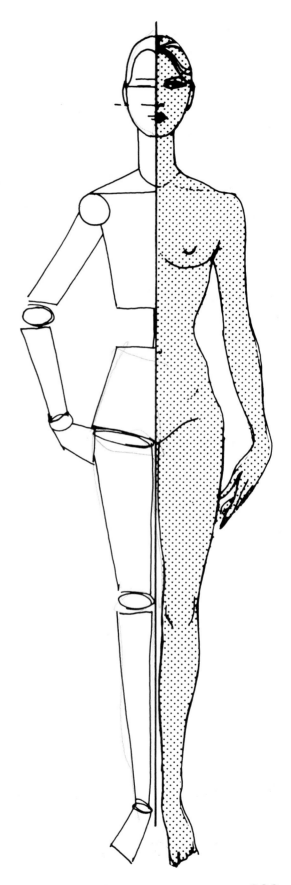

233

framework. Remember to make the figure fashionable by omitting any excess bulk. A fashion model should have a slender body that emphasizes bone structure.

As you draw the fleshed-in figure, constantly visualize the framework of the body. Think about the immovable sections of the body, and consider the joints.

MOVEMENT AT THE WAIST

The waist is the most flexible part of the body. It can move from side to side or backward and forward. The fashion model's waist is slender and supple.

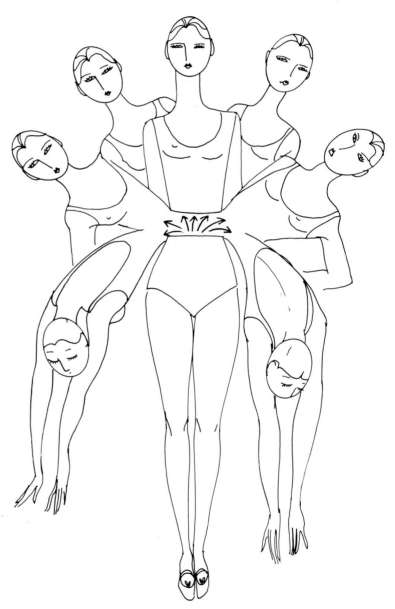

When it is fashionable to have a small waist, women wear foundation garments that cinch in the waist and make it smaller. Gradually a person's waist will constrict even when the corset is not worn because no rigid bone structure determines the waist size. When fashion deemphasizes the waist, women abandon their corsets and waist cinchers. Then the waist returns to its normal size of about a 10-inch drop (the difference between the waist and the hip).

MOVING THE FIGURE

Moving the figure adds drama and personality to a sketch. The one-leg stance (or S curve) is a typical sketching device to move a figure. The weight is balanced on one leg. Follow the arrow in the following illustrations and you will discover the rule about the center of gravity: *The supporting leg must always fall under the chin to avoid drawing a leaning figure.*

235

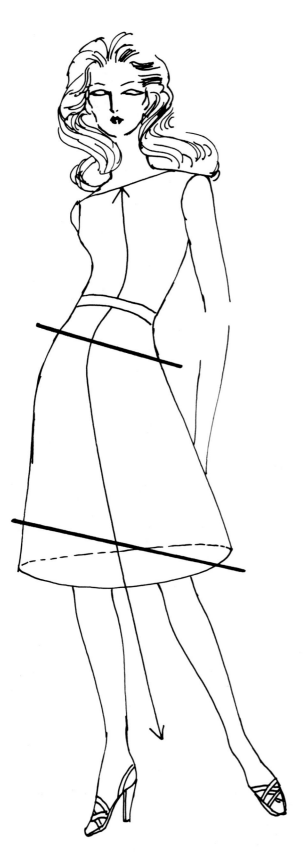

Analyze the slant of the shoulders in the illustrations. Notice the opposition of the shoulders and hips in the central figure in the three-figure illustration. This stance is particularly good for displaying garments because the figure is in action, yet the clothing can be shown with little visual distortion.

Begin now to sketch from life. Analyze the slant of the shoulders and hips before beginning a sketch. Try drawing from photographs you find in magazines. Photographs are preferable to illustrations because you can see actual body movements and poses without becoming caught up in the artist's style.

THE THREE-DIMENSIONAL FIGURE

The three-dimensional figure adds another aspect to drawings of clothes and the human body. This stance is particularly important for illustrating an interesting sleeve or construction details on the side of the garment. The shaded areas in the illustration show the plane of the figure moving away from the center front part of the body. Again, the angle of the shoulder is an important first step in sketching. The center front line of the figure is altered considerably as the body turns (notice the dotted line on the center figure).

The center figure illustrates the torso and the hips moving in two different directions. Both body blocks can be aligned, as shown in the illustrations on either side.

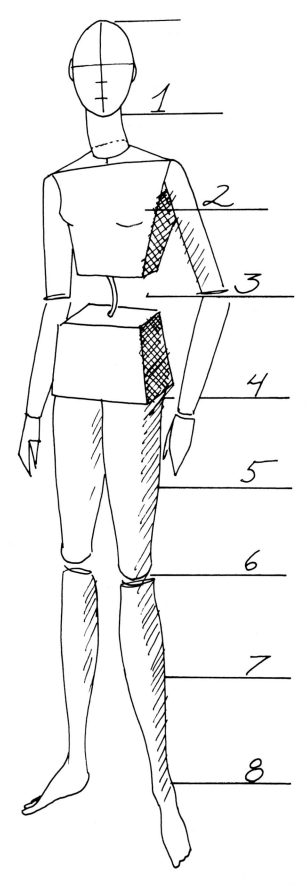

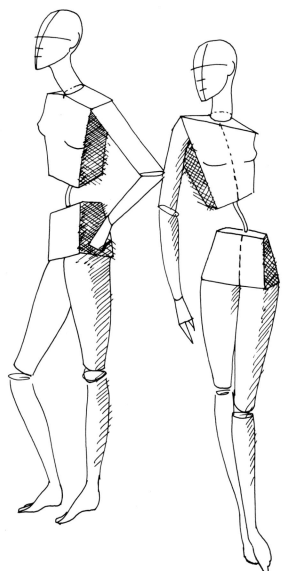

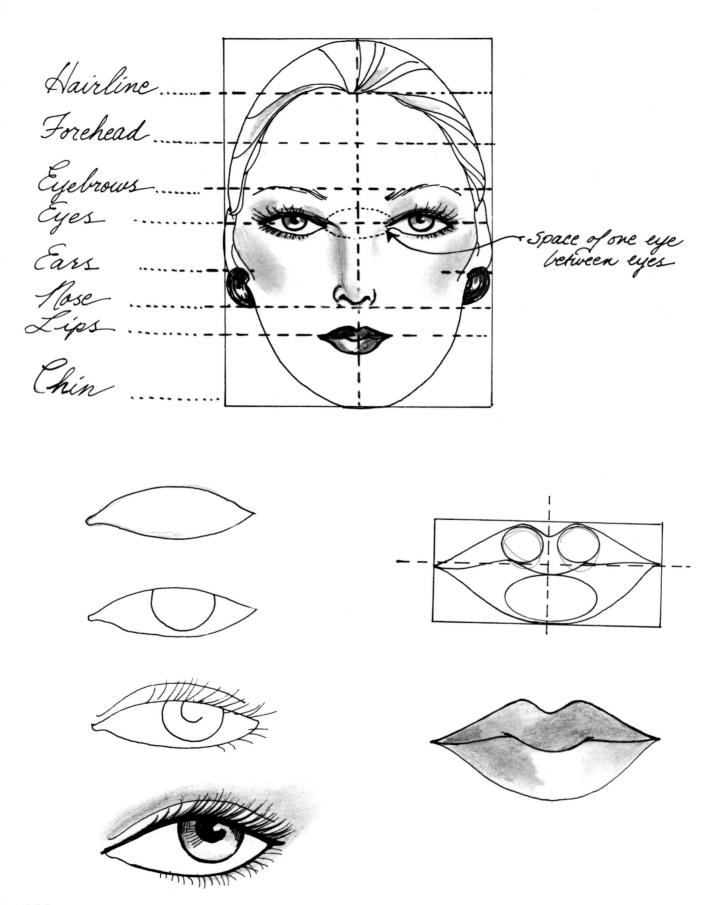

Hairline
Forehead
Eyebrows
Eyes
Ears
Nose
Lips
Chin

space of one eye
between eyes

238

Continue to sketch from life. Analyze each figure to locate the forefront line of the body (the one closest to you). Study the angle of the hips and shoulders and determine which body planes are receding. As your sketches become more complicated, do not lose sight of basic body proportions.

DRAWING THE FACE

The face is oval, with features symmetrically arranged on either side of a central line. Study the sketches here carefully, and practice drawing the shape of the head only. Then draw the components (eyes, mouth, and so forth) several times until you feel comfortable drawing them. Practice many diagrammatic sketches of the face and outlined features. When you have perfected the placement of the features, begin to sketch from photographs. Avoid exaggerated eyes and hairdos, which are common pitfalls for the beginner. When the face and hairstyle are drawn simply and elegantly, they do not detract from the clothes.

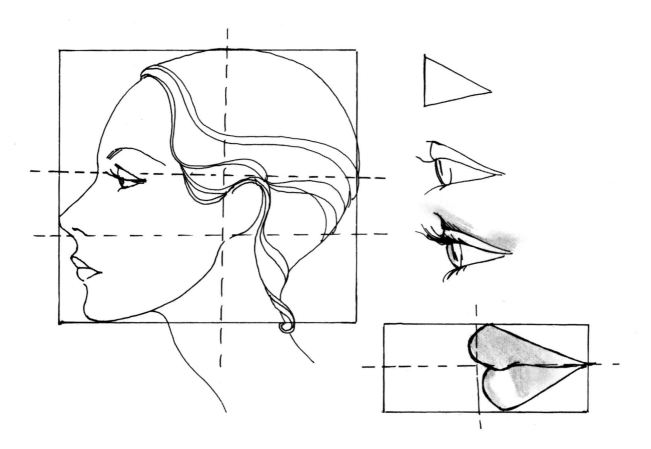

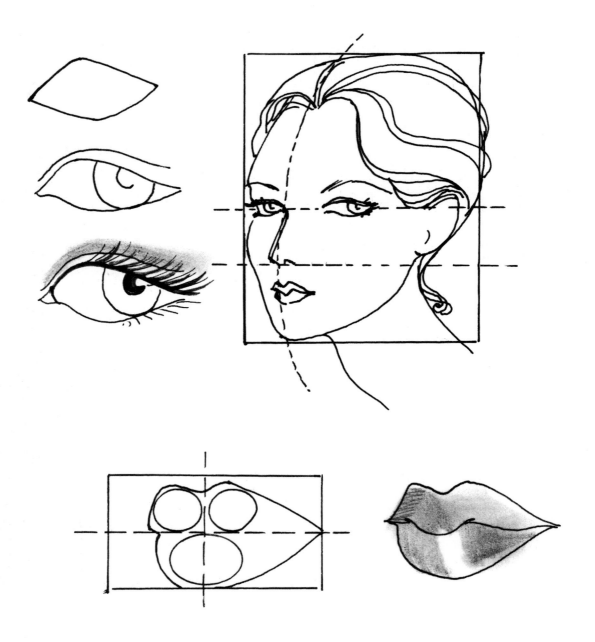

DRAWING HAIR

The face and hairstyle in a fashion sketch should be
compatible with the garments illustrated. Young
clothes should be shown on a model with a young
face and a simple hairstyle. Casual clothing will look
out of place if the model has an elaborate hairstyle.
Nothing makes a garment look more unfashionable
than a model with a dated hairstyle that is inappropriate for the clothing illustrated. Save examples of
hairstyles, poses, and faces that give you ideas for
sketches.

Heavier eye makeup – shading
of lash and eyebrows more
detailed – hairstyle more
defined, cheekbones more
pronounced, lips more
defined, a more serious
look – more jewelry

Light makeup, less
eyebrow emphasis,
perky nose – softer, fuller
lips, simple, softer
hairstyle, softer
cheekbones, a sweeter
look

242

Spirals—with Marker—Stresses Movement

Contour drawing—Strong line

Ink line and wash with Brush—Fluidity

MEDIA

After a sketcher masters the basics of proportion and movement and is able to flesh out a figure with a lead pencil, he or she should begin to experiment

Fine
line,

delicate,
elegant—
ink for
felt pen

Charcoal—
Sophisticated
feeling

with other media. Media are tools and materials that create line and tone. Seven basic media to experiment with are

1. Prisma pencils. Black, grays, and colors are available. Very easy to use. A wide variety in the quality of the line is possible, from very delicate to broad shadows and tones.
2. Marking pens. Many textures and qualities of line are available in colors and black. Mix several kinds in one drawing to add interest. Among others, fine line, hard point, soft fine line, and broad tipped are available.
3. Ink. May be applied with a brush or various kinds of pens. Very fine lines can be made with a Rapidograph pen. Broad, bold lines can be made with broad pen nibs. Use a brush for washes.
4. Water color and gouache (opaque water color). For adding colors and white to sketches. Applies with soft brushes, which should be purchased in a variety of sizes and shapes to handle lines and washes. Novelty effects can be obtained by using a toothbrush to splatter paint or by adding salt to a wet wash for an interesting texture.
5. Transparent dyes. Excellent for color sketches, they may be applied with brushes or ink pens. Intense transparent color is an easily obtainable effect.
6. Charcoal, crayons, pastels. Soft, textured markers give a smudgy look and great character of line and shadow. These markers are easily smudged and blended, so they should be sprayed with a fixative to protect the finished sketch.
7. Textured and colored papers. They give an added dimension to the lines and tones drawn on them. Colored paper allows for the use of white accents and highlights.

Combination of Media

Combining several media in a sketch can create a dramatic visual statement. Contrasting tones and several kinds of line add dimension and interest. Fernando R. Flores, a professional illustrator, used several different media in the illustration shown next. He enhanced the garment by sketching it on a sophisticated model in an unusual pose, resulting in a sketch with great charter.

California
Apparel
News

May 1, 1976 Vol. 32 No. 16 California Apparel News

Collagedress
See Page 2.

Sketch by Fernando R. Flores

(Courtesy of Fernando R. Flores and *California Apparel News*.)

DRAWING GARMENTS

Fashion sketching uses the body to show garments. No matter what his other talents, including pattern-making, a designer must be able to sketch ideas. The following pages illustrate basic methods of drawing specific garments. Because fashion changes so rapidly, basic styles have been chosen as examples. These exercises should be developed to encompass current fashion trends.

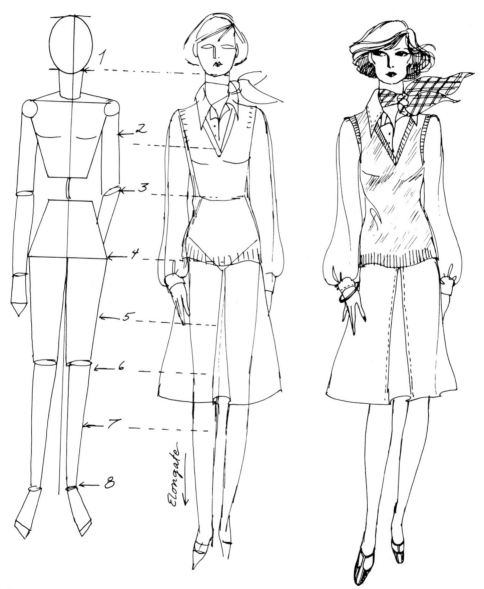

One way of drawing a finished garment. This drawing demonstrates how light guidelines indicating the figure are sketched first. The second step is lightly drawing in the lines of the garment. Finally, draw in the definite lines and final details. This is an excellent method for the beginner because it reinforces the idea of body proportions and closely relates garments to parts of the body. However, the finished sketch can become overworked and soiled.

This drawing shows a rough sketch that has been drawn over on a sheet of tracing paper, or vellum. Semitransparent paper is an excellent tool for producing a finished, well-drawn, neat sketch. Using this type of paper allows the designer to quickly do several versions of a garment from one sketched pose. To preserve the tissue, mount it on a piece of opaque paper.

Darts

A *dart* is the part of a flat piece of fabric that is taken into a seam to make the fabric conform to body curves. The excess fabric may be made into one dart or divided into several darts.

The "point of bust" is the center point of the bust. A standard dart will end 1 inch from the point of bust no matter where on the perimeter of the pattern piece the dart comes from. Darts are frequently used to remove the excess fabric between the waist and the fullest part of the hips. These darts taper to nothing about 6 inches below the waist. Small darts are used at the back shoulder line to shape the fabric over the shoulder blades.

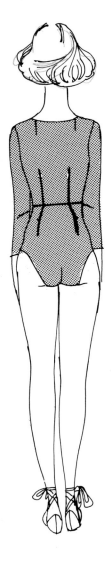

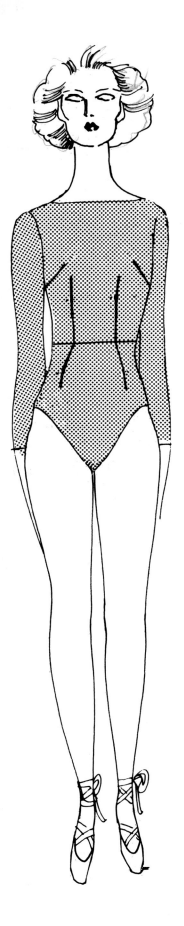

There are many different kinds of darts. Most often darts are used for stiff, structured styles. Garments styled in softer fabrics will not have darts, producing a more casual, less fitted look.

Gores and Yokes

Gores are vertical divisions of the bodice and skirt. *Yokes* are horizontal divisions of the bodice and skirt. If a seam, either vertical or horizontal, passes over the point of bust, no dart or ease is necessary because the fabric can be contoured to fit by remov-

250

ing ease and shaping the pattern piece. As the seams of the gore or yoke move further from the point of bust, the amount of ease or the size of the dart increases. Gores and yokes are often used in combination with ease and darts to extend flexibility.

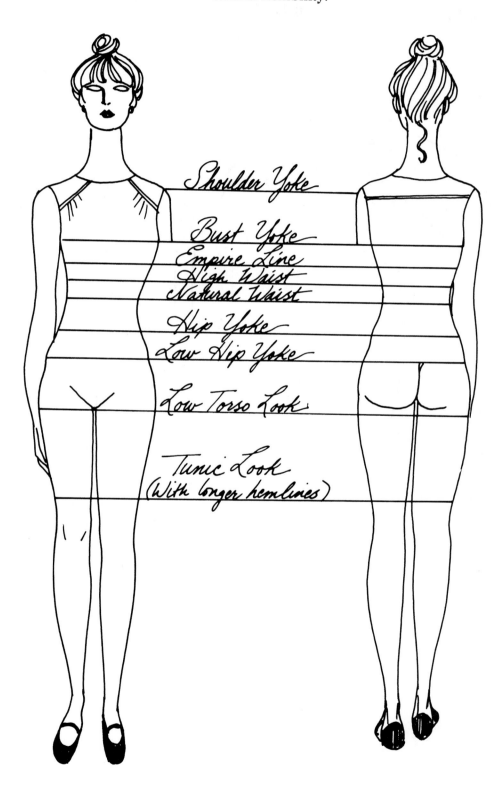

Shoulder Yoke

Bust Yoke

Empire Line

High Waist

Natural Waist

Hip Yoke

Low Hip Yoke

Low Torso Look

Tunic Look
(with longer hemlines)

Gores

Yoke and
Pin Tucks

Empire
Bodice

Yoke

Gathers

Waist
Belt

Hip
Yoke

Multiple
Yokes

Ease and
Shaped Yoke

253

Sleeves

Sleeves are tubes of fabric that surround the arm. On a fashion sketch, every seam in a set-in sleeve should be drawn. The standard placement for the seam of a set-in sleeve is on the top of the shoulder socket, before the arm curves into the bicep. A dropped arm's eye is a style variation that gives a smoother look to the shoulder. This sleeve usually has a looser fit. When the shoulder seam is closer to the neckline, the shoulders look narrower and more youthful.

Sleeves that incorporate a part of the bodice are shown in the accompanying illustration. Note that these sleeves are much looser than the standard set-in sleeve, especially under the arm.

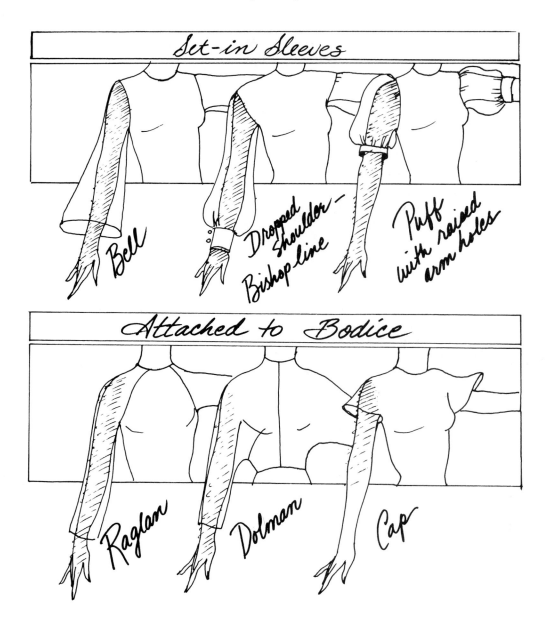

Set-in Sleeves

Bell

Dropped shoulder—Bishop line

Puff with raised arm holes

Attached to Bodice

Raglan

Dolman

Cap

Belts

In the illustrations, observe how belts gather fabric to the waist or hip. Notice too the way different fabrics are affected by belts. The silhouette of a fitted garment will have changed very little when belted, but the silhouette and proportion of a loose garment will change radically when belted.

Belts at the waistline and above should have a slight upward curve. Belts placed below the waist should have a slightly scooped curve.

Belt CIRCLES The Body

Waist and above are upward curves

Hips are downward curves

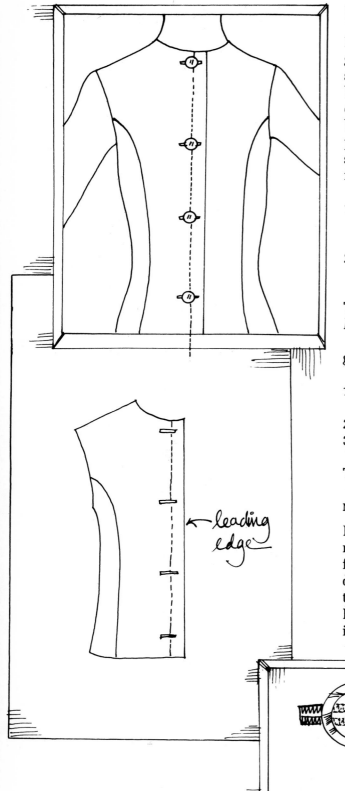

← leading
edge

Button Plackets

Buttons should line up on the center front line of a garment. To do this, the buttonhole must extend slightly beyond the center front of the garment. The button that endures the greatest stress will pull to the end of its buttonhole, and this will line up all the buttons with the center of the garment. The button placket extension is wider than the buttonhole. The size of the button placket extension depends on two factors:

1. The larger the button, the wider the placket will be. The button should always look balanced, which means it should be surrounded by fabric.
2. When a heavy fabric is used, the extension is larger.

The front edge of the button placket is called the *leading edge*.

Buttons should be placed on the bodice where the greatest stress is exerted:

1. The top of the bodice or where the collar begins to roll
2. The bustline, opposite the point of bust
3. At the waistline

The buttons should be evenly spaced on the placket.

NOVELTY BUTTON PLACKETS

Novelty button plackets require slightly different methods. The loop buttonhole is placed on the center front line of the placket. The side of the bodice that carries the buttons has an extension. When buttoned, the buttons and loops line up with the center front. Because they tend to gap, loops are placed at smaller intervals than standard buttonholes.

↓center front

Double-breasted garments have pairs of buttons placed symmetrically on either side of a center front line. Horizontal buttonholes are generally used.

Buttonholes may be placed vertically, especially when a band placket is used. The placket may be so narrow that horizontal buttonholes would be awkward. Horizontal buttonholes are the most functional because the button will position itself on the center front of the garment by fitting into the end of the buttonhole.

Collars

Collars encase the column of the neck. They should be drawn to appear as if there is a back as well as a front. The collar is usually symmetrical, and both sides should be drawn evenly. Practice with guidelines, but drop them gradually as your sketching improves.

The *stand* is the part of the collar that rises from the base of the neck to frame the face. *Lapels* are part of the bodice, but they have been incorporated into a standard collar. Notice how the collar is controlled by the top button on the placket. Note also how the collar flows into the leading edge of the buttonhole placket.

Round collars frame the face evenly by forming a symmetrical curve that extends from the base of the neck. This basic shape can be varied in many ways. For example, when the basic shape moves away from the base of the neck toward the shoulders, it becomes a bateau neckline.

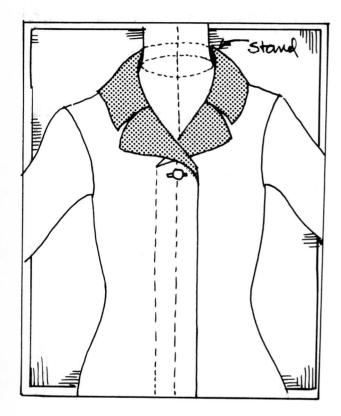

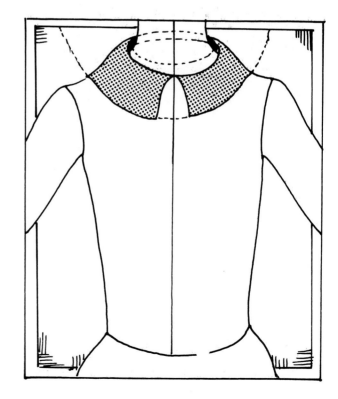

Skirts

A skirt is a tube of fabric that encircles the body from the waist down. When drawing a skirt, the two most important factors are the silhouette and the length. The silhouette refers to the shape of the skirt, which depends on the amount of ease (extra fabric) in the skirt and the kind of fabric. The shape of the pattern pieces for the skirt will also affect the silhouette. Skirts are styled in three basic shapes: straight, flared (wider at the hem, flaring from a slim waist), and pegged (tapered at the hem).

The sheath skirt is relatively easy to draw because it follows the shape of the body. However, the kind of fabric will greatly alter the shape of the skirt. A full skirt in a crisp fabric will be more flared than a skirt made from the same pattern but in a soft fabric.

Be careful that your skirt sketches have the correct length for the prevailing fashion. Proportion of the skirt to the figure is essential if you are to sketch the proper length, so be sure to indicate the knee and relate the hemline to it. When fashion is experimenting with skirt lengths, try several lengths and relate the skirt proportion to the look of the garment as a whole.

TYPES OF SKIRTS

A *sheath skirt* should have almost no curve to the hemline. The side seams fall straight, perpendicular to the hem.

A *dirndl skirt* has straight side seams, but a great deal of ease has been added to the waistline. Some dirndls have as little as 4 inches of ease added at the normal waist, whereas others have many, many inches of ease, resulting in a full, free-flowing silhouette. Dirndls make the hipline look bulkier. The dirndl is the typical skirt used for European folk costumes.

The *pleated skirt* is a variation on the straight skirt. Most pleated skirts have a straight silhouette because the ease has been controlled in crisp, vertical style lines. A pleated skirt is easier to wear than a straight skirt because added fabric allows for more movement.

A *circular skirt* is the ultimate flared skirt. For a very full effect, several complete circles can be sewed together and gathered to make a combined dirndl-flared skirt. For novelty, ruffles and uneven hemlines can be used with a circular skirt 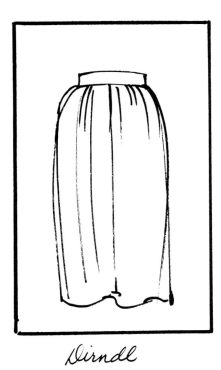 (see p. 261).

Sheath

Dirndl

Flare in a
crisp fabric

Flare in a
soft fabric

A line flare
in a stiff
fabric

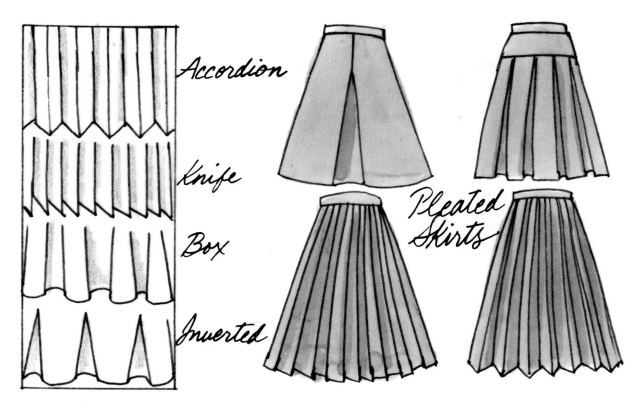

Accordion

Knife

Box

Inverted

Pleated Skirts

circular ruffle

straight ruffle

handkerchief hem

Pants

Almost always, pants are constructed with a center front and center back seam forming the crotch. These seams should be sketched. Do not drop the crotch below the midpoint (fourth head) of the figure, or the figure will look matronly.

The pants style depends on the amount of ease that is added at the hipline and hemline. Many silhouettes are possible by fitting or flaring the pants.

The length of pants varies just as skirt lengths do. Be sensitive to the shoes that are worn with pants, because they alter the proportions of the figure by adding height to the leg.

Knits

Knits take on the body's shape without the use of darts or seams (except side seams and armholes). Knits range from the finest denier jersey, which reflects every line and curve of the body, to bulky, crunchy sweaters, which may partially conceal body shape with their texture and dimension. To draw knits successfully, begin to observe photographs and renderings of knit garments. Visualize the fabric before you draw the figure, and imagine how the garment will look on the body. Knits, even the bulkiest, tend to fit more snugly than wovens.

Bulky Knit

Soft Knits

264

Jackets and Coats

To allow for underlayers made of bulky fabrics, outerwear garments fit the body more loosely than standard clothing. Heavier fabrics look bulkier, so when you are sketching a heavy fabric, draw corners with a slightly rounded line. This gives the impression of weight needed in sketches of jackets and coats.

THE DESIGNER SKETCH

Designers develop unique sketching styles that reflect their personalities. Often the kind of apparel a designer creates affects the style of the sketch.

Gayle Baizer designs active sportswear for Jantzen. Her breezy, sporty models complement the crisp, no-nonsense quality of her garments.

(Courtesy of Gayle Baiser.)

Michael Calderón's stylized, sophisticated figures fit the contemporary dresses he designs so well. He is concerned with the chic details that are essential to practical but feminine garments.

A designer sketch should be understood easily and include all essential construction details. The unique and appealing personality of a sketch adds great zest to the designer's inner vision.

KNIFE PLEATED CREPE BLOUSE & SKIRT

RUSSIAN

RIBBON TRIM....

RAYON FLOSS BELT & TIES

CALDERÓN

(Courtesy of Michael Calderón.)

REVIEW

Word Finders

Define the following terms from the chapter you just read:

1. Charcoal
2. 8-head figure
3. Guache
4. Illustration
5. Media
6. Prisma pencil
7. Rapidograph
8. Three-dimensional figure
9. Wash
10. Working sketch

Discussion Questions

1. What is the rule for balancing a fashion figure drawn in the S-curve position?
2. For an 8-head figure, what is the vertical midpoint?

9.
bodices, blouses, jackets, coats

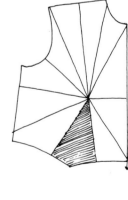

The *bodice* is the part of the garment that covers the body from the waist up. Bodices can be fitted to the body in several ways.

DARTED BODICES

Darts are V-shaped wedges that take in the excess fabric around the outer edge of the pattern and taper to nothing about 1 inch from the point of bust. The back darts taper to nothing about 1 inch from the fullest part of the back. If the pattern piece extends beyond the waist, the darts may not reach to the edge of the fabric. A dart that starts and ends within the pattern piece without touching the pattern edge is called a *fisheye* or *double-ended* dart. Darts always end at the fullest part of the figure. Darts make the flat piece of fabric fit the body's curves.

The top bodice in the illustration is a standard two-dart bodice. (The three drawings are seen from

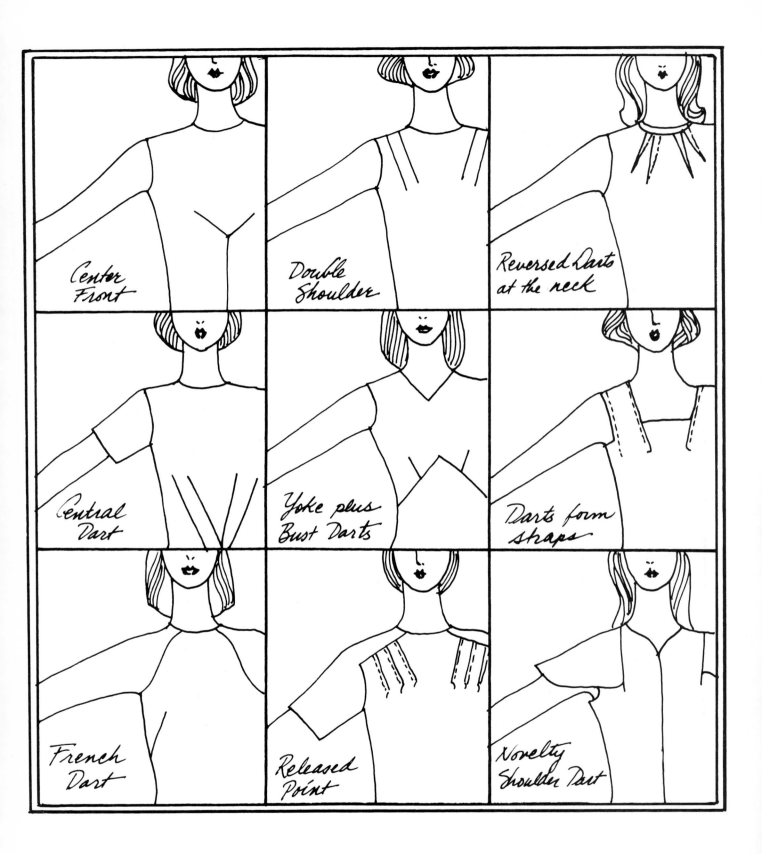

Center
Front

Double
Shoulder

Reversed Darts
at the neck

Central
Dart

Yoke plus
Bust Darts

Darts form
straps

French
Dart

Released
Point

Novelty
Shoulder Dart

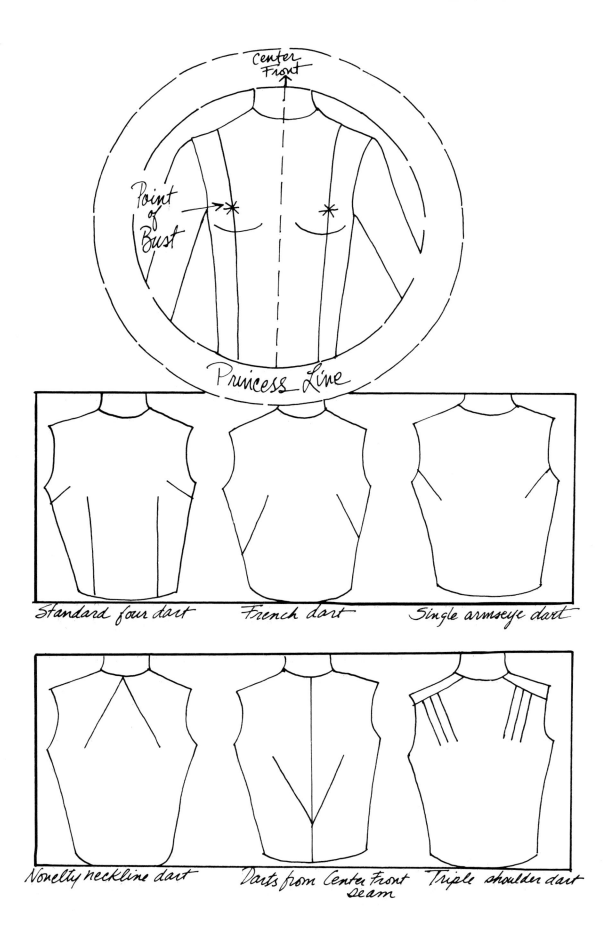

Center
Front

Point
of
Bust

Princess Line

Standard four dart

French dart

Single armseye dart

Novelty neckline dart

Darts from Center Front seam

Triple shoulder dart

271

center front.) The second drawing shows a bodice front, where the shaded area contains all the ease; the lines show the other popular dart positions. The dart can radiate to any area of the bodice's outer edge. The bottom drawing shows a fisheye dart and a bust dart.

Multiple-Darted Bodices

Darts can be used singly, in pairs, or in multiples (either darts or tucks). The illustrated examples here are the components of many possible styling variations. The variations could be incorporated into tops, blouses, or jackets.

Gathered or Eased Bodices

Instead of sewing it into a dart, excess fabric can be gathered into a seam. This is a very flattering way of fitting a garment and a simpler way because ease does not have to fit as precisely as a dart. Also, ease has a soft look that is particularly appropriate for knits and soft wovens. When a dart is used with sheer fabric, the excess fabric taken in by the dart may show through, but no shadow is visible when a fabric is eased. (A fabric that *shadows* means a fabric transparent enough for seams and details to show through.)

Yoked and Gored Bodices

A garment can be shaped by horizontal divisions (yokes) and vertical divisions (gores) in the pattern pieces (see p. 274). Gores are adaptable because they can be shaped in many ways. A gore fits a garment very closely to the body (if this is desired) because it can be shaped to the body's contours at closer intervals than a dart can. Gores and yokes can be combined with ease and darts to achieve the best fit.

Gathered or Eased Bodices

Yoke plus Ease

Slash and Ease

Inset with Ease

Neck Yoke and Ease

Sweetheart neck and Center Front Ease

Cossack Yoke

Peasant Blouse

Center Front Ease

Surplice Wrap with Ease

Yoked and Gored Bodices

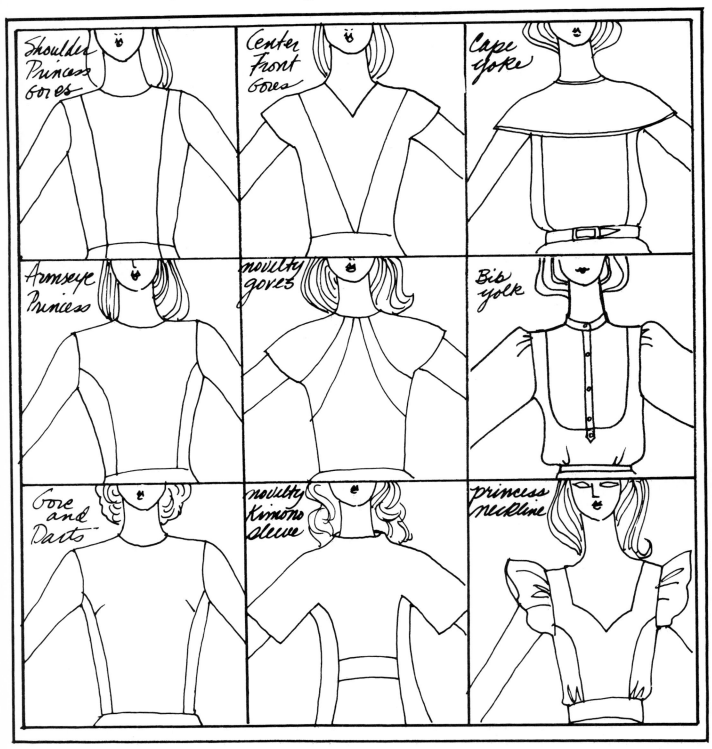

Shoulder Princess Gores

Center Front Gores

Cape Yoke

Armseye Princess

novelty gores

Bib yolk

Gore and Darts

novelty Kimono sleeve

princess neckline

FIT

The *fit* of garments is determined by the standard fit for each category of merchandise and by current fashion. A junior garment and a missy garment in a similar style will fit in two different ways. The junior garment will have a shorter back neck-to-waist measurement. Compared with a missy garment, measurements for the shoulders and bust are usually smaller, and the garment fits with less ease. A contemporary garment will fit a youthful figure, and the styles will emphasize the avant-grade in current fashion. For example, if blousons are the current style, the contemporary version would be the fullest and most exaggerated blouson on the market. The junior style would modify the blouson, possibly by taking out some fullness and adjusting the length so it will look better on a shorter figure. The missy style would change the blouson to flatter a more mature figure, possibly preserving the look only in a looser top that is belted to give a fuller look at the natural waistline.

Price also determines how a garment fits. Inexpensive, "downstairs" (budget and chain store) manufacturers take out all excess fabric to cut the cost of the garment, but they use enough yardage to suggest the original silhouette. Often these garments look skimpy because an inexpensive fabric is substituted for the original and most ease is taken out.

In moderately priced garments too, construction is designed to conserve fabric. Generally a manufacturer of moderate garments will not remove so much fabric that the garment loses its style. The customer feels that a garment must look worth the money and will resist purchasing a skimpy-looking or poorly fitted garment, despite its moderate price.

Usually the appeal of expensive garments is based on styling and construction details. The customer buys these garments because they are the essence of high fashion. Cost is less of a consideration when a garment has the latest nuance of fit and detail. More expensive garments tend to be closest to forward fashion's current ideal of fit.

CLASSIC STYLING

Classic styling is that style that is repeated over and over during different fashion cycles. A particular style may fall from fashion for a period of time, but it is almost always revived. The name and appearance of each style is part of the basic visual and verbal vocabulary of every person employed in fashion—from the designer and merchant to the copywriter.

The classic tops and jackets illustrated here show only one version of each style, but many are possible. The examples are basic, but they should help you to recognize the styling details that occur in current fashion.

Blouson

Polo Shirt
(often knit)

Overfold
at waist
or
dropped
torso

Bandeau

Peasant

Halter

Bare
Midriff

T Shirt

Smock

Kimono

Chinese Mand- arin

Peplum (short skirt like addition)

Chanel Jacket

Cardigan (often knit)

epaulet

Safari Jacket

Bolero

Double breasted Blazer

Eisenhower or Battle jacket

Shirt Jacket

Pea Jacket

worn by sailors

Tuxedo

Parka

satin lapels

Smoking Jacket

Loden Coat

Hacking or Hunting

Cape

(Can be lengthened to coat length)

Poncho

Knit Styling

Many classic styles can be made in knit fabric as well as woven fabric. Some styles are made only in knits. The two commercial methods for manufacturing knit garments are cut-and-sew and full fashioned.

Cut-and-sew refers to the method by which a garment is made from knit yardage. The manufacturer purchases the knit yardage and then cuts and sews it just like a woven piece of goods. *Stabilized* knits are finished to react like wovens. This type of knit garment will require fitting and pattern techniques similar to the woven garment, except that the fit will be snugger because the fabric stretch compensates for some ease allowance. Specially designed knit braids and ribbed bands can be purchased to give the cut-and-sew garments a custom-made look.

Full-fashioned knits are knit in pieces that roughly correspond to the shape of the pattern piece. Darts and ease are rarely used, but these garments fit because their construction is very elastic. Many full-

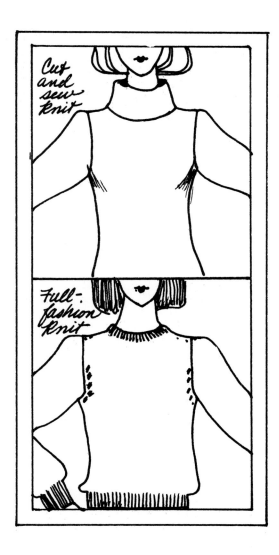

fashioned knits are made in the Orient, where labor costs are low, which makes possible a reasonably priced garment. Domestic full-fashioned knits are usually more expensive.

The most expensive knit garments are hand-knitted or crocheted. These garments take the most time to construct, but they have the greatest variety of stitches and detailing. Hand-knit garments for commercial distribution are made abroad, where labor is cheaper and more readily available.

Many classic bodies can be made in knits. Those in the illustrations that are traditionally made only in knits are indicated.

Classic Coats

Classic coats are reinterpreted frequently during fashion cycles. Lengths are changed to conform to current hemline trends, and collars and details are

The double-breasted coat can be styled with a great variety of collars. A clutch coat is any unbuttoned coat. Clutch coats are often reversible. The trench coat is a classic raincoat. The smock coat resembles an artist's smock.

The Inverness cloak is a Sherlock Holmes-type coat, with pelerine (cape) over the sleeves. Another version of a chesterfield is trimmed in black velvet, as shown here. The balmacaan is another classic raincoat. The princess coat has a fitted A-line shape.

Double Breasted

Clutch Coat

Trench Coat

Smock Coat

Inverness Cloak

Chesterfield

Balmacaan

Princess Coat

modified. The fashion cycle for coats is slower than the cycle for dresses or sportswear. The customer invests more money in a coat and wants it to last for several seasons, so she will buy a more classic garment.

Coats must fit with more ease if they are to accommodate clothes worn underneath. Often coats are made of bulky fabric, so a looser fit, especially in the sleeves and chest, is essential for freedom of movement.

Many times raincoats are made from a lightweight fabric, such as poplin, that has a water-resistant finish. These coats should be roomy because they are not warm and underlayers must be added in cold weather. The only truly water-repellent fabrics (those that allow no water penetration) are vinyls. These fabrics do not breathe, so vinyl garments are generally constructed with air holes under the arms to allow some air to circulate. Vinyls can be quite stiff, so the designer must add ease to allow for movement.

In outerwear, pockets and collars should be functional. Pockets are used to warm the hands or hold gloves and scarves, so they should be large and conveniently located. Often hoods are incorporated into collars, or extra flaps are added at the neck as a windbreak. Linings and zip-out extra-warm liners are built into cold weather outerwear. Outerwear should be both functional and fashionable.

REVIEW

Word Finders

Define the following words and terms from the chapter you just read:

1. Balmacaan
2. Bandeau
3. Blouson
4. Cut-and-sew knits
5. "Downstairs" manufacturer
6. Ease
7. Fisheye dart
8. Full-fashioned knit
9. Inverness cloak
10. Kimono
11. Peplum
12. Shadow
13. Smock
14. Water-repellent
15. Vinyl

Discussion Questions

1. How does the fit of outerwear compare with the fit of regular clothing?
2. Discuss the construction methods that can be used to make a flat piece of fabric conform to the body shape.
3. What factors affect fit, and does each factor modify a garment's fit?

10. skirts

BASIC SKIRT SHAPES

Four basic skirt shapes recur in fashion cycles: straight, flared, pegged, and circular. First, we will generally discuss and illustrate the types, and then we will consider each type in detail.

Straight Skirt

The side seams of a straight skirt are aligned with the straight grain of the fabric, and the cross grain runs across the hips from side seam to side seam. The drop, or difference between the size of the hips and the waist, is removed with darts or gathers. Variations on the straight skirt include the dirndl, pleated skirt, sheath, and straight wrap skirt.

Flared or Gored Skirt

The pattern pieces in a flared skirt are wedge-shaped. They taper at the waistline and gradually flare over the hips to greater fullness at the hemline. The gored skirt can be made in as few as two pieces, a front and back. Most fullness will be added to the side seams in this type of flared skirt. A more attractive flared skirt is made with more gores, which allows fullness to be added at regular intervals. Gored skirts can have from 2 to 16 gores or even more. Inverted pleats and trumpet gores are possible variations.

Pegged or Draped Skirt

A pegged skirt is wider at the waistline, and the excess fabric is gathered or draped into a waistband. The side seams are tapered at the hemline. Varia-

Straight skirt

Flared or gored skirt

Pegged or draped skirt

tions include the sarong, asymmetrical drape, and hobble skirt.

Circular Skirt

This skirt can be a half-circle, a full circle, or, for the most exaggerated look, several full circles sewed together. Of all skirts, this one is the widest at the hemline. It has a small waist, and the skirt pattern looks like a doughnut.

STRAIGHT SKIRTS

Sheath

The basic sheath pattern has four front darts to reduce the excess fabric between the waist and the fullest part of the hip. This pattern is often used as the basic sloper from which other skirt variations are made. Usually this skirt has a center back seam, two darts in the back, and a slit or release pleat to make walking easier.

Dirndl

The dirndl can have a minimum amount of ease, with a slim silhouette where the excess fabric, or drop, is eased into the waistband. This dirndl would look like a sheath, except the hipline would be slightly bulkier. The typical dirndl, however, has much fullness eased into the waistband. The amount of ease depends on prevailing fashion and the kind of fabric used. The more body a particular fabric has, the less fabric should be used for the dirndl because a stiff fabric emphasizes the natural fullness of the hips. This skirt is the traditional style for many ethnic costumes, and the word *dirndl* is taken from the name of the skirt in an Austrian folk costume.

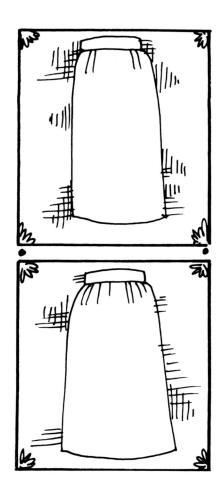

Gored

This skirt substitutes seam lines for darts, but the side seams are straight. The seam lines may conceal pockets. This style is very slenderizing. The gores may be arranged in many ways—for example, a plain darted front and three gores in back for smooth fit. Other variations include a style that buttons in front or a skirt that wraps to the side front. More ease can be added if a dirndl-like skirt is desired. Inverted pleats or large box pleats can be added to the seamlines. This is a versatile way of making a sheath skirt.

Gathered

The gathered skirt is the simplest kind of skirt to make and consequently is often a beginner's first sewing project. Much of this skirt's character is determined by the kind of fabric used to construct it. A stiff fabric will accentuate the hips and hang away from the body. A soft fabric will cling to the body and create a more natural silhouette. This skirt is much fuller than a dirndl.

Pleated

Generally pleated skirts are straight pieces of heat-sensitive fabric that are pleated commercially. Best for pleating are fabrics made from fibers that do not decompose under high heat, such as polyester, tria-cetate, acrylic, or blends of these fibers. Wool, cotton, and linen can be pleated, but not permanently. The pleats will have to be reset every time the garment is cleaned. Both knit and woven fabrics can be pleated.

A special contractor is used for most commercial pleating. Frequently the skirt will be seamed and hemmed before it is sent to the contractor. Often inexpensive garments will be pleated with a very small underfold, and the shallow pleat will sit out. This is a way of saving fabric. The designer determines the style and size of the pleat. Then the contractor makes a manila paper pattern that is scored in the dimension of the pleat and the underfold. A graduated pleat can be made. From the hip upward, more fabric is taken out of each pleat so that the skirt will fit the curve of the body. When the skirt is sewed into the waistband, it will fit smoothly at the waist, yet it will not strain or spread awkwardly at the hipline.

Pleated skirts can be made from circular-shaped patterns, but the majority are constructed from

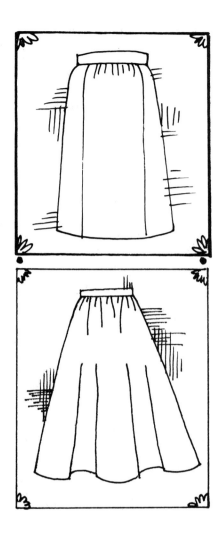

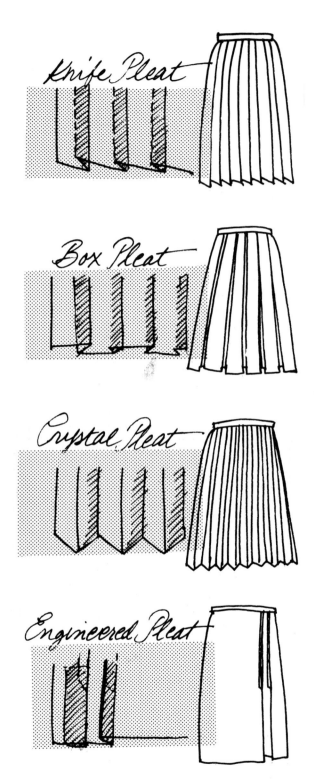

straight pieces of fabric. After the skirt length has been placed in a hot oven that sets the pleats, thin strips of masking tape at the hemline and waist hold the pleats in place until the skirt can be sewed to a waistband or bodice. As the pleats are sewed, the tape is removed.

Variations can be made by pleating only the top of the garment (unpressed or released pleats), top stitching the pleats over the hip and releasing them on the rest of the skirt, or setting the pleated skirt on a yoke or a low torso dress.

KINDS OF PLEATS

Knife, straight   A straight pleat is easily graduated to compensate for the drop between the waist and the hips. The pleats may be any size, from a quarter of an inch to several inches wide. This pleat will look crisp and tailored in a sporty fabric, yet it can look dressy in a soft fabric.

Box   The box pleat has a sporty look, as does the inverted box pleat. The box pleat is particularly appropriate for plaids because one pleat can emphasize one color of the plaid and the contrast plaid can be used as the underfold. A box pleat is difficult to graduate at the waistline.

Accordion, crystal   The larger version of this style is called an accordion pleat; the small, fine version is called a crystal pleat. This style has no underlay, but the pleats are gathered into a seam or the waistband. Crystal pleating is effective with sheer fabrics and has a dressy look. This type of pleat is difficult to show on a hanger because the pleat tends to collapse. When the garment is worn, the pleats are held out by the body and drape nicely.

Engineered   This kind of pleat is planned for an individual garment. It can be a constructed pleat, built into the pattern and pressed by hand rather than constructed by a contractor. Sometimes commercially pleated fabric can be combined with straight fabric to simulate the look of an engineered pleat.

FLARED SKIRTS

A flared skirt is wider at the hem than at the waist; this slims the waist and hips. The side seams slant outward from the fullest part of the hip. Because the side seams are not on the straight grain, the skirt is

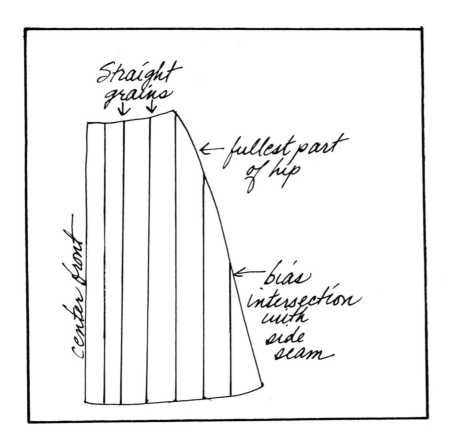

cut partially on the bias, which influences the way it hangs. When bias fabric hangs, it tends to sag. For this reason, flared skirts are often gored so the grain line can be controlled by a seam in the individual segment of the skirt. Multiple gores can add body and fullness to the skirt because the seams stabilize the way the skirt drapes. Furthermore, gores can be shaped to add fullness to specific areas of the skirt. For example, the trumpet gore fits smoothly over the hips and thighs and flares at any point thereafter, depending on the designer's preference.

Novelty effects can be achieved by cutting all gores on the true bias. This is particularly effective for stripes and plaids, but the patterns should match exactly when more than four gores are used, and this is difficult to engineer.

A gored skirt often has a center back seam (with a zipper opening) that divides the back into two gores. A single panel in front makes a classical three-gore skirt. A gored skirt is named by counting the number of gores. A gored skirt does not have to be divided equally in the front and back. Sometimes the back is simplified by using two gores, although the front may have more divisions. All gored skirts can be altered by adding more fullness to each panel. Or the design

can be varied by adding more fullness to the center panel and easing the excess into the waistband. Another common styling device is to put the gored skirt on a hip yoke or a low torso dress. An inverted pleat can be added to the gores of a flared skirt to give added fullness to the hemline.

PEGGED AND DRAPED SKIRTS

The pegged skirt visually enlarges the hip area because the skirt is tapered at the hemline. This skirt may be coupled with a snugly fitted bodice, a combination that makes the waist seem very small. The first example (below) shows a straight skirt that has been tapered slightly from the fullest part of the hips. If the taper is not too exaggerated, it will give the skirt a slender look. As the skirt becomes tighter at the hemline, it must be slit, or a pleat must be added so that the wearer can walk. The second example is a draped skirt. Concentrating the ease at the center of the waist exaggerates the size of the hips.

During periods when physical movement and active life-styles are fashionable, this silhouette is not found in daywear and appears only occasionally in evening wear. When fashion stresses the feminine

aspects of womanhood (as it did between 1912 and 1915), this silhouette is popular.

The sarong and other asymmetrically draped skirts were popular during the late 1940s. They were worn for street wear as well as evening wear. The wrap sarong over a bathing suit has become a classic.

The harem skirt (also worn as full, ankle-length, bloomerlike pants) is a novelty that is revived occasionally as lounging apparel.

CIRCULAR SKIRTS

Circular skirts are rarely made commercially because very wide fabric is required if the skirt is to be cut from a single piece of goods. When the fabric is not wide enough for a full circle, the skirt must be pieced or gored. The circular skirt also wastes a great deal of fabric. And the skirt is difficult to hem because it is mostly on the bias; a very small hem must be used. During the 1950s, circular felt skirts were popular, particularly those trimmed with whimsical appliqués. Felt is the ideal fabric for circular skirts because it has no grain line, is very wide, and does not have to be hemmed because it will not ravel.

When a very full skirt is desired, especially for evening wear, several circular shapes can be put together for a dramatic effect.

Perhaps the half-circle skirt is the most wearable of all the silhouettes. It has a modified and graceful flare that is more easily cut from fabric of average width. Waste fabric (called *fallout*) is still a consideration.

Full circle with seam to demonstrate piecing

Half circle skirt

Multi-circular skirt

Mini Skirt

Above Knee

Knife Pleat — Slightly above Knee

Just below Knee

Maxi Skirt

floor length

SKIRT LENGTHS

Raising and lowering hemlines has been a major occupation in fashion since the beginning of the twentieth century. The length of skirt affects the other components in a costume or dress because any change in hemline, even a few inches, alters the garment's balance. Greater variety is possible with a skirt that covers the knees because the skirt shape is emphasized by greater length.

When a particular length is the accepted fashion for a period of time, the eye becomes accustomed to the established proportion. A radical change led by a few fashion leaders may be necessary to start a more moderate change of hemline. Gradually designers and a few consumers experiment with the new length, and complementary accessories are developed. Leg coverings and shoes are the accessories most relevant to a change in length. Eventually the general public begins to recognize the new look as high fashion. More people ask for and buy the newer length. Usually the consumer does not discard an existing wardrobe, but will gradually add new items in the fashionable length.

Fashion magazines reinforce the new look and sometimes give suggestions on how to make older garments look more contemporary. Bit by bit the less radical versions of the newer length are accepted by the general public. Accessories that enhance the new look become available at lower cost and in more stores. Now the new length is widely accepted. Many variations are designed around the new fashionable proportion, and then the variations become more important than the new length. As endless variations are designed and the general public wears them, fashion leaders look for something new. Hemlines change once more, giving designers a new proportion to experiment with. The cycle has returned to the starting point, and once again length is the fashion question.

The cycle requires several years, but economic and social factors that alter life styles often affect the speed with which the cycle completes itself.

REVIEW

Word Finders

Briefly define the following terms from the chapter you just read.

1. Accordion pleat
2. Box pleat
3. Circular skirt
4. Crystal pleat
5. Dirndl
6. Gored skirt
7. Graduated pleat
8. Harem skirt
9. Knife pleat
10. Maxiskirt
11. Miniskirt
12. Pegged skirt
13. Sarong
14. Sheath
15. Straight skirt

Discussion Questions

1. Discuss the various types of straight skirts. Which allow more freedom of movement?
2. How do gores affect the styling of a flared skirt?
3. What are the technical difficulties in styling a skirt that is a full circle? What fabric is particularly suitable for circle skirts?

11.
dresses

The traditional definition of a dress is a single garment that covers the torso and legs. Merchandising policies of department and specialty stores are flexible enough to incorporate a broader range of garments into the dress department when fashion dictates variety. Dress departments may also include costumes and two-piece garments as well as the traditional dress. Merchandising trends today divide dresses by age, use, and price range, based on the theory that the customer will recognize the merchandise that appeals to her and wants to find it conveniently located in one area. Some innovative stores may group better and designer dresses in a specialized department featuring one company or designer. The merchandise has to have significant consumer recognition and be able to sell a large number of units to support an individualized department.

JUNIOR DRESSES

Junior dresses tend to be less expensive than missy dresses, and their prices fall in the moderate to budget range. The designer of junior dresses must analyze customers in the following ways: by age, occasion, fit, and hot items.

Age

The average age of the junior dress customer is 14 to 25 years. Younger girls purchase their dresses and sportswear in the teen and children's departments. Typically, the junior customer is in junior high, high school, or college. Some young businesswomen are included in this category.

The junior dress department boomed in the 1960s and 1970s when the bulk of the baby-boom genera-

tion dominated the economy. Junior departments continue to appeal to the young consumer, but are planned to be less of a volume factor at retail during the coming decades as the baby-boom generation moves into middle age.

Occasions

One of the most important occasions to consider when designing for this customer is school or work life. Because the majority of these customers are in school, trends at high school and college campuses are crucial. Dress codes, or the lack of them, influence dress departments. When it was compulsory to wear dresses or skirts to school, many more of these items were sold. When the community has many schools where uniforms are mandatory, the daytime junior dress business will be radically affected. Some businesses maintain a dress code that requires dresses or skirts, but the trend toward more casual garments has discouraged many customers from wearing dresses during the day.

The junior dress designer should be constantly aware of what the student is wearing, her life-style, and the events she attends. A special category of dresses has emerged in the junior department—the occasion dress. This is a long, fancy dress that is priced from $50 to $125. The junior customer wears this dress to proms, weddings (often as the bride or bridesmaid for casual weddings), sweet sixteen parties, and other special occasions. She may buy one or two of these garments per year. Spring and summer are especially popular times to purchase and wear these dresses. In general, the garments are made of delicate cottons, prints that mix and match, and eyelets trimmed with lace and ribbons. More sophisticated party dresses, made of slinky knits or other body-conscious fabrics, are also popular in long and short versions.

Fit

Fit restrictions for this category are fewer than for missy garments. The more youthful figure tends to have fewer fitting problems than a more mature one. The designer should make samples using a typical junior fitting model.

Hot Items

Trends are important in this market. Many items and fads make this a fast-moving, constantly changing classification. Many trends come from junior and contemporary sportswear. For example, when T shirts became a hot item in junior sportswear, dress manufacturers quickly incorporated them into junior dress departments, teaming the shirts with a skirt and pricing the combination as a unit. Occasionally a dress item will become an important sportswear item—for example, jumpsuits. Jumpsuits were a hot item in the dress department, and sportswear manufacturers included them in their lines as soon as they checked (sold well).

CONTEMPORARY DRESSES

The contemporary category is relatively new to the department store. This category was developed so the latest fashion could be included in the merchandising mix. The contemporary customer emerged in the 1970s when a large number of young women grew out of traditional junior apparel. More often than previous generations, these women tended to pursue careers and delay marriage and childbearing. This created an audience of fairly affluent women who were figure-conscious because of society's emphasis on diet, active sports, and a more mobile lifestyle. This customer was unable to find fashion merchandise in the missy area unless she paid very high prices for famous designer clothes. The new contemporary division concentrated on moderate- to better-priced garments featuring forward-looking styles.

Many retailers have added petite departments for the small adult customer who cannot find clothes that are sophisticated enough for the work world in the junior departments, yet needs garments styled for a figure under 5 feet, 3 inches. These departments feature contemporary garments and have been very successful.

Age

The average age of this customer ranges from the sophisticated 17- or 18-year-old to women in their forties and fifties, if they have the proper figure and frame of mind.

Occasions

The contemporary customer, more than consumers in other categories, tends to put less emphasis on occasion and more on the flexibility of her wardrobe. The total look of the outfit is more important than its formality. Because the category is new and not traditionally divided among established departments, there is more room for experimentation in the merchandising of contemporary garments.

Many contemporary designers choose the boutique method of grouping garments, disregarding whether the items are dresses or separates. Some stores follow suit by putting similar looks together to give the impression of a contemporary department. They hope to capture the customer's attention with a small, well-defined selection of merchandise. For many years boutiques and specialty shops have concentrated on the look of the merchandise and not tried to be all things to all people. If the boutique approach is successful in the contemporary category, department stores may use that method to merchandise all apparel in the future.

Location

This is an important consideration for the contemporary designer. Generally the most advanced fashion appeals to the urban dweller, especially the resident of a large city.

Fit

Contemporary garments should be less affected by fit restrictions and concentrate more on pure fashion. If the style is supposed to fit snugly, the contemporary garment should not compromise. If the full, long blouson is the current fashion, the most exaggerated version will be found in the contemporary area. Contemporary garments are usually limited to small sizes. Rarely do they go over size 12.

Hot Items

This is the testing ground for new fashions and colors. All other categories look to this area for retail items. Often a contemporary designer will capture the fashion essence of the most current life style. These designers will be emulated in lower price ranges and will set the pace for many different design areas.

MISSY DRESSES

Missy dresses is a traditional category that is well represented in several price ranges in most department stores. Typically, a department store will have budget or inexpensive, moderate, and better missy dress departments and a designer dress department. Often a sport dress department, which sells casual dresses, shifts, and pantsuits, will also be included.

Age

The ages covered are 18 through the seventies, but missy fashion tends to be a state of mind and figure more than an age.

Occasions

A great range of activities is covered by this category of dresses, from housework to office work. Occasion dresses, such as short cocktail dresses, long formals, and MOB (mother of the bride) costumes, are traditional in the missy category. Generally a manufacturer will specialize in dresses in a limited price range and for one type of occasion. The buyer will select from many vendors to stock a variety of garments. Some seasons will place emphasis on different kinds of merchandise. For example, the holiday season will require a larger stock of cocktail and dressy dresses. The knowledgeable buyer will have a selection of formals on hand for conventions and black tie dinner dances. In the spring and during holiday seasons, the dressy costume suitable for a wedding sells well.

Fit

The missy dress category has many fit restrictions because this customer with a mature figure may have some figure problems to disguise. Forward fashion is distilled and modified so it will fit the customer who wishes to look up to date. The missy dress customer wants to look neat, fresh, and fashionable in easy-care garments that pack and travel well. Polyester fabrics, or fabrics blended with polyester, are particularly popular in this category because they are easy to care for.

This missy customer usually wants the upper arm covered because it may be heavy or flabby. Thus there are few bare and sleeveless looks. Overblouses and tunics are flattering for many figures. Loose dresses that have separate belts are very successful because the dress can be worn by a short- or long-waisted person. The shirt dress, styled in a heavy shirting fabric with a crisp collar, front button placket or zipper, and casual styling details, is a consistent best seller. Moderate hemlines are most successful in this area. Changes in skirt length are usually tested in other categories before there is a change in the missy department.

All these dress categories constitute the bulk of the department and specialty store business. Special categories of dresses are also manufactured. These specialties offer the manufacturer a limited market, but there may be less competition within the specialty.

SPECIALTY CATEGORIES

Sportswear

Most often this is a missy classification that combines casual, easy-care dresses that travel well with more sporty items, such as pantsuits and shifts. The lightweight polyester print costume in a knit fabric sells well in this department.

Bridal

Bridal departments feature dresses for brides and formal dresses suitable for bridesmaids, proms, graduations, and other formal occasions.

Half-Size Dresses

This category carries missy dresses for the matronly figure. Larger sizes are featured in classic, subdued styling. The half-size garment is styled for the shorter, bulkier figure and is usually available in budget, moderate, and better price ranges.

Tall Size

Dresses in this category fit women who range in height from 5 feet 8 inches to over 6 feet. Most often this apparel is sold in specialty shops that can completely outfit the taller woman.

Large Size

Large sizes fit the stout woman and are available in sizes 18 to 52. The larger woman has many fit restrictions that must be taken into consideration when designing. Price is a factor because this category of apparel is difficult to manufacture at budget levels. The specialty store is best qualified to cater to this customer.

Maternity

Pregnant women have to buy clothing that will fit their temporarily expanded figures, but they will not wear the garments for long. Thus maternity clothes are moderately priced and easy to care for. Generally maternity clothes are made in youthful styles because the expectant mother is usually under 35. Dresses are a minor category because separates are more versatile. Specialty stores are most successful with maternity wear, so many department stores are gradually phasing it out.

Hawaiian and Resort

Hawaiian merchandise includes both sportswear and dresses. The fashions are styled in cottons and easy-care fabrics that feature unique prints in bright colors. These specialty manufacturers produce summer and resort clothes year-round. The garments are sold in areas where winters are warm and in northern cities for women who vacation for the winter in warmer areas.

TRADITIONAL DRESS CONSTRUCTION

Horizontal Divisions

A dress may be divided horizontally at any point on the body. Three typical divisions are illustrated: the empire, natural waistline, and low torso. These divisions can be applied to long or short dresses or other one-piece garments.

1. Shoulder yoke. This horizontal seam controls bust ease and is a classic styling device for shirt-dresses.
2. Empire line. This is especially popular for junior dresses because it is a youthful proportion. An empire line makes the person seem taller, especially when the line is used on a long dress.
3. Natural waist. The natural waist is the traditional and most natural division between the bodice and the skirt. This style line may be emphasized with a belt, sash, or jacket that ends at the waist.

Low Torso   **Natural Waist**   **Empire**   **Shoulder Yoke**

4. Low torso or hipline. This is the proportion of overblouses and jackets, sweaters over skirts, and dresses with a dropped waistline.

Horizontal Divisions and One-Piece Dresses

Dresses may be styled with no horizontal divisions. This style emphasizes height and may slenderize the figure if the garment is divided into gores. The two typical kinds of dresses without horizontal divisions are the princess line dress and the shift. The princess line can fit the body very snugly or skim the figure. The shift fits loosely. Like bodices and skirts, dresses are shaped by darts, gores, and ease.

Often the waist of a loose dress will be defined by a belt. Knit garments are often undarted and ungored. They cling to the body because of the nature of the fabric.

Some traditional gored variations of one-piece dresses and other one-piece dresses are illustrated. These traditional styles have countless variations, but the classics are reinterpreted during various fashion cycles.

Sheath   Shift or Float   Tent A-line or Trapeze   Two-piece

Coatdress

Tent
Shirt
dress

Batwing
Sheath

Jumper

Costume
or
Dress-
maker
suit

Blouson
with
asymmetric
neckline

Smock

Soft Princess
(with ruffle
detail)

T Shirt
dress
(Rugby
shirt)

Dropped
torso

Wrap
or
Surplice

"Prairie
Dress"

Peasant

Caftan

Cocktail dress

Gown

REVIEW

Word Finders

Define the following terms from the chapter you just read:

1. Costume
2. Dress
3. Half-size
4. Hawaiian apparel
5. Junior occasion dress
6. Large size
7. Maternity dress
8. Missy dress
9. MOB
10. Princess line
11. Sportswear dresses
12. Shift

Discussion Questions

1. What factors affect sales of junior day dresses? Consider the life-style of the customer.
2. Characterize the contemporary dress customer.
3. What fit restrictions apply to missy dresses?

12.
sportswear and pants

Sportswear is a twentieth-century word. The merchandising definition of sportswear is separate garments, priced individually, that are worn for casual occasions or participation in active sports.

Active sportswear is worn for playing active sports. Designers of active sportswear are most successful if they participate in and understand the demands of the sport for which they design. Function is the most important aspect of active sportswear, with easy care as the important second requirement. Often competitive sports set rigid limits on the kind of apparel and the colors that are acceptable. Active sportswear is less influenced by fashion, yet it frequently influences the styling of spectator sportswear. For example, the hacking jacket and jodhpurs of the British equestrian and the denim jeans, riding boots, and cotton shirts of the cowboy have been adopted for casual wear. Jogging suits and sweatshirts have inspired lounge and sportswear. The simple tank suit of the professional swimmer has been adapted into a one-piece suit. Tennis dresses are acceptable as resort wear, and sportswear colors are now accepted on the tennis courts.

Originally, spectator sportswear was designed for attending a sporting event. When a casual life-style became common in the United States and working people gained more leisure time, spectator sportswear was adopted for any casual occasion. This evolution was logical because sportswear is colorful, comfortable, and easy to care for.

HISTORY OF PANTS
AND SPORTSWEAR

Sportswear for women is a recent development. Amelia Bloomer's attempt to liberate women from the cumbersome and unhealthy corsets and full skirts popular during the mid-nineteenth century was a failure. Pants for women were forgotten until the beginning of the twentieth century. At that time active sports became more popular and women became increasingly interested in them. The sports that first allowed women to wear pants were horseback riding and bicycling. These sports required the legs to be free. The first riding suits had man-tailored

1850 -1860 Bloomers

1901 Cycling Costume

Knickerbockers

Jodhpurs

1910 To Present

1920s Lounging Pajamas

jackets, much like the formal riding jackets of today, and baggy pants, which allowed the rider to sit astride the horse. Bicycling pants were full bloomers styled like the skirt fashions of the times.

Separate skirts and blouses became fashionable about this time, and women began wearing elaborately embroidered and trimmed blouses with basic skirts. These garments were more easily mass produced than dresses because fit was less difficult and the items could be sold at a lower price. Waist shops (blouse shops) were the first to sell separate, ready-made garments.

The first pants and sportswear for women emulated men's wear. This theme is popular in women's sportswear even today. Women borrowed the battle jacket, pleated pants, tailored shirts, blazers, tuxedo jackets, jeans, and cardigan sweaters from men's wear.

World War I stimulated the development of sportswear. Pants were worn for activities other than active sports, although the skirt and dress remained dominant. Perhaps because sportswear was a new development in clothing, it was most affected by the social climate of the period.

During the Depression of the 1930s, women returned to the housedress. This fashion trend reflected the national desire to create jobs for men. The war was over and the nation's work force swelled with returning soldiers, so it was back to housework for women. As unemployment became widespread, the housedress was the prevalent look. The long skirt and somber colors further emphasized that times were hard.

Working outside the home became a necessity during the 1940s as World War II drained men from the work force. Rosie the Riveter, the symbol of the female factory worker, wore no-nonsense pants, overalls, or a jumpsuit to work. Now pants were here to stay. Women had tasted the freedom and flexibility of pants and so they became an integral part of their wardrobes, although they were still worn only for specific activities.

After the war, a nation tired of strife looked to its heritage for a simpler, more wholesome life-style. Women discovered Western wear, and casual cottons were developed into sportswear.

During the 1960s, the youth movement was in full swing as the postwar babies entered young adulthood. Influenced by warfare in Vietnam, youths adopted military uniforms and battle jackets in the original khaki. This was the beginning of the anti-

1942
Pleated
Pant

1943
Work-
Jumpsuit

1945
Pedal
Pusher

1947
Western
Pant

society hippie movement. Inspired by American idealism, youths adopted the pioneer uniform of denim work clothes. Jeans and long hair became the badge. Meanwhile, high fashion was engrossed in the future, fascinated by scientific technology and moon walks. Pared-down fashions evolved into the micro-miniskirt, often made from shiny, structured fabrics and worn with boots.

Some young people disdained mass-produced, stylized fashions. Instead, they wore natural fabrics, wrinkled and faded to a pale indigo blue. These young adults popularized antifashion apparel that minimized the differences between the sexes.

Denim jeans survived the antifashionable sixties to become a basic apparel item worn by almost all catagories of consumers. Famous designers stepped in to establish the jean as status fashion by affixing their names and logos to the back pockets. Expensive designer jeans sell along with the classic basics, making the basic five-pocket jean a classic style.

Recycling clothing was an important innovation as

youth became increasingly concerned about ecology and commercially induced obsolescence.

The casual life-style of the 1960s became high fashion during the 1970s. Design from the streets was the catchword of designers, and the casual look invaded all levels of fashion, even the couture collections. Changing life-styles affect fashion radically. The contemporary 1970 fashion emphasized comfortable and flexible clothing dyed with natural colors and spiced with the fantasy of hand-crafted ethnic items. Worldwide imports supplemented American clothing production. Sweaters from the Orient, Indian gauze and sheetings, embroidery from the Near East, and African native prints joined the traditional European fashion imports in American stores. (Imports are generally single items or components of an outfit, so they are sold in sportswear departments and boutiques.) These fashions were particularly popular with the young and avant-garde. Freedom of choice was the motto for this fashion revolution. Pants broke the occasion barrier, and they are now acceptable fashion almost everywhere.

The more conservative customer continues to purchase standard polyester knits and traditional sportswear components. For this customer, fashion is still dominated by the mass-produced look that emphasizes easy care and reasonable prices.

What about future apparel trends? This is a continuing question in the mind of the creative designer. Designers must be sensitive to changes in life-styles. They must stay in constant touch with the particular customer who buys their designs. Larger social trends often indicate what apparel will be popular in the near future. Finally, distribution of the population in terms of age, career, habitat, and increased leisure time greatly affects purchasing habits.

The designs of the future have their roots in the present. Apparel designers must heighten their awareness of life-styles and customer demands.

MERCHANDISING SPORTSWEAR

Commercial sportswear lines are usually organized in one of three ways.

Items

Items are garments sold as separate units. Generally items are trendy and change constantly as the customer seeks novelty. Price depends on the specific garment, so there is no typical price range. Junior sportswear departments carry many items, most of which are inexpensive. Items are easy for a store buyer to move in and out of—that is, to buy for a limited time. Characteristically, items are more popular during prosperous times and when innovative fashion is important. Many import lines fall into this category.

Separates

Garments that are unusual enough in design to be purchased singly are called *separates*. Unlike items,

Separates A popular and typical separates item in most categories of men, women's, and children's sportswear departments is the classic knit polo shirt, often with an identifying manufacturer's logo or name. The separates item is usually offered in many colors, but the line has fewer, more basic styles.

1954 Toreador Pants

1957 Clam Diggers

1960 Short Shorts

1961 Stretch Pants

separates generally fit into a group of styles that can be worn together and are made of complementary fabrics.

A manufacturer may organize the whole line around separates or offer buyers a separates group. These items may tie in with each other, but each item has such a definite style that it can be sold alone. This is a flexible way to purchase apparel because the store does not have to buy a group of styles in a range of colors and sizes, which would be a large investment. Instead, the store can buy more garments in the current hot category and fewer garments in the less important categories.

Separates buying is advantageous when layering is popular because the choice of separates gives the customer many options. Selecting separates requires a rather sophisticated customer, able to coordinate an outfit from many optional pieces. She may have to search in other departments or stores for matching components. Generally the misses customer who

1964
Culotte

1967
Bell
Bottoms

1970
Gaucho

1969
Knickers

shops in department stores is not this sophisticated. Coordination can be made easier by training salespeople and increasing the displays of coordinated separates. In the end though, the customer must put together the final look.

Coordinates

A closely developed group of garments, carefully linked by color or detailing, is a typical description of *coordinates*. These garments are designed in an interrelated group to encourage the customer to complete an outfit by buying several pieces. A typical coordinated group may consist of overtops—bulky sweaters or jackets—or undertops—shirts, pullover sweaters, and T-shirts. Bottoms may include pants—both a basic and a novelty version—and skirts—again a basic and a novelty version.

The group can be rounded out by adding shorts, halters, and bandeaus during the summer and pantsuits, long skirts, and tunics in the fall. Current hot items will be adapted for the coordinated group. To buy this complete package, the buyer will select many components so that the customer will have several possible outfits from which to choose. Each component will be bought in several colors and in a range of sizes. This will be an expensive purchase that will consume much of the *open to buy.*

The buyer usually purchases coordinated groups from large manufacturers who can ensure delivery and provide cooperative merchandising programs. The buyer saves a small percentage of the budget for items and fashion merchandise. This buying trend encourages large manufacturers to concentrate on safe, coordinated sportswear groups. Small and medium-sized vendors handle the fashion merchandise, items, and separates. One problem with purchasing coordinates is that some odd pieces are left unsold. After most components of a group have been sold, the remainder must be marked down.

Coordinated Groups Typical coordinated groups are based on a theme and offered in a limited color and fabric range. All the bottoms and tops are coordinated so the customer is encouraged to purchase several pieces of the group to wear together. The colors of the tops and bottoms must match exactly.

SPORTSWEAR CATEGORIES

Sportswear is manufactured for junior, contemporary, and missy customers in the same way that dresses are. Both active and spectator lines are designed for each category.

Junior sportswear is usually more item-oriented and less expensive than missy sportswear. The junior customer is more likely to experiment with her clothing purchases, but staples are still the cornerstone of the department. Prices range from budget to moderate. Special active sportswear and swimwear are created for this customer.

Contemporary sportswear tends to be the most experimental of all the categories, putting many items that are not traditionally considered sportswear into the merchandising mix. Fashion is the crucial factor in this category. Items are important, and prices range from moderate to high.

Missy sportswear tends to be conservative. It is manufactured in all price ranges, from budget

1971 Hot Pants.

1972 Palazzo Pants

1974 Pajamas

1973 Rehearsal Shorts

1973-74 Baggies

through expensive designer categories. Large manufacturers dominate missy sportswear, and items decrease in importance. Easy-care synthetic staples are emphasized in this category.

COATS AND SUITS

Gradually this traditional merchandising category is being incorporated into general sportswear, especially the suit. A traditional, tailored suit had much hand tailoring, which was done by skilled people. People skilled in hand tailoring are becoming rarer, and handwork in the American market is expensive. Because cost is such an important consideration, many customers select less structured sportswear components or combine a jacket with a matching skirt or pair of pants for a suit look.

Coats and outerwear jackets still constitute a separate category of merchandise. The contemporary customer may find some outerwear in a sportswear de-

Balloon Pant with Ties

Drawstring Pant

1975-76

Jumpsuit

Cigarette Jean

partment, but coat manufacturers still sell to junior and missy coat departments. Increasingly, handwork is being eliminated in all coat categories. Fusible interfacings have replaced time-consuming hand padding. Also, expensive fabrics are simulated by bonding inexpensive goods to stiff backings so the fabrics are bulky enough for outerwear. Hand-bound buttonholes are reserved for the most expensive apparel. In almost every case, mass production techniques have replaced the skills of the hand tailor in women's outerwear.

The sportswear jacket or skirt is usually more complicated in construction than the comparable item produced by a dress house. The item must stand on its own and be purchased as a separate unit, so it must be more detailed. The jacket as a dress component depends on companion pieces to sell the whole outfit, so the jacket may be less tailored in its detailing.

The designer must be aware of merchandising trends and social changes. Merchandising trends af-

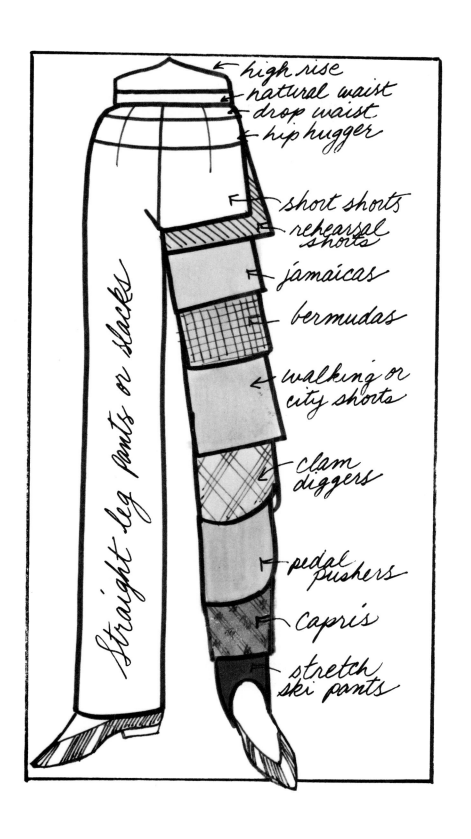

high rise
natural waist
drop waist
hip hugger

short shorts
rehearsal shorts
jamaicas
bermudas
walking or city shorts
clam diggers
pedal pushers
capris
stretch ski pants

Straight leg pants or slacks

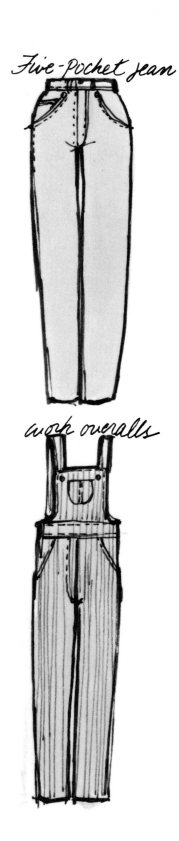

Five-pocket jean

work overalls

fect short-term fashion trends, particularly hot items and popular categories of merchandise. Social trends affect the long-term evolution of fashion cycles, including merchandising trends. Buyers and fashion reports for retailers are good sources of merchandising information. Designers in all categories of merchandise should constantly review these sources. *Clothes* is an important magazine that analyzes merchandising and social trends in light of the garments currently offered by vendors and stores.

REVIEW

Word Finders

Define the following terms from the chapter you just read:

1. Active sportswear
2. Bloomers
3. Coordinates
4. Culotte
5. Items
6. Jodhpurs
7. Jumpsuit
8. Life-style
9. Merchandising trends
10. Outerwear
11. Separates
12. Social changes
13. Spectator sportswear
14. Tailored jacket
15. Waist shops

Discussion Questions

1. Discuss the three ways a sportswear line can be organized.
2. What items are included in a typical coordinate sportswear group?
3. Name five garments that were designed originally for active sportswear but have been adapted for spectator sportswear.

13. sleeves

There are two categories of sleeves: (1) set-in sleeves and (2) sleeves that are cut in one piece with the bodice or incorporate part of the bodice into the sleeve. The *set-in sleeve* is used most often. This sleeve is a separate piece of fabric that joins the bodice at the armseye. A correctly made set-in sleeve allows enough ease for free arm movements. The arm is the most mobile part of the torso, so free movement is essential.

Usually the basic sleeve is drafted from standard measurements or measurements based on the cir-

Set-in sleeve

Sleeve cut in one with the bodice

cumference of the armseye. Then this basic sleeve sloper can be divided, expanded, or manipulated to make most other sleeve styles. A sleeve can be draped, but this method is less accurate.

Finishing the sleeve end is an important part of sleeve design. There are many ways of finishing a sleeve, and these methods apply to both set-in and bodice-incorporating sleeve styles.

FIT FOR A SET-IN SLEEVE

A standard set-in sleeve should smoothly cover the upper arm and shoulder socket. The armhole seam should fall on the shoulder where the socket joins the arm. If the sleeve droops, it will look matronly, If it is too snug, it will impede the movement of the arm and the fabric will pull.

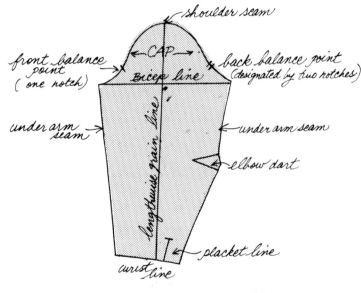

Move the armhole seam toward neckline; raise the underarm seam. Effect: neat, small shoulder that gives the bodice a youthful look. This diminishes the size of the shoulder. This device is often used in junior clothing and is especially effective for styling a full or puff sleeve.

Parts of the Set-in Sleeve The shoulder seam is connected to the armseye of the garment. The front and back balance points control the amount of ease and its distribution as the sleeve is sewn in. The cap covers the top of the arm at the shoulder joint and must have a small amount of ease in rigid fabrics to allow for movement. The bicep line is the measurement of the circumference of the arm at the underarm point. The underarm seams are joined to form the sleeve body. The elbow dart allows for movement of the lower arm in a fitted sleeve in a rigid fabric. The placket line should follow the wristbone up the arm and is open in a fitted sleeve to allow the hand to enter the sleeve.

322

The cap of a standard sleeve has from ¾ inch to 1¼ inches of ease. This amount is small enough to be eased into the armseye without gathers or bunches.

The underarm seam should fit comfortably under the armpit. In garments that will be worn over other clothes, the armhole is enlarged and dropped slightly.

The designer may wish to vary the position of the armseye seam at the top of the cap to achieve a certain effect. Modifications in the armseye can be combined with all variations of the set-in sleeve to produce a great variety of sleeve treatments, as the following series of illustrations will show.

Bishop Sleeve and Puff Sleeve Variations

Ease may be added to any area of the sleeve to achieve different effects. The illustrations show the variations possible in a bishop sleeve and a puff set-in sleeve. The *bishop* is a classic sleeve style often

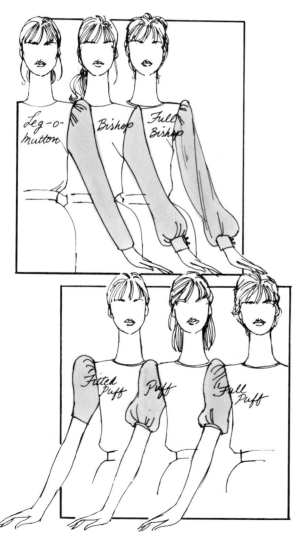

Lowered armhole seam: Shoulder seam has added fabric, and the cap has less height, making the armhole seam rather shallow. Effect: greater ease of movement and a sporty casual look. This sleeve can have a novelty seam treatment like a flat-felled seam because the top of the sleeve has a shallow curve. This detail is typical of men's wear and is called a drop shoulder.

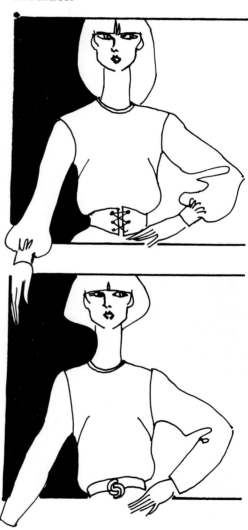

Dropped under armseye seam: Shoulder seam remains the same, but the armhole is much deeper. Effect: tends to look mature. Extra fabric must be added to the underarm seam or the sleeve will limit movement.

used in all categories of women's apparel. The *puff* sleeve is used less widely because of its youthful look. Think how these sleeves could be further modified by varying the finish on the sleeve end or changing the placement of the armhole.

Two-Piece Set-In Sleeves

SHOULDER SEAM

This two-piece sleeve has the usual underarm seam, but it also has a seam from the top of the cap to the center of the wrist. Ease can be taken out of the sleeve cap with this upper seam, and a snugly fitted sleeve will be the result. This extra seam is rarely added for fashion styling interest. The two-piece sleeve forms the basic sloper, which is developed into all attached-to-the-bodice sleeve styles.

TAILORED SLEEVE, UNDERARM PANEL

The tailored two-piece sleeve has no underarm seam. Instead, it has a panel that covers the under-

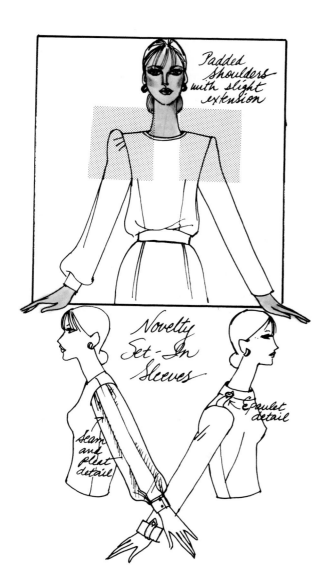

arm area. This sleeve is particularly good for coats and jackets made from bulky fabrics because the sleeve can be fitted quite snugly and the elbow dart can be eliminated. The underarm panel should be narrow enough to be inconspicuous from both the sleeve front and the sleeve back.

SLEEVES INCORPORATING PART OF THE BODICE

Raglan Sleeve

A *raglan* sleeve is separate from the bodice and has an underarm seam, like the set-in sleeve. It qualifies as a sleeve cut with the bodice because it fits the shoulder to the neckline as well as covering the arm.

When styling a raised neckline, the raglan sleeve is a natural choice because the seams running to the neckline can be curved in many ways. Frequently the raglan has a slightly deeper armseye so that the arm will not be impeded by the fitted shoulder. The shoulder curve can be shaped by a large dart or by a seam down the center of the sleeve, from shoulder to mid-wrist.

Kimono Sleeve

The classic Japanese kimono sleeve is a simple rectangle of fabric. When laid flat, a garment with *kimono* sleeves forms a T shape. The sleeves fall gracefully from a lowered shoulder line. The underarm seam is also considerably lower than in a set-in sleeve. Garments with kimono sleeves are made in many different styles and fabrics for men, women, and children. Although the fabric and style may differ, the basic shape of the garment and sleeve remains constant. People in many early cultures had costumes in this basic T shape.

Western contemporary styling has modified the kimono sleeve, resulting in many variations. Often the shape of the variation bears little resemblance to the Japanese kimono sleeve. When long kimono or dolman sleeves are styled from fabric 45 to 55 inches wide, there must be openings or seams in the center back and center front of the garment. The pattern pieces would not fit if they were undivided.

Dolman and Kimono Sleeves

Kimono sleeves and dolman sleeves are cut in one piece with the bodice or incorporate part of the bodice into the sleeve. They lack the armhole seam of the raglan or set-in sleeve. Classic dolman and kimono sleeves have an unbroken line from the bodice to the sleeve end, so they are well suited to plaids and stripes, which can be difficult to work with if a style has too many seams. Underarm seams are sometimes used on a bodice with a kimono shape to save fabric. The shaded area in the illustration represents a typical dolman sleeve pattern. If the arm is raised higher

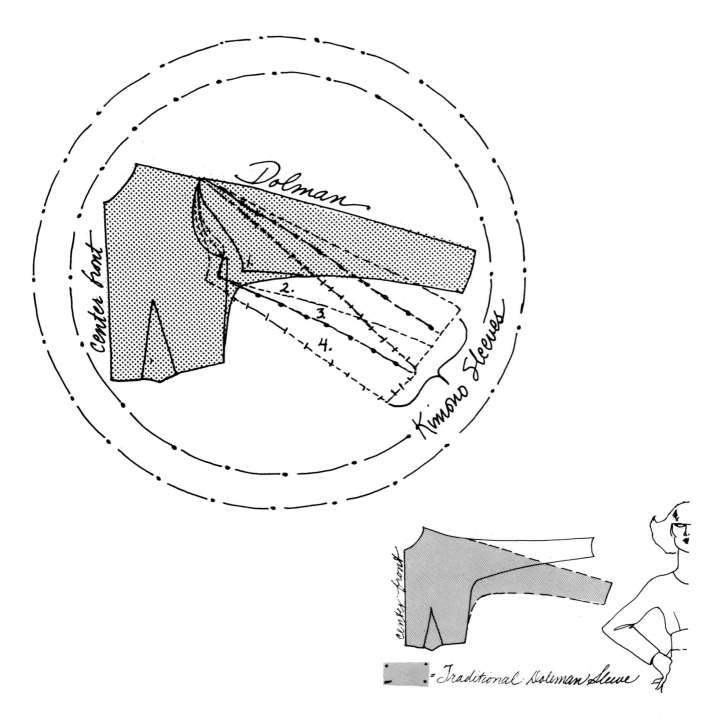

= Traditional Dolman Sleeve

than the shoulder line, the rest of the garment is pulled out of shape. To allow the maximum movement, the underarm seam has been extended. When the arm is in repose, the added fabric at the underarm seam falls in graceful folds. A true dolman sleeve adds bulk to the torso and bust.

The shoulder line may be fitted to conform to the curve of the arm when the arm is in repose. As the angle of the shoulder becomes more exaggerated, the movement of the arm is more restricted. To allow for the movement of the sleeves illustrated in positions 2 to 4, a gusset must be added to the underarm seam. A *gusset* is a diamond-shaped piece of fabric, cut on the bias, that is inserted in a slash in the underarm area which roughly corresponds to the armpit. This fabric should be inconspicuous while the arm is at the side of the body. The gusset compensates for the fabric that was removed when the shoulder was shaped. The gusset need not be a separate piece of fabric. It can be incorporated into a gore of the bodice.

Styled Kimono Sleeve

Another way to shape the kimono sleeve without using a gusset is to raise the shoulder seam. This automatically allows the underarm seam to grow, increasing mobility of the sleeve. The underarm area fits more snugly than in traditional dolman or kimono sleeves. This style is important for two reasons. First, it allows for upward movement of the arm by raising the shoulder slope; second, it increases the length of the underarm seam, also permitting more movement. This was a favorite sleeve of the American sportswear designer Claire McCardell.

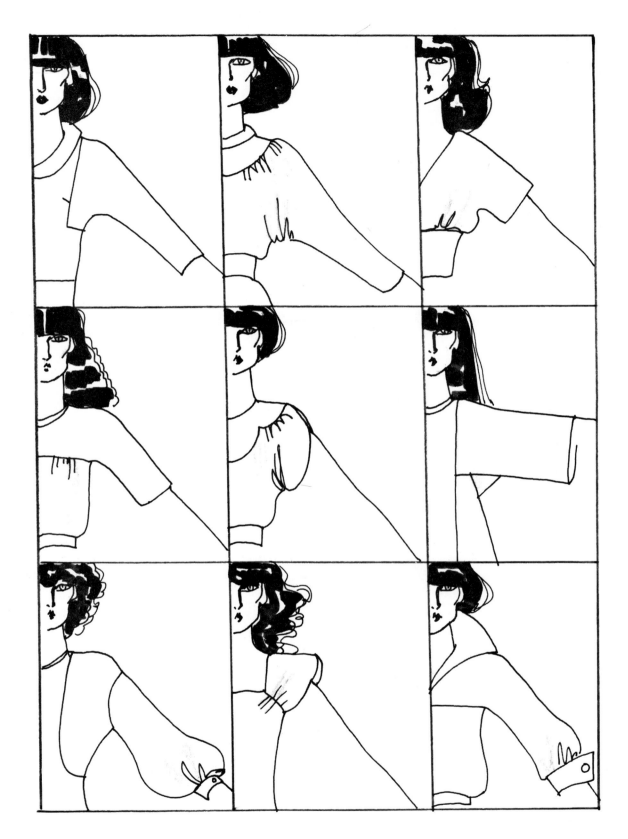

Novelty sleeves incorporating part of the bodice.

Sleeve Finishes

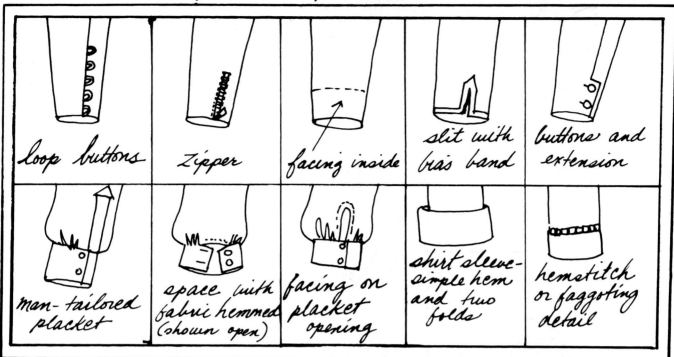

loop buttons	zipper	facing inside	slit with bias band	buttons and extension
man-tailored placket	space with fabric hemmed (shown open)	facing on placket opening	shirt sleeve-simple hem and two folds	hemstitch or faggoting detail

Cuff and Sleeve Endings

gathered over elastic in a casing	elastic stitched to sleeve forming a ruffle	turn back cuff with a notch detail	French cuff (double) with cuff links	convertible cuff (single layer)
band cuff	novelty ease	long fitted cuff	long, turned back cuff	knit rib that stretches

The cuff treatments, position of the armhole and underarm seams, and fullness added to the sleeve at various places are factors governing the different kinds of sleeves. Think of the many modifications possible by altering these elements in any of the basic sleeves.

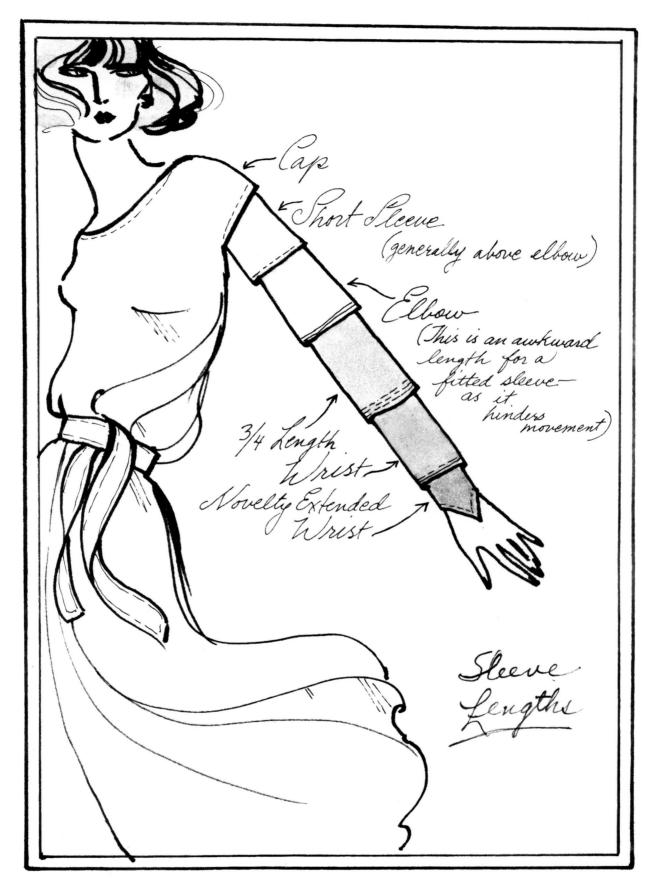

Cap

Short Sleeve
(generally above elbow)

Elbow
(This is an awkward
length for a
fitted sleeve—
as it
hinders
movement)

3/4 Length
Wrist
Novelty Extended
Wrist

Sleeve
Lengths

REVIEW

Word Finders

Define the following terms from the chapter you just read:

1. Basic sleeve sloper
2. Bicep line
3. Bishop sleeve
4. Dolman sleeve
5. Drop shoulder
6. Gusset
7. Kimono sleeve
8. Lantern sleeve
9. Leg-of-mutton sleeve
10. Petal sleeve
11. Puff sleeve
12. Raglan sleeve
13. Set-in sleeve
14. Two-piece tailored sleeve
15. Three-quarter sleeve

Discussion Questions

1. Describe the standard fit of a set-in sleeve. How much ease is added to the cap of a basic set-in sleeve?
2. Describe and diagram the parts of a set-in sleeve.
3. What are the basic sleeves that are cut in one piece with the bodice?

14.
collars

A *collar* is an added piece of fabric that surrounds the neck and is attached to the neckline of a garment. The collar is an important part of the garment because it frames and directs the eye toward the face. The edge of the garment that surrounds the neck or shoulders is the neckline.

The four styling factors that determine how a collar looks are the following:

1. Distance between the neckline and the base of the neck
2. Height of the stand (that is, how far the collar stands up)
3. Shape and depth of the fall
4. Revere or lapel, if included, and its size and shape (this is an optional styling device)

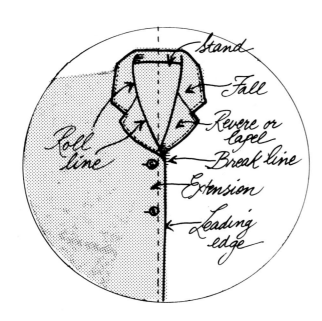

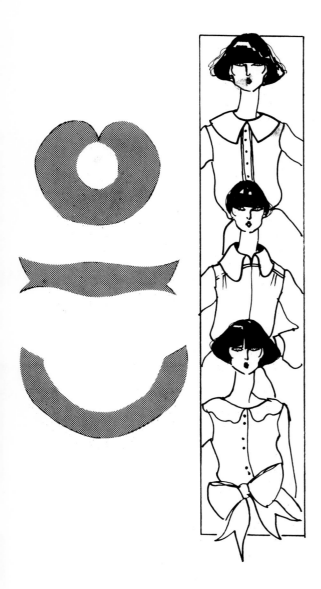

COLLAR SHAPES

The shape of the collar and the neckline seam will determine how the collar lies.

1. Collars with the same curved shape as the neckline of the garment will lie flat with no stand. The outer edge of the collar and the neck edge of the garment are exactly the same size at this point, so the collar falls flat over the garment. This type of collar is like a facing on the outside of the garment.
2. As the neckline curve of the collar becomes straighter (it can be a straight piece of fabric if it is cut on the bias), the stand becomes taller. Fabric is added to the neckline curve to build the stand. The outer edge of the collar is much smaller than the garment, so the collar stands up higher on the shoulder.
3. The greater the outside curve on a collar piece, the fuller the collar will be, almost like a ruffle. The expanded outside edge allows for ripples or ruffles. The surface area of the collar is much larger than the area of the bodice it covers. There will be no stand on this collar. Rather, the height will be at the outer edge. This type of collar may be gathered into the neckline for a very full look.

There are many types of collars. Each type can be modified by varying the four principles that govern collar styling. The possibilities of varying a collar by using these modifications can be illustrated by changes in a simple bias band collar. Many of these modifications can be used for any of the following collar illustrations, and others can be made if trims or contrast fabric are introduced into collar styling.

Straight Band Collars

A *straight band* collar may be cut on the straight grain line. It has a slightly curved neckline, stands straight, and has no fall. Usually this collar is quite narrow because a high band would be uncomfortable. The first two examples show classic band collars. The mandarin collar is a shaped band that is typical of Chinese costume.

The third example shows a man-tailored shirt with a mechanical stand. The band and the top collar are made separately and then sewed together. The stand holds the collar rigidly in place, which is particularly

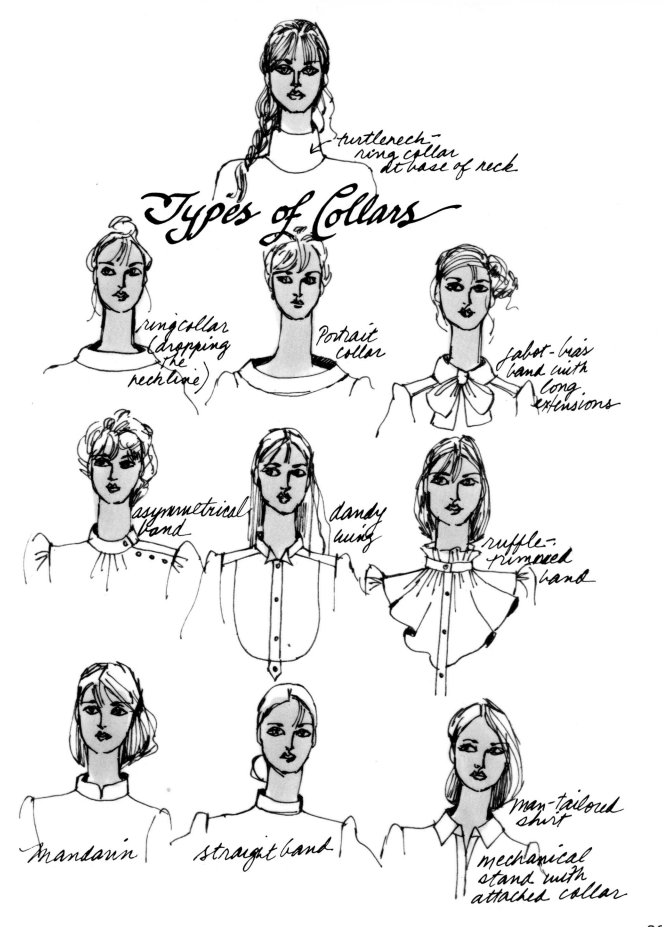

Types of Collars

turtleneck—
ring collar
at base of neck

ring collar
(dropping
the
neckline)

Portrait
collar

jabot—bias
band with
long
extensions

asymmetrical
band

dandy
wing

ruffle—
rimmed
band

Mandarin

straight band

man-tailored
shirt

mechanical
stand with
attached collar

337

desirable if the shirt will be worn with a tie or if it is made in a soft fabric. The top collar may have any shape.

The band collar is usually interfaced with a fabric that is stiffer than the outer fabric, further reinforcing the stand. Most collars are interfaced. The designer can choose from a wide variety of woven and nonwoven interfacings that vary in stiffness and weight. To make the collar pieces easier to handle, interfacings are often fused (bonded to the outer fabric by a machine that applies heat and pressure to both fabric layers). The interfacing reinforces the drape and shape of the collar. It is essential if the garment is to preserve its original look after washing or cleaning.

Bias Straight Band

A soft bow at the neckline is a popular collar for blouses and dresses. Generally this collar is cut on the bias to give it the maximum softness and drape. The ends of the tie can be finished in a variety of shapes. Separate bows are often tied under shirt collars. Alternatively, ties can be set into the shoulder seams so the ties cannot be detached from the garment.

Revere Collars

A *revere* collar has part of the bodice fabric incorporated into the lapel or underlapel. The jacket front facing is an extra facing piece that can be extended to incorporate the back collar as well as the revere (as in the Italian collar).

Peter Pan Collars

Peter Pan collars are youthful and casual. Like the bias band collar, Peter Pan collars can be varied in many ways. When a Peter Pan collar is worn close to the neck, it is particularly youthful. This collar is used quite a bit in children's wear.

The *Buster Brown* collar has the look of an old-fashioned school uniform or an artist's smock. The tie is characteristic of this collar. The Buster Brown collar varies in size from medium to large, depending on the size of the bow, whereas the Peter Pan collar varies greatly in size.

The *Puritan* collar has its ancestry in the cartwheel ruffs worn during the sixteenth century. Gradually the ruff softened and the lace trim became less

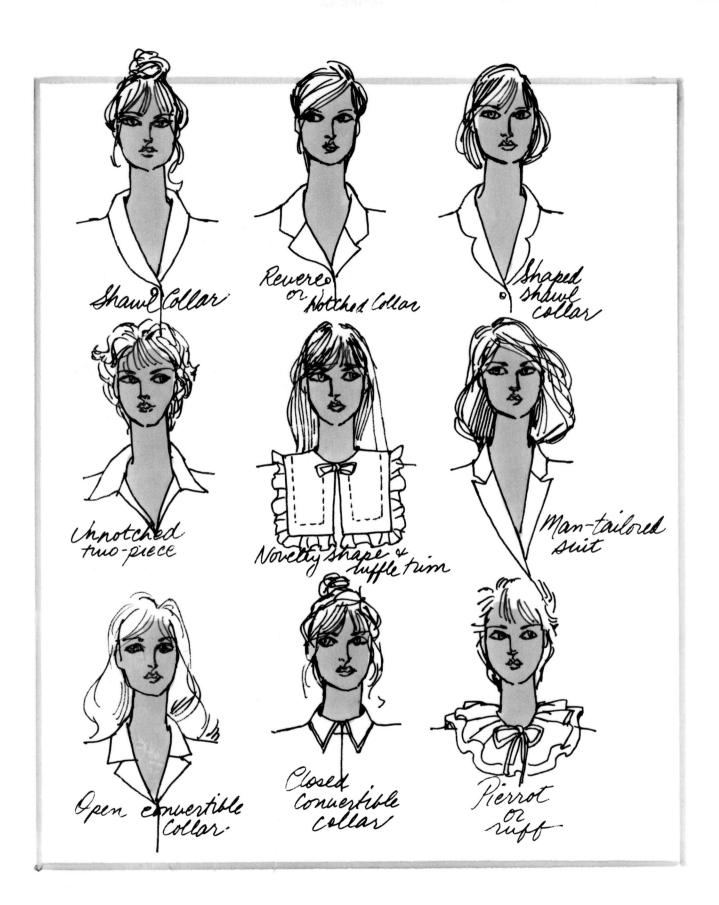

Shawl Collar

Revere or Notched Collar

Shaped shawl collar

Unnotched two-piece

Novelty shape & ruffle trim

Man-tailored suit

Open convertible collar.

Closed Convertible collar

Pierrot or ruff

Peter Pan

Buster Brown

Puritan

**Bermuda
(Semiconvertible)**

elaborate. During the seventeenth century, the sober "fallen collar" became the fashion among Protestants. Early settlers carried the collar to America, where it was firmly associated with the Puritans and early Americans. This type of collar is generally quite large.

One modification of the Peter Pan collar is the *Bermuda* collar, which is used mostly on casual day garments. It can be made with a band placket, which holds the collar firmly away from the neck in a slight V. The Bermuda collar may be shaped like the Peter Pan collar.

Cowl Necklines and Collars

A *cowl* neckline is draped on the bias grain. It is a graceful, soft neckline that resembles the drape of a Greek *chiton*, but it is named after the priest's robe, which also has a draped neckline. When the designer is planning a cowl, she or he usually drapes it in the garment fabric rather than muslin because of the need to determine precisely how the cowl will drape and how much fabric will be required for the perfect look. Soft, pliable knits and wovens are best suited to this style because they fall naturally into graceful folds. A cowl can be draped high on the neck with only one fold, or more ease can be added to create a deep cowl with several folds. A cowl can also be draped at the armseye.

A cowl collar can also be draped in soft, pliable fabric. The collar is a separate piece of fabric attached to the garment that is draped instead of draping part of the bodice.

High Cowl

Deep Inset Cowl

Pleats to hold a deep Cowl

side view

Middy or Sailor Collars

Traditionally, a sailor collar is used on a seaman's uniform. Typical trim would be two bands of soutache braid sewed around the edges and two stars at the back corners. When authentically duplicated, this collar is worn with a tie. Nautical colors of white, navy blue, and red are particularly effective. This is an ageless collar, appropriate for both young and old. The size and shape of the collar can be altered for novelty variations.

Middy or Sailor

Bertha or Cape Collars

The *bertha* collar resembles a small cape and can be designed in several novelty styles. This collar tends to be bulky, so this style may not be appropriate for heavy fabrics. The *pelerine*, a cape sleeve, is closely related to this collar. (See the illustration of the Inverness cloak in Chapter 9.)

Mitered Corners

A *mitered corner* is two pieces of straight fabric sewed together at a 45-degree angle. This effect produces a square neckline. The mitered pieces may be sewed to the garment like a band, or they can be a separate collar. This is the most effective way of adding a straight strip or band to a garment.

Bertha

Bertha Variation

Hoods

Hoods are effective as outerwear collars. Many times they are as attractive worn down around the neck as they are worn over the head. A soft knit makes the most successful one-piece hood. When a stiffer, bulkier outerwear fabric is used, the hood should be fitted to the head and gracefully lie on the back when not covering the head. The parka almost always utilizes a hood.

Necklines

The neckline does not have to be finished with a collar. It can be faced. A facing is a piece of fabric that corresponds exactly to the shape of the neckline and is sewed on to finish the neckline's raw edge. Then the facing is secured to the interior of the garment so the facing is not visible. Necklines may also be finished with piping or bias binding. Knits are often finished with ribbed bands.

Many neckline shapes and variations are possible. Some basic necklines are illustrated here and on the facing page.

REVIEW

Word Finders

Define the following terms from the chapter you just read:

1. Bermuda collar
2. Bertha collar
3. Bias band collar
4. Boat neckline
5. Break line
6. Buster Brown collar
7. Cowl
8. Interfacing
9. Jewel neckline
10. Mandarin collar
11. Mechanical stand
12. Middy collar
13. Mitered corner
14. Neckline
15. Peter Pan collar
16. Puritan collar
17. Revere collar
18. Stand
19. Straight band collar
20. Sweetheart neckline

Discussion Questions

1. What four factors determine how a collar will look?
2. What are the possible variations of a Peter Pan collar?

342

Jewel or basic Neckline

V Neck

Square Neck

Scoop Neck

Bateau Neck

Princess Neck

Built-up Neck

Elasticized Neck

Off the Shoulder

index